MUSIC'S FOURTH WALL AND THE RISE OF REFLECTIVE LISTENING

AMS Studies in Music

GURMINDER KAUR BHOGAL, *Series Editor*

Editorial Board

Nancy Yunhwa Rao, *Chair*
Amy Beal, *ex officio*
Gurminder Bhogal, *ex officio*
Mark Clague, *ex officio*
Walter Clark
Sarah Clemmens Waltz
Georgia Cowart, *ex officio*
Valeria de Lucca

Olga Haldey
Jake Johnson, *ex officio*
Inna Naroditskaya
Benjamin Piekut
Pamela Potter
Colin Roust
Siovahn Walker, *ex officio*

Conceptualizing Music:
Cognitive Structure, Theory, and Analysis
Lawrence M. Zbikowski

Inventing the Business of Opera:
The Impresario and His World in Seventeenth-Century Venice
Beth L. Glixon and Jonathan Glixon

Lateness and Brahms:
Music and Culture in the Twilight of Viennese Liberalism
Margaret Notley

Music, Criticism, and the Challenge of History:
Shaping Modern Musical Thought in Late Nineteenth-Century Vienna
Kevin C. Karnes

Jewish Music and Modernity
Philip V. Bohlman

The Critical Nexus:
Tone-System, Mode, and Notation in Early Medieval Music
Charles M. Atkinson

Changing the Score:
Arias, Prima Donnas, and the Authority of Performance
Hilary Poriss

Rasa:
Affect and Intuition in Javanese Musical Aesthetics
Marc Benamou

Josquin's Rome:
Hearing and Composing in the Sistine Chapel
Jesse Rodin

Details of Consequence:
Ornament, Music, and Art in Paris
Gurminder Kaur Bhogal

Sounding Authentic:
The Rural Miniature and Musical Modernism
Joshua S. Walden

Brahms Among Friends:
Listening, Performance, and the Rhetoric of Allusion
Paul Berry

Opera for the People:
English-Language Opera and Women Managers in Late 19th-Century America
Katherine K. Preston

Beethoven 1806
Mark Ferraguto

"Taken by the Devil":
The Censorship of Frank Wedekind and Alban Berg's *Lulu*
Margaret Notley

Songs of Sacrifice:
Chant, Identity, and Christian Formation in Early Medieval Iberia
Rebecca Maloy

Representing Russia's Orient:
From Ethnography to Art Song
Adalyat Issiyeva

Healing for the Soul:
Richard Smallwood, the Vamp, and the Gospel Imagination
Braxton D. Shelley

Sacred Sounds, Secular Spaces:
Transforming Catholicism Through the Music of Third-Republic Paris
Jennifer Walker

French Musical Life:
Local Dynamics in the Century to World War II
Katharine Ellis

Where Sight Meets Sound:
The Poetics of Late-Medieval Music Writing
Emily Zazulia

Musical Genre and Romantic Ideology:
Belonging in the Age of Originality
Matthew Gelbart

Music's Fourth Wall and the Rise of Reflective Listening
Mark Evan Bonds

MUSIC'S FOURTH WALL AND THE RISE OF REFLECTIVE LISTENING

MARK EVAN BONDS

OXFORD
UNIVERSITY PRESS

Oxford University Press is a department of the University of Oxford.
It furthers the University's objective of excellence in research, scholarship,
and education by publishing worldwide. Oxford is a registered trade mark of
Oxford University Press in the UK and in certain other countries.

Published in the United States of America by Oxford University Press
198 Madison Avenue, New York, NY 10016, United States of America.

© Oxford University Press 2025

All rights reserved. No part of this publication may be reproduced, stored in a retrieval system, transmitted, used for text and data mining, or used for training artificial intelligence, in any form or by any means, without the prior permission in writing of Oxford University Press, or as expressly permitted by law, by license or under terms agreed with the appropriate reprographics rights organization. Inquiries concerning reproduction outside the scope of the above should be sent to the Rights Department, Oxford University Press, at the address above.

You must not circulate this work in any other form
and you must impose this same condition on any acquirer.

Library of Congress Cataloging-in-Publication Data
Names: Bonds, Mark Evan, author.
Title: Music's fourth wall and the rise of reflective listening / Mark Evan Bonds.
Description: [1.] | New York : Oxford University Press, 2025. |
Series: AMS studies in music series | Includes bibliographical references and index. |
Identifiers: LCCN 2025004465 (print) | LCCN 2025004466 (ebook) |
ISBN 9780197806371 (hardback) | ISBN 9780197806401 |
ISBN 9780197806388 (epub)
Subjects: LCSH: Music—Philosophy and aesthetics. | Listening (Philosophy)
Classification: LCC ML3845 .B6 2025 (print) | LCC ML3845 (ebook) |
DDC 780.1—dc23/eng/20250206
LC record available at https://lccn.loc.gov/2025004465
LC ebook record available at https://lccn.loc.gov/2025004466

DOI: 10.1093/9780197806401.001.0001

Printed by Marquis Book Printing, Canada

The manufacturer's authorized representative in the EU for product safety is
Oxford University Press España S.A., Parque Empresarial San Fernando de Henares,
Avenida de Castilla, 2 – 28830 Madrid (www.oup.es/en).

In memory of my father,
Joseph Elee Bonds (1920–2011),
and his brother,
Robert Mason Bonds (1922–43)

Contents

Acknowledgments	*ix*
List of Abbreviations	*xi*
Introduction	1
1. The Pleasure of Resonance	17
Resonant Listening	18
The Pleasure Principle	24
2. Resonance Subverted	31
The Framework of Oratory	34
Breaking the Fourth Wall	42
Beyond Haydn	58
3. The Pleasure of Reflection	67
Before Kant	68
Kant	76
After Kant	83
4. The Prestige of Reflection	101
From Oratory to Poetry	101
Learning to Listen	105
Social Prestige	118
Epilogue: The Resilience of Resonance	124
Notes	*133*
Works Cited	*193*
Index	*217*

Acknowledgments

A year-long fellowship at the National Humanities Center in 2021–22 provided much of the time, space, and resources to write this book. I am grateful to Francesca Brittan, Tim Carter, Annegret Fauser, and Stefan Litwin for their helpful feedback over many conversations. The graduate students in my Spring 2021 seminar on the history of listening (Drew Borecky, Ken Ge, Kari Lindquist, Bri Nave) also helped me develop a number of ideas for this book. Michael Morse and Nicole Grimes were their usual generous selves in reviewing portions of an earlier draft of the manuscript. Jennifer Walker gave sage advice on the finer points of translations from French. Gurminder Bhogal, editor of AMS Studies in Music, guided this book through a process that included the immensely helpful suggestions of anonymous reviewers and members of the Publications Committee. And as always, Dorothea, Peter, and Andrew assisted in ways both known and unknown to them.

Abbreviations

19CM	*19th-Century Music*
AmZ	*Allgemeine musikalische Zeitung*
BAmZ	*Berliner Allgemeine musikalische Zeitung*
BJA	*British Journal of Aesthetics*
CJ	Kant, Immanuel. *Critique of Judgment*. Trans. Werner S. Pluhar. Indianapolis: Hackett, 1987.
CPJ	Kant, Immanuel. *Critique of the Power of Judgment*. Ed. Paul Guyer. Trans. Paul Guyer and Eric Matthews. Cambridge: Cambridge University Press, 2000.
JAMS	*Journal of the American Musicological Association*
JM	*Journal of Musicology*
KdU	Kant, Immanuel. *Kritik der Urtheilskraft*. Ed. Preussische Akademie der Wissenschaften. Berlin: Georg Reimer, 1913. (His *Gesammelte Schriften*, 5.)
M&L	*Music and Letters*
OHML	*The Oxford Handbook of Music Listening in the 19th and 20th Centuries*. Ed. Christian Thorau and Hansjakob Ziemer. New York: Oxford University Press, 2018.
OHWMP	*The Oxford Handbook of Western Music and Philosophy*. Ed. Tomás McAuley, Nanette Nielsen, Jerrold Levinson. New York: Oxford University Press, 2021.

Unless otherwise noted, all translations are my own, and all emphases are in the original. Orthography has been modernized silently in cases that might be read as typographical errors (e.g., "Zweck" for "Zwek," "sowohl" for "sowol"), but not in the case of common earlier spellings (e.g., "thun," "Würkung").

Introduction

In a moment of remarkable candor, the composer Aaron Copland once confessed that drama moved him more deeply than music.

> Contrary to what you might expect, I do not hold that music has the power to move us beyond any of the other arts. To me the theater has this power in a more naked form, a power that is almost too great. The sense of being overwhelmed by the events that occur on a stage sometimes brings with it a kind of resentment at the ease with which the dramatist plays upon my emotions. I feel like a keyboard on which he can improvise any tune he pleases. There is no resisting, my emotions have the upper hand, but my mind keeps protesting: by what right does the playwright do this to me? Not infrequently I have been moved to tears in the theater; never at music. Why never at music? Because there is something about music that keeps its distance even at the moment that it engulfs us. It is at the same time outside and away from us and inside and part of us. In one sense it dwarfs us, and in another we master it. We are led on and on, and yet in some strange way contemplate it at the same instant that we are swayed by it.[1]

The difference between the theater and the concert hall, for Copland, is that drama exercises its emotional power by virtue of what is commonly known as its "fourth wall." This imagined barrier separates actors on the stage from their audience and allows spectators to more readily forget that what they are watching is a carefully calculated act. The fourth wall ordinarily goes unnoticed until actors, following the direction of playwrights, break through this invisible partition to draw attention to the fact that they are indeed actors. They typically do this by addressing their audience directly, thus acknowledging its presence and thereby calling

Music's Fourth Wall and the Rise of Reflective Listening. Mark Evan Bonds, Oxford University Press.
© Oxford University Press 2025. DOI: 10.1093/9780197806401.003.0001

attention to the artificiality of the entire enterprise. A broken fourth wall shatters any possible illusion in the minds of spectators that the events onstage are somehow "real." It is precisely this illusion that could bring Copland to tears. The moment he stepped back and reminded himself of the fourth wall was the moment he became annoyed and not a little resentful toward the playwright for having been able to tug at his emotional heartstrings so easily.

The fourth wall is the default assumption of theatergoers in general. And it is very much an assumption: spectators routinely take it for granted and rarely give it any thought. Left undisturbed, the fourth wall allows theatergoers the opportunity to be taken out of their daily existence, even if only for a brief interval, and transported to an altogether different time and place. If spectators forget they are watching a play—if they forget they are watching actors act, performing lines a playwright has written—they are far more likely to be moved.

Music has its own fourth wall, and it, too, is the default assumption of many, if not most, concertgoers today. If listeners forget they are listening to musicians performing what a composer has written, the emotional response is likely to be all the more immediate and powerful: listeners can more readily become "lost" in the music. This is what Copland could not do. His profound knowledge of music's technical elements made it effectively impossible for him to forget the art's fourth wall for very long, and it was his awareness of it that prevented him from weeping in the concert hall.

At the same time, Copland scarcely qualifies as a typical concertgoer, who is someone far more likely to approach a musical performance in the way Copland approached drama, which is to say, as someone who accepts—unconsciously—the premise of a fourth wall. Under these assumptions, the music is more likely to "engulf" listeners. These are powerful moments, moments when music is "heard so deeply," as T. S. Eliot put it, "that it is not heard at all, but you are the music / While the music lasts."[2]

This is what I call "resonant listening," a type of listening in which we forget that what we are hearing is an object.[3] It is the aural counterpart

INTRODUCTION

to Paul Valéry's alleged definition of seeing as "forgetting the name of the thing one sees."[4] It is impossible to measure this phenomenon in any meaningful way, but it is equally impossible to deny its existence. In the case of music, a loss of reflective self-consciousness and a sense of transport are common enough for psychologists, neuroscientists, philosophers, and historians to have given this reaction a variety of names. Some call it the "chill phenomenon," that moment when we respond to music in a way that creates chills or goosebumps, while others speak of "flow" or "musical frissons."[5] One particularly extensive study has documented "the strongest (most intense, most profound) experience with music" of more than a thousand participants of various ages and backgrounds. Individual reports of these responses typically include depictions of total absorption, a forgetting of time and space, a state of transcendent being, a merging with the music, or an out-of-body experience.[6] Even professional critics speak of unusually powerful performances by using such terms as "magical," "captivating," "ravishing," "mesmerizing," or "spell-binding."

Such imagery reflects music's ability to induce a trance-like state in listeners that, in its most extreme form, amounts to ecstasy, a term derived from the Greek word meaning "to be taken outside oneself." We go into the concert hall willing, if not actively hoping to be transported to a state beyond our everyday existence, else why bother going to the concert in the first place? And it is that experience of transport—what might be called a stylized trance—that listeners are most likely to recall long after the fact.

At the other end of the spectrum lies what I call "reflective listening," an awareness that what we are hearing is an object, an event or a phenomenon outside of and apart from ourselves. To invert Eliot's formulation, we are *not* the music while the music lasts. Reflective listening is more basic than what has come to be called "structural listening," an awareness of a given work's technical elements, such as its form, harmony, rhythm, texture, or timbre. All structural listening is reflective, but not all reflective listening is structural. The much lower threshold for reflective listening amounts to a simple awareness of the act of

4 INTRODUCTION

listening itself, which is to say, an awareness that what we are hearing is an object.

In practice, of course, few if any acts of listening are purely resonant or purely reflective: even Copland's account reflects elements of both. We can slip in and out of these two modes easily enough, oscillating between being lost in the music and being aware of its existence as an object. But it is not possible to listen in both ways at the same time, for if we are truly lost in the music, we cannot at the same instant be conscious of it as an object, and if we are aware of it as an object, we cannot be lost in it. Taken together, these two modes of listening might be thought of as the aural counterpart to Necker's cube or Wittgenstein's duck-rabbit figure. Granted, there are different degrees of being lost, but that is in the end a function of the speed of oscillation between the two modes of listening.

I will have much more to say about these two modes of listening— resonant and reflective—in the chapters that follow, but for the moment, I would point out that they provide useful coordinates for tracing a fundamental change in listening practices that took place in Western concert halls in the late eighteenth and early nineteenth centuries. It was during this time that reflective listening became the preferred mode of perception among lay audiences, for reasons that were both aesthetic and social. This was not a new way of listening: composers, professional musicians, and connoisseurs had been listening reflectively long before. But by the middle of the nineteenth century, lay audiences had, for the most part, accepted the idea—even if it was only an idea—that they listen in this way as well. Reflective listening became the new standard for the concert hall, even if that standard often remained more aspirational than real. Consciously or not, and regardless of whether they acted on it or not, concertgoers came to assume an obligation to grasp what the creator of any given piece was trying to "say," to listen with an awareness of the composer's agency. They may or may not have approved of what they heard, but they perceived what they heard as an object. Music was no longer just an experience but an object as well. Resonant listening, while not necessarily rejected, was no longer considered sufficient in and of itself.

INTRODUCTION 5

Music's Fourth Wall and the Rise of Reflective Listening traces the origins of this new standard by examining the changing assumptions about what it meant to listen in the concert hall between roughly 1750 and 1850. The evidence is invariably indirect, for by their very nature, assumptions are rarely articulated. But they do reveal themselves if we read between the lines of enough commentaries from a sufficiently wide range of sources. These include philosophical and aesthetic treatises, fiction and poetry, reviews of publications and performances, essays, program notes, and "how to listen" guides aimed at lay audiences. For all the diversity of their approaches and intended readerships, these sources trace a trajectory that moves from an earlier ideal of resonant listening to a later ideal of reflective listening. The evidence, I grant, is circumstantial: critics of the time did not use these terms, but the concepts come through clearly enough in other ways, and circumstantial cases ultimately rest on an accumulation of evidence that consistently points in the same direction. It is for this reason that I have called so many witnesses to the stand.

All of these witnesses can be problematic in their own ways, to be sure. Music and the experience of listening famously resist verbal description. The written accounts that have come down to us, moreover, transmit only a tiny fraction of actual responses to music, and aside from the occasional letter or diary entry, we must rely for the most part on the judgments of professional critics with their own personal and ideological agendas.[7] In the face of so many challenges, perhaps the best we can do is attend to the assumptions behind each of these responses and trace the way in which those assumptions gradually changed.

The most revealing of these witnesses address the nature of instrumental music. From the perspective of lay listeners, vocal music posed no particular challenge, for it was understood as a projection of the particular text being sung. The words provided a ready point of entry for listeners, for they understood the music as being "about" the words in more than one sense. "Characteristic" or program music, although purely instrumental, provided a similar kind of help. Through distinctive and descriptive titles ("The Battle of David and Goliath," "Winter,"

"The Storm"), listeners could associate what they heard with the images suggested by such titles, in contrast to works whose titles were strictly generic ("Symphony," "Sonata," "Concerto") and which gave audiences little if any sense of what a work might be "about." In the eighteenth and early nineteenth centuries, non-programmatic instrumental music was an inherently abstract art form at a time when abstract art of any kind could scarcely be imagined. The oft-repeated question attributed to the eighteenth-century French philosophe Bernard Le Bovier de Fontenelle, "Sonate, que me veux-tu?" ("Sonata, what do you want of me?") captures the frustration shared by many of his contemporaries: he would never have put such a question to an aria, a motet, or vocal music of any kind, or even to a work of program music, for the answer would have been obvious.[8] But music without a text or paratext resisted explanation, and it was for this reason that writers of Fontenelle's time, almost without exception, regarded vocal music as the clearly superior form of the art. Noël-Antoine Pluche summarized this consensus succinctly in his enormously popular *Le spectacle de la nature*: "The most beautiful melody, if it is only instrumental, almost necessarily becomes cold and then boring because it expresses nothing. It is a fine suit of clothes separated from a body."[9]

Johann Georg Sulzer, in his widely read encyclopedia of the fine arts (1771–74), was slightly more sympathetic to music that lacked words but ultimately maintained that the art could realize its full potential only when united with language.[10] The composer and critic Johann Nikolaus Forkel concurred, putting it this way in 1783:

> The amateur [listener] must have a translator to make the expression of the art understandable: poetry serves this function. It therefore remains incontestably true, that as far as impact, effect, and value are concerned, instrumental music ranks in every respect far behind vocal music. In the latter, all the powers of art are united; in the former, only a few, and only the weakest.[11]

A few years later, Immanuel Kant would famously declare in his *Kritik der Urteilskraft* that without a text, music is more a matter of pleasure

INTRODUCTION 7

than of culture on the grounds that it leaves nothing for the mind to contemplate.[12]

By 1800, however, a growing number of critics were beginning to regard instrumental music as aesthetically equal, if not superior, to vocal music precisely because of its semantic openness. This story has been told from a variety of perspectives many times in recent decades, most recently in the work of Roger Mathew Grant, who traces the changing conceptions of affect over the course of the eighteenth and early nineteenth centuries as culminating in the idea that an "attuned" listener, resonating sympathetically with the music, could value instrumental music just as highly as vocal music.[13] Grant's thesis complements my own notion of resonant listening, though I would argue that this latter mode of perception was firmly established in practice long before it came to be articulated by critics and philosophers.

The rise of reflective listening—the very opposite of resonant listening—has gone largely unrecognized to date, however, and as I argue in this book, it was this phenomenon that served as an even more powerful catalyst for the growing prestige of instrumental music. Reflective listening was encouraged by a combination of the music being written at the time—most pointedly in works that violated music's fourth wall—and by changing assumptions about the nature of aesthetic experience in general.

Chapter 1 of *Music's Fourth Wall* examines resonant listening, in which listeners approach music as an experience rather than an object. Resonant listening lies at the heart of every myth or legend about the power of music. Orpheus overcame the boundary between the living and the dead not through the words he sang—Caron and Pluto had heard such pleas many times before—but through melody and the sound of his voice and lyre. Alexander the Great, having vanquished all his enemies, was himself vanquished by his musician, Timotheus, who was able to manipulate the mood of his otherwise omnipotent master like a puppet by performing a succession of different kinds of music, from gentle to warlike. Comparable accounts from real life abound. Samuel Pepys, for example, noted in his diary on 27 February 1668 that the music (now lost) to the play he had just seen that evening—*The Virgin Martyr* by Thomas Dekker and Philip Messinger—had moved him beyond all measure:

> That which did please me beyond anything in the whole world was the wind-musique when the Angell comes down, which is so sweet that it ravished me; and indeed, in a word, did wrap up my soul so that it made me really sick, just as I have formerly been when in love with my wife; that neither then, nor all the evening going home and at home, I was able to think of anything, but remained all night transported, so as I could not believe that ever any music hath that real command over the soul of a man as this did upon me.[14]

Two centuries later, Hector Berlioz, one of the most literate of all composers, insisted that "one's self must vibrate *with* the instruments and voices and *because* of them in order to experience genuine musical sensations."[15] And he described those sensations in graphic detail:

> Upon hearing certain pieces of music, my vital forces seem at first to double in strength; I feel a delicious pleasure in which the reasoning faculty has no share; the habit of analysis arises spontaneously later and brings forth admiration; emotion, increasing proportionately with the energy or loftiness of the composer's inspiration, soon produces a strange commotion in my circulation; my arteries throb violently; tears, which ordinarily signal the end of the paroxysm, often only indicate an advancing condition that is far from having reached its peak. In such cases, there are spasmodic muscular contractions, a trembling of all the limbs, a *total numbness of feet and hands*, a partial paralysis of the optical and auditory nerves; I cannot see, I barely hear; vertigo . . . a half-swoon . . . One may well imagine that feelings heightened to such a degree represent a rare occurrence . . . .[16]

Accounts like these remind us that music is more than simply powerful: it is dangerous, for resonant listening leaves us weak and vulnerable. When music possesses us—"ravishes" us, as Pepys put it—we are not in full control of ourselves. We risk losing our personal autonomy, and personal autonomy was something of an obsession for Enlightenment thinkers.

It seems more than merely coincidental, then, that composers began to violate music's fourth wall when they did, for works that foreground

INTRODUCTION 9

the signs of their own production subvert resonance and compel us to listen reflectively. Examples of such works are the focus of Chapter 2. They are both a symptom and a cause of changing assumptions about listening in the closing decades of the eighteenth century and early decades of the nineteenth. By far the best-known example of a work that encourages reflective—distanced—listening is Joseph Haydn's String Quartet in E♭, op. 33, no. 2, popularly known as "The Joke" because of its finale. By playing with and against the conventions of musical closure, Haydn makes us aware of his agency and steps out from behind the music, as it were, to expose the artificiality of his art and his role as the creator of what we are hearing. The effect is to puncture the premise of aesthetic illusion and self-forgetting that is the essence of resonant listening. We cannot "lose" ourselves in a work of music that goes out of its way to remind us that it is a work of music. By violating music's fourth wall, Haydn compels us to listen reflectively. We cannot lose ourselves in the experience of such works because we are so forcefully reminded that we are in the process of having that experience.

Many other works achieve this same effect in ways that are subtler yet cumulatively no less effective. Contemporaneous responses to the music of Haydn, Carl Philipp Emanuel Bach, and Beethoven make it clear that certain of their works encouraged listening from a distance, and the music of late Schubert, Berlioz, and early Schumann reinforced this attitude so strongly that by the middle of the nineteenth century reflective listening had come to be accepted as the proper (and more socially prestigious) mode of listening, at least in the concert hall. Audiences began to make an effort to understand what they were hearing, and they began to perceive the emotions they heard in the music as an expression of composers' own personal emotions: Beethoven's "Pastoral" Symphony was no longer a portrayal of nature but *Beethoven's* portrayal of nature; Berlioz's *Symphonie fantastique* was not about an unhappy love affair but rather *Berlioz's* unhappy love affair; and Schumann's *Carnaval* amounted to a series of fragments from a wordless autobiography.[17] It is largely for this reason that overt violations of music's fourth wall went more or less underground for more than two generations in the middle of the nineteenth century: once listeners assumed that the music they were hearing was autobiographical, they necessarily heard it as sincere. This also helps explain the well-known critical bafflement over Beethoven's late works, especially the string quartets, which violate the fourth wall repeatedly. A sense of emotional distance would eventually re-emerge in the works of such later composers as Gustav Mahler, Eric Satie, Charles Ives, Sergei Prokofiev, Igor Stravinsky, and Kurt Weill, all of whom seem to have delighted at times in drawing overt attention to their agency. But these composers were operating in an environment quite different from that of a century before. By 1900, audiences had long since accepted reflective listening as an aspirational norm, which meant that openly self-reflective music was no longer the novelty it had once been. That turning point in the history of listening was already well behind them. Music that calls attention to its own artificiality (by John Cage, Luciano Berio, Helmut Lachenmann, and Johannes Kreidler, among many others) has since become so common that it no longer seems in any way extraordinary, precisely because the perception of music as an object has become so firmly embedded in our framing of the concert-hall experience. The focus of Chapter 2, then—and for that matter of this entire book— is on the century between 1750 and 1850.

Chapter 3 traces the rise of reflective listening through the prism of philosophy and aesthetics, with special emphasis on changing conceptions of pleasure and beauty. Immanuel Kant and the post-Kantian philosophers are the key figures here. It was around 1800 that the conceptual framework for listening to instrumental music began to move from one based on persuasion to one based on judgment, itself a form of reflection. Instrumental music's elevated status in the early nineteenth century came about in part through the recognition that it was the one art most capable of integrating the mind and the senses. The question here is not when composers began writing instrumental music worthy of reflection—they had been doing that for quite some time—but rather when the music-consuming lay public began to accept reflection as part of its responsibility. That acceptance was crucial to the rapid rise of instrumental music's aesthetic status. As long as music was regarded as the

INTRODUCTION 11

"language of the heart"—the standard view throughout the eighteenth century—there was no need to know anything about the art in order to enjoy it. One simply experienced it. But once beauty became the *sine qua non* of the fine arts, reflection displaced resonance as the primary source of pleasure in music, at least in theory.

Chapter 4 surveys the growing prestige of reflective listening over the first half of the nineteenth century. This was a time when listening came to be regarded as a skill, a technique that could be learned and developed. Publishers recognized the growing demand for writings that would help members of the general public cultivate (and display) that skill. This literature proliferated in the form of journals, how-to-listen books, composer biographies, and explications of an increasingly canonic repertory. François-Joseph Fétis' enormously successful *La musique mise à la portée de tout le monde: Exposé succinct de tout ce qui est nécessaire pour juger de cet art, et pour en parler sans l'avoir étudié*—"Music Made Accessible to the Entire World: A Concise Account of Everything Necessary to Judge this Art and Discuss it Without Having Studied it"—became a model for virtually every subsequent music appreciation book.[18] These texts have all shared a common goal: to help audiences better understand and judge what they were hearing. Perhaps the most enduring legacy of the divide between resonant and reflective listening is the overt distinction that arose around this time between two kinds of repertories, broadly conceived of nowadays as "popular" and "classical." These constructs rest less on styles of composition than on modes of perception, with resonant listening typically associated with the former (known revealingly in German as *Unterhaltungsmusik*, "entertainment music") and reflective listening associated with the latter (*ernste Musik*, "serious music"). It is in fact possible to listen to any kind of music in either way, even if the repertorial distinction seems all but intractable.

This book's epilogue considers the resilience of resonant listening over and against the price of listening from a distance. Many histories of concert-hall listening practices, it must be said, adopt a covertly triumphalist narrative. It is a good thing, we read, when audiences began to fall silent, sit still, and pay close attention to what they were hearing, and when program notes, pre-concert lectures, and composer biographies began to provide those listeners with even deeper insights. In certain respects, these were and remain welcome developments, but they have come at a cost. Does a heightened awareness of craft necessarily lead to a superior aesthetic experience? Is losing oneself in a performance really such a bad thing? By its very nature, reflective listening inhibits our access to a higher realm of Pepysian consciousness, a state of mind embraced by the idealists of the early nineteenth century and later by Schopenhauer, Wagner, and Nietzsche. The ecstatic, transcendental experiences so frequently described in response to music of all kinds are a product of resonant listening. Thus, while reflective listening had established itself as the accepted standard in the concert hall by the middle of the nineteenth century, resonant listening continued—and continues—to offer its own alternative form of superiority.

* * *

I make no claim of novelty for the idea that music has a fourth wall. In his monumental *Oxford History of Music*, Richard Taruskin offered an illuminating discussion of the phenomenon in the music of the early twentieth century (Prokofiev in particular), and Nancy November has since associated it in varying ways with Beethoven's string quartets.[19] Without using the term itself, Dean Sutcliffe has recognized that the ending of Haydn's "Joke" Quartet carries implications that go far beyond its obvious humor. "The 'seriousness' of what Haydn has done" in this finale, Sutcliffe points out, "could not be greater. This is a eureka moment in the history of Western art music—revolutionary in the way in which it alters the balance of power between composer and listener, in which it acknowledges the existence of a listener whose participation is essential to the meaning of the music." Sutcliffe goes on to offer many examples of other composers contemporary with Haydn who also played with and against listeners' expectations, all the while connecting these instances to the broader theme of music's inherent sociability in the second half of the eighteenth century.[20]

INTRODUCTION

Although the history of concert-hall listening has attracted considerable attention in recent decades,[21] the rise of reflective listening has gone largely neglected by scholars, including myself. In my *Wordless Rhetoric: Musical Form and the Metaphor of the Oration* (1991), I was at a loss to explain the precipitous decline of oratory as a framework for understanding instrumental music, beginning around 1810; I now think I have a better of idea of why this happened, and why it happened so quickly. I also now recognize that my *Music as Thought: Listening to the Symphony in the Age of Beethoven* (2006) focused almost exclusively on resonant listening and the philosophical Idealism with which it is so closely associated. In *Music's Fourth Wall*, I make the case for a parallel trajectory of reflective listening that contributed just as much, if not more, to the elevation of instrumental music's prestige around the turn of the nineteenth century. The present book also complements my more recent *The Beethoven Syndrome: Hearing Music as Autobiography* (2020), in which I trace the evolving perception of Beethoven's music as a sonic diary of his life. Toward the end of writing that book, I came to realize that to hear music as a reflection of a composer's inner self rests on the even more fundamental act of perceiving that music as an object rather than as an experience.

While *Music's Fourth Wall* builds on the work of many earlier scholars, I am particularly indebted to the writings of Lydia Goehr, Judith Becker, and Carolyn Abbate. Hearing the musical work as an object is both an impetus for and a byproduct of what Goehr has called the "work-concept." This concept, as she notes in her influential *The Imaginary Museum of Musical Works* (1992), "evolved over many decades" around 1800, and it "marked a transition . . . away from seeing music as a means to seeing it as an end."[22] Exactly. I would go beyond this to argue that the work-concept is itself predicated on reflective listening, in that before a work can be thought of as a work, it must first be thought of as an object. In this sense, *Music's Fourth Wall* offers yet another perspective on how and why perceptions of concert-hall music changed so fundamentally around the turn of the nineteenth century.

Judith Becker's *Deep Listeners: Music, Emotion, and Trancing* (2004) emphasizes the epistemological value of a mode of listening that Western critics have been largely reluctant to embrace. "Deep listening," as Becker explains, "is a kind of secular trancing, divorced from religious practice but often carrying religious sentiments such as feelings of transcendence or a sense of communion with a power beyond oneself." This stands in marked contrast to "a Cartesian, rational, disengaged self" that resists trancing. The Western notion of a "bounded, unique, inviolate self," Becker argues, "may hinder the trance experience of the surrender of self and consequently the ability to imagine trance as a reasonable, natural phenotypic kind of consciousness." Becker defines trance as "a bodily event characterized by strong emotion, intense focus, the loss of the strong sense of self, usually enveloped by amnesia and a cessation of the inner language." Following William James, she identifies trance as "an event that accesses types of knowledge and experience which are inaccessible in nontrance events."[23] Trance may seem an extreme manifestation of what I call resonant listening, but the two share basic features: an all-consuming response, a blurring between subject (the listener) and object (the music), and an *oubli de soi*. Becker's work, which focuses on non-Western cultures, has direct applicability to the Western concert hall.

Carolyn Abbate's essay "Music—Drastic or Gnostic?," also from 2004, identifies two approaches to listening that overlap in certain ways with what I call resonant (drastic) and reflective (gnostic). Abbate points out the general unwillingness of scholars to deal with the former and notes just "how ingrained" their "clinical voice can be, as the only proper voice" when talking about music.[24] The gnostic approach manifests Western culture's long-standing "devaluation of physical or ephemeral phenomena in intellectual culture, as well as that culture's reservations about immediacy and pleasure."[25] Yet subjective, emotional responses, as she notes, are precisely why most people listen in the first place. Abbate thus identifies a fundamental binary in present-day listening practices, and *Music's Fourth Wall* seeks to place that binary within a historical context, even if my terminology and focus differ from hers in certain respects. As to terminology: I prefer "resonant" and "reflective" to

INTRODUCTION

Abbate's "drastic" and "gnostic" (which she adopts from the Russian-French philosopher Vladimir Jankélévitch). "Resonant" captures what Veit Erlmann, in his important 2010 book on theories of hearing, calls "the collapse of the boundary between perceiver and perceived." Erlmann characterizes resonance as "the complete opposite of the reflective, distancing mechanism of the mirror. While reason implies the disjunction of subject and object, resonance involves their conjunction."[26] "Reflective," in turn, is the term used by eighteenth-century philosophers, most notably Kant, to describe the relationship of the observer to the observed. "Gnostic," moreover, implies knowledge and interpretation, which are at least one step beyond the more fundamental perception of music as an entity outside of the self.

The recognition of these two very different kinds of listening under different names has been noted by others as well. Nicholas Cook, for one, distinguishes between "musical" and "musicological" listening, the former carried out "for purposes of direct aesthetic gratification," the latter "for the purpose of establishing facts or formulating theories."[27] Here, however, I would maintain that the perception of music as an object fundamentally shapes the nature of aesthetic gratification. Even the relatively simple process of "following" the music from moment to moment, locally as opposed to globally—what the philosopher Jerrold Levinson has helpfully termed "concatenationism"—rests on the more basic premise of music as an object of cognition.[28]

I should also make clear that my arguments about music's fourth wall make no claims to universality. In terms of repertory, my focus is squarely on what has come to be known as Western art music, a repertory that is in practice overwhelmingly presentational rather than participatory, that is, produced specifically with non-performing listeners in mind.[29] I use the terms "concert hall" and "concert-hall listening" as shorthand for any performance offered to any sort of audience, including those in the more intimate setting of the private salon. Often under the purview of women, the salon was indeed particularly conducive to a type of listening that could be intense and all-consuming, as many accounts from the time demonstrate.[30]

In the end, however, the particular configuration of any social setting (e.g., public vs. private, large vs. small) is less important than the more basic distinction between performers and listeners. And while performers are of course also listeners, they are listeners of a very different kind and not my central concern here.[31] My focus is also squarely on instrumental music: violations of the fourth wall in opera, a staged genre, are in principle no different from those in the theater of the spoken word.[32]

Finally, one last note on sources: Although the eighteenth- and nineteenth-century texts on which I have drawn come largely from German-, French-, and English-language sources, German ones necessarily predominate, in part because it was composers from German-speaking lands who more than any others cultivated instrumental music during this time, in part because it was philosophers and critics from those same lands who speculated at greater length than anyone else about the challenges posed by this kind of music. France and Italy vied for supremacy in opera, but no one of that time questioned the intensity with which composers from German-speaking lands cultivated instrumental music. Stendhal, an outsider to this tradition and thus ideally positioned to observe it, put it this way in his typically incisive, sardonic fashion in 1824: "In our own time, the talent for instrumental music has altogether taken refuge in peaceful and patient Germany. In the midst of its forests, the beauty of sounds, *even those without melody*, is enough for these dreaming souls to redouble the pursuit and pleasures of their wandering imaginations."[33] "Imagination," as we shall see in Chapter 3, is the key word here: it is the faculty that allows for a reflective—and thus more distant—relationship between listeners and what they were hearing, one that did away with music's fourth wall. This book traces the rise of that mode of listening in the European concert hall.

1

The Pleasure of Resonance

> Loud applause at the end of a concert is the surest proof that only the sense of hearing was engaged. Music that penetrates the heart must make us forget that we have hands.
>
> —Anonymous (1783)[1]

Resonant and reflective listening are best understood as contrasting yet complementary modes of perception. Critics have long recognized the two by a variety of terms, describing resonant listening as visceral, naïve, non-conceptual, immersive, and drastic, while portraying reflective listening as aesthetic, structural, conceptual, and gnostic. The advantage of "resonant" as a term is that it avoids characterizing a phenomenon in terms of a binary opposition (non-conceptual/conceptual, visceral/intellectual, naïve/sophisticated). More importantly, it avoids any implication of a mind-body dichotomy, for music always passes through the mind when it is perceived, even if we do not reflect consciously on what we hear. "Resonant" also captures the sense of a spontaneous and immediate connection between subject and object: the whole of the listener resonates in sympathy with the music. "Reflective," in turn, points to a distinction between the listener and the object being heard, even while avoiding implications about structure or meaning, which are only two of many possible features to which reflective listeners might attend.

Music's Fourth Wall and the Rise of Reflective Listening. Mark Evan Bonds, Oxford University Press.
© Oxford University Press 2025. DOI: 10.1093/9780197806401.003.0002

Resonant Listening

Resonant listening is not the same as passive listening: it can, in fact, be quite draining. Wilhelm Heinrich Wackenroder's account of the "remarkable musical life" of the fictional musician Joseph Berglinger, published in 1799, gives eloquent voice to resonant listening's psychic and physical demands. Whenever the young Berglinger attended concerts, Wackenroder tells us, he sat in a corner and listened with great intensity:

> Not the slightest tone eluded him, and by the end he was quite limp and fatigued from strained attention. His perpetually malleable soul was altogether a play of tones. It was as if his soul had been liberated from his body and was flittering freely around it, or at the same time, as if his body had merged with his soul, so freely and lightly was his entire being embraced by the beautiful harmonies, and the finest bends and inflections of the tones left their impressions on his tender soul.[2]

The listening subject oscillates here between melding with the music and perceiving the "bends and inflections of the tones." In this respect, Wackenroder's prose captures the mixed nature of most listening. Our experience of music, after all, is rarely entirely immediate or entirely detached. It more typically resembles a back-and-forth between what the literary theorist Hans Ulrich Gumbrecht, in a broader context, has more recently called "presence effects" and "meaning effects," the former immediate and non-conceptual, the latter reflective.[3]

These contrasting modes of perception are applicable to all the arts, *mutatis mutandis*, and to all music, but they play a particularly important role in the case of instrumental music, which stands out as the only art form that is at once intangible, ephemeral, and unrelated to language. This makes it far easier for us to "lose" ourselves in it than in any other kind of art. Arts that depend on vision, either wholly or in part, confront us directly with a tangible object of some kind, be it a printed page, a painting, or actors and scenery on a stage or screen. The very possibility of losing oneself in these arts depends on our ability to repress the material presence of whatever it is that transports us out of our daily

THE PLEASURE OF RESONANCE 19

existence. And it is this sense of transport that is a hallmark of the most intense aesthetic experiences. It is nothing short of a cliché to say that the ideal novel is one that makes us forget we are reading a book, or that the ideal drama is one that makes us forget we are watching actors on a stage. Even if we are in the presence of musical performers, we can close our eyes and still experience what we hear just as well, if not better; indeed, a good many listeners claim to hear best with their eyes shut.

The presence of a text does not preclude resonant listening. We always have the option to ignore the words being sung, and if they are in a language we do not understand, it becomes that much easier to listen resonantly, though we are likely to have in the back of our minds the knowledge that the music is in fact "about" something, even if we do not know the details of what that something is. At the other extreme, we can be so familiar with a text that we hear it essentially as a single entity with the music or as an element of lesser aesthetic importance. It is no happenstance that, as texts, the librettos of operas on the whole make for rather dreary reading. Arthur Schopenhauer, for one, pointed to the operas of Rossini as capable of providing access to a higher state of consciousness not because of their texts but in spite of them (more on this in the Epilogue). Moments of transcendence ultimately hinge on the music, as opposed to the meaning of the words being sung, which by themselves would be unlikely to induce a sense of ecstasy. Saint Augustine was famously familiar with this phenomenon and chastised himself for being more attracted to the music of a chanted psalm than its words. The many myths attesting to music's power reflect this same imbalance: Caron and Pluto, as noted earlier, had heard countless pleas for mercy at the gates of the underworld, and it was his music, not the eloquence of Orpheus' verbal plea, that made them yield.[4]

Instrumental music, then, has a ready-made advantage when it comes to the immediacy of sensation, for there is no physical entity to repress and no language to process. Cognition takes a back seat to sensation. Philosophers and critics of the eighteenth century recognized this mode of perception, even if they did not describe it in these particular terms. Johann Georg Sulzer, for example, in his influential encyclopedia of the fine arts published in 1771–74, distinguished cognition (*Erkennen*) from sensation or feeling (*Empfindung*) by noting that "feeling involves our inner state in an unmediated manner, for with every new feeling we are aware of a change within ourselves; cognition is directed toward something we regard as separate from ourselves. In cognition, we are spectators to whatever is happening; in feeling we are ourselves the thing that is in the process of happening, and we do not observe what is happening as something apart from us but rather as something that lies within our capacity to bring it about."[5] The verbs Sulzer uses here and elsewhere in his encyclopedia to describe cognition (*erkennen, fassen, begreifen, wahrnehmen*: to cognize, grasp, comprehend, perceive) were in his time almost never used to describe listening to music, whereas the verb he consistently employs to describe sensation (*empfinden*: to sense, to feel) is the one he and other writers routinely used to describe the act of listening.

Sulzer was one of many Enlightenment writers who emphasized the materially seductive power of music. It is not possible, he maintained, to hear well-constructed dance melodies "without being controlled by the spirit that lies within them; one is compelled, against one's will, to express through gesture and movement that which one feels," for "nature has endowed an altogether unmediated connection between hearing and the heart . . . Hearing is thus by far the sense most capable of arousing the passions."[6]

Resonance—an immediate and intimate connection between the aural and the physical—had long been the pre-eminent explanation of music's power over the soul. According to Pythagorean doctrine, the entire universe, including both music and the human form, consists of manifestations of number: sounding music thus resonated with the human body, causing it to vibrate sympathetically with the motions of air. This line of thought continued in a more or less unbroken line down through the Enlightenment. Hearing itself was long regarded as based on the mechanism of resonance.[7] Resonance permeates Johann Gottfried Herder's many commentaries on the art. "Music plays in us a clavichord that is our own innermost nature." "The 'sensations aroused

THE PLEASURE OF RESONANCE 21

by music do not come from without,' but rather from within us, within us."[8] The ear is the organ "closest to the soul, precisely because it is an *interior* feeling." "The sensuality of music lies buried deep within us: it acts through intoxication."[9]

> So it is with the pleasure of fragrances, and indeed of tones. We draw them into us, we drink the stream of their sensuality with long tongues. And only then, when it melts our heart, when it becomes one with the inner play on the strings of our feelings, do we say that we *savor* music. The stream of pleasurable sound, no matter how fine, is in the meantime *devoured*: it lasts only as long as the harmonic effects and in the pleasurable vibrations it has made on us.[10]

The theory of resonant listening continued to flourish even as reflective listening began to gain prestige in the early decades of the nineteenth century. The critic Friedrich Ludwig Bührlen observed in 1815 that "what music expresses can never appear before us as distant, reduced, cold; it approaches us and compels our psyche to extend itself with it harmoniously. It arouses our feelings, and it works in such a way that we must as it were melt into the object . . . By its nature, music penetrates directly into the soul."[11]

Nor was the idea of aesthetic "melting" an experience limited to music. In his *Elements of Criticism* (1762), the Scottish philosopher Henry Home, Lord Kames, called this phenomenon "ideal presence." In a chapter devoted to "Emotions and Passions," Kames noted that "in contradistinction to real presence, ideal presence may properly be termed *a waking dream*; because, like a dream, it vanisheth the moment we reflect on our present situation."

> Hence the pleasure of a reverie, where a man, losing sight of himself, is totally occupied with the ideas passing in his mind, the objects of which he conceives to be really existing in his presence. The power of language to raise emotions, depends entirely on the raising [of] such lively and distinct images as are here described: the reader's passions are never sensibly moved, till he be thrown into a kind of reverie; in which state, forgetting himself and forgetting that he is reading, he conceives every incident as passing in his presence, precisely as if he were an eye-witness . . . When ideal presence is complete, we perceive every object as in our sight; and

the mind, totally occupied with an interesting event, finds no leisure for reflection of any sort . . . Upon the whole, it is by means of ideal presence that our passions are excited.[12]

Although Kames did not apply ideal presence specifically to music, the transfer is made easily enough: replacing "reader" and "reading" in the passage above with "listener" and "listening." provides a good description of resonant listening.

Ideal presence was, in any case, central to the experience of drama. Save for productions openly billed as farce or parody, a sense of illusion—a willing acceptance of what we now think of as the fourth wall—remained central to the theater. Sulzer, for one, insisted that

in any dramatic performance, viewers must forget that they are seeing something produced through art. Only when they have absolutely no sense of the playwright or of the actor as actor will they enjoy the pleasure of the performance. The moment the slightest thing causes them to consider whether or not the playwright or the actor has remained within the bounds of nature is the moment when they are transported from a setting in nature to a stage created by art, and in the process they are turned from spectators into critics. Every impression the play makes on them is thereby suddenly weakened, for they have been transported from an actual world into an imagined one.[13]

At this point, Sulzer sends readers to his entry on "Natural," in which he observes that works of art "must deceive in order for us to believe that we perceive their reality."[14]

Other writers of the time made a similar case for the importance of aesthetic self-forgetting. Under the rubric of *Phantasie* in his *Theorie der schönen Künste* (1774), the critic Friedrich Just Riedel identified "fantasy"—imagination—as the faculty that leads us in an "idealized manner" into the presence of whatever it is we are beholding. This "mental presence" is a form of "deceit or illusion," in that we forget, when we are deceived, that what we are imagining is nothing more than an imitation or an arbitrary fabrication. "Our fantasy transports us into the scene the artist has portrayed for us."[15] Karl Philipp Moritz, in a widely read essay of 1785, extolled "the *pleasurable forgetting of our self* in the contemplation

THE PLEASURE OF RESONANCE 23

of a beautiful work of art," maintaining that "it is precisely this loss, this forgetting of our self, that is the highest degree of pure and disinterested pleasure afforded us by beauty."[16] And in the inaugural volume of his *Betrachtungen der Mannheimer Tonschule* (1778), the composer and theorist Georg Joseph Vogler gives an extended account of ideal presence in listening. His otherwise sober prose becomes suddenly rhapsodic at this point:

> The power of harmony elevates us to a sphere where we hear the angels singing—we sing with them—there the radiance of the Almighty flows and we are altogether blinded, blinded by the radiance—by the caprice of the mighty harmonist—if the omnipotent creator of tones wills it, we fall, roll, rumble in the abyss, in the depths of the deep—we hear the devils howl, howl with despair—and what is appalling—if we are perhaps not those devils ourselves—is that it was only an illusion, a captivating illusion that robbed us of our powers of understanding simply to think with a full heart, to think feelingly, and rather than think, to feel . . .[17]

All of these accounts, and many others like them, rest on the conception of music first and foremost as an experience and not as a mind-independent object of perception. This distinction helps explain the marked contrast between Enlightenment and nineteenth-century theories about the nature of music. Earlier commentary tends to focus on the experience, sometimes frustratingly so: in the process of waxing rhapsodic about the music they hear, Wackenroder and his collaborator Ludwig Tieck rarely cite specific composers, much less specific works. And for all the attention London critics of the 1790s gave to the twelve symphonies Haydn wrote there, they showed little interest in going to the trouble of identifying *which* particular symphony they were praising. What counted was their reaction to what they heard.

The tendency to think about what Christopher Small called "the presumed autonomous 'thingness' of works of music" has become so deeply ingrained in Western musical thought that it is easy to overlook.[18] It is a manifestation of what Nicholas Cook has dubbed "Plato's curse," the idea of performance as the audible presentation of a notated text, an approach he aptly labels "Page-to-Stage."[19] The work is the realization of an ideal to be cognized and understood. If, on the other hand, we allow the music we hear to resonate within us, we give in to it and would not think to interrogate it. Indeed, the very idea of interrogating the music is utterly foreign to resonant listening, which is altogether an act of the moment, a realization of John Dewey's notion that the "uniquely distinguishing feature" of aesthetic experience is that "no . . . distinction of self and object exists in it," for "the two are so fully integrated that each disappears."[20] Philosophers and critics, as we shall see, have long regarded music as the art with the greatest potential to elicit this kind of response.

The Pleasure Principle

Eighteenth-century critics consistently identified pleasure as the goal of all the arts, including music. "The perfection of the arts," Montesquieu observed in an essay written in the 1750s, "is to present us with those things that provide as much pleasure as possible."[21] Across the Rhine, Sulzer took this same position, declaring the fine arts to be "the most noble implements for the bliss of mankind."[22]

Enlightenment thinkers regarded pleasure, in turn, as one of the chief catalysts of happiness. For John Locke, "every intelligent Being really seeks Happiness, which consists in the enjoyment of Pleasure, without any mixture of uneasiness."[23] And happiness was more than a state of mind: it was a moral and ethical virtue, a noble end in its own right. As the historian Ritchie Robertson points out, "the pursuit of happiness, long before Thomas Jefferson used the phrase in drafting the American Declaration of Independence, was the overriding purpose of enlightened thought and activity."[24] Thomas Kavanaugh has similarly argued that for France, the eighteenth century "was a century of pleasure . . . The period's major figures, novelists and artists, *philosophes* as well as *libertins*, set out to describe, analyze, and systematize the multiplicity of pleasure." Pleasure was "consecrated as a force driving individual action and constituting the essence of existence."[25] Or as the Marquise du Châtelet declared in her *Discours sur le bonheur*, published in 1779,

THE PLEASURE OF RESONANCE 25

"we have nothing more to do in this world than to procure for ourselves pleasurable sensations and sentiments. The moralists who say to human-kind: 'If you want to be happy, suppress your passions and master your desires' do not know the way to happiness."[26]

Not surprisingly, then, Enlightenment philosophers and critics con-sistently identified sensory pleasure as the ultimate basis on which to judge the experience of music. A work of music, the composer and theorist Johann Mattheson declared in 1739, might adhere to all rules and conventions of the art and might even exhibit genius, but if it does not give pleasure, it has failed in its purpose.[27] David Hume, in his *Treatise of Human Nature* (1739–40), similarly maintained that "a good composition of music and a bottle of good wine equally pro-duce pleasure; and what is more, their goodness is determin'd merely by the pleasure."[28] Almost five decades later, Charles Burney was still defining music as "the art of pleasing by the succession and com-bination of agreeable sounds," which meant that "every hearer has a right to give way to his feelings, and be pleased or dissatisfied without knowledge, experience, or the fiat of critics."[29] Mozart himself made music and pleasure virtually synonymous, declaring that "music must never offend the ear, but must please the listener, or, in other words, must never cease to be music."[30] This was not an original idea. Kames, among others, had said as much two decades before: "No disagreeable combination of sounds is entitled to the name of music: for all music is resolvable into melody and harmony, which imply agreeableness in their very conception."[31]

Sulzer's entry on "Music" in his *Allgemeine Theorie der schönen Künste* (1771–74), provides a good summary of late eighteenth-century thought on pleasure as the benchmark of musical quality.

> Music in general affects people not according to how they think, nor through their powers of imagination, but rather by the extent to which they feel. Thus any work of music that does not arouse feeling is not a work of true music . . . The listener, for whom a work of music is made, can in any case decide if a piece is good or bad, even if he understands nothing of the art; but he must have a sensitive heart. If his heart does not

understand it, then he may say unapologetically that the piece does not achieve its goal and is good for nothing. But if his heart feels itself engaged through it, then he can without a second thought declare it as good, for it has achieved its goal.[32]

Some critics of the time, mostly French, insisted that if it was to make any claims to artistic value, instrumental music had to represent something before it could please. Many of Pluches' contemporaries agreed with his comparison of instrumental music to "a fine suit of clothes" without a body. Jean-Baptiste Du Bos's *Réflexions critiques sur la poësie et sur la peinture* (1719) and Charles Batteux's *Les beaux-arts réduits à un même principe* (1746) were particularly influential in propagating the idea that all arts are essentially representational. Batteux maintained that "all music and all dance must have a meaning, a sense," while the encyclopedist Jean Leronde d'Alembert opined that "composers who write instrumental music will produce only trifling noise unless they intend to paint an event or an expression of feeling."[33] This attitude encouraged audiences to listen reflectively, comparing what they heard against what a work through its title claimed to represent.

It is all the more revealing, then, that so many of the most intense arguments in favor of pleasure explicitly refute the aesthetics of mimesis, for the mimetic conception of music, by associating sounds with objects, ideas, or specific passions, compelled listeners to hear in a manner that was inherently reflective. This, as a number of German observers pointed out, vitiated the pleasure of the art. The composer-critic Christian Gottfried Krause, writing in 1752, was quite explicit on this point when in 1752 he contrasted music with the visual arts. The latter, he maintained, oblige us to compare the depicted subject matter with our knowledge of the external world, whereas "music touches us immediately and in this way infinitely surpasses painting . . . When listening to a piece of music, one does not worry about whether or not it imitates some motion in the corporeal world but rather only whether or not it is beautiful, pleases, and moves. Our inner self, our entire soul, wants to partake of it."[34] The composer-critic Johann Adam Hiller made much the same point a few years later:

THE PLEASURE OF RESONANCE

> Music has secret portals to our hearts which we have not yet discovered and which we are not able to defend. There are sentiments that are better felt than expressed . . . One should pay attention to what transpires in the heart while hearing certain music. One is attentive, it pleases. The music seeks to arouse neither sorrow nor joy, neither compassion nor rage, and yet we are moved by it. We are moved by it in a way so unnoticed, so softly, that we do not know what it is that we feel; or to put it in a better way, that we can give no name to that which we feel. This feeling of tones is unknown to us but it awakens delight in us, and for us that is enough. Not everything that is captivating in music can in fact be named or assigned a specific rubric. For this reason, music has certainly fulfilled its duty if it has satisfied only our heart.[35]

Hiller would go on to point out that even Batteux had conceded this last point, quoting him as saying that "the heart . . . has its own way of understanding that does not depend on words; and if it is moved, then it has comprehended everything."[36]

Again around mid-century, the north-German composer Caspar Ruetz ridiculed Batteux's preoccupation with mimesis and listeners' supposed desire to identify the "meaning" of each and every turn of music:

> This is the worst kind of listener one could possibly have, one who wants to have everything explained instead of giving himself over to his feelings. What does this phrase mean? . . . What kind of passion is conveyed in this figure? What does this progression mean? For anyone who cannot or does not want to feel a piece of good music, the meaning of this or that phrase might mean a great deal. Let someone invent ahead of time a language in which one could name each and every feeling and differentiate it from all others.[37]

Ruetz's closing suggestion drips with sarcasm, for it was a commonplace of the time to acknowledge that music could convey emotions that resisted identification through the blunt instrument of language.

The writer known simply as Boyé (probably a pseudonym) agreed. "The principal object of music," he declared in 1779, "is to please us physically, without the mind bothering to take pains to look for pointless comparisons for it. One must regard music absolutely as a pleasure of the senses and not of intelligence."[38] The critic and composer Carl Ludwig Junker, writing in 1786, likewise recognized that any attempt to identify the emotions experienced while listening would inhibit a listener's pleasure in the experience of that work.

> Give yourself over, then, to pure pleasure! Just feel. In moments of pleasure, never parse individual concepts or consider the share that the intellectual powers of your soul partake in delight. Never try to clarify the feelings you perceive into pure, distinct ideas. You must situate yourself in a certain degree of confusion that eliminates the desire to calculate! Leave the business of analysis to philosophers and aestheticians in their study rooms. For this is an eternal truth: a feeling parsed into its individual units ceases to be that feeling, and the delight of pleasure rests on obscure feelings.[39]

Along similar lines, the philosophe Jean-François Marmontel observed in 1787 that while one could reasonably demand a "faithful imitation" of the words in a work of vocal music, instrumental music operated under an entirely different principle, for if it "flatters the ear without suggesting any distinct image or identifiable feeling to the soul . . . that is enough."[40]

Sensory pleasure was not without its problems, however. As a measure of judgment, it made instrumental music vulnerable to the charge of being a "merely" sensuous art on the same level as objects of taste, touch, and smell, and therefore inferior to the representational arts, which by their very nature demanded at least some degree of cognition and reflection. The senses provided a gateway to the mind, to be sure, but if instrumental music could effectively bypass cognition, it could never stand on equal footing with vocal music. Worse still, an exclusive reliance on the senses posed a threat to personal autonomy, for it left the self vulnerable to external forces. Plato had warned repeatedly of music's danger if indulged in to excess, perhaps nowhere more pointedly than in Book 3 of *Republic*, where he cautioned against the "sweet, soft, and plaintive" sounds of the flute (*aulos*), or in other words, instrumental music.

> Therefore, when someone gives music an opportunity to charm his soul with the flute and to pour those sweet, soft, and plaintive tunes we mentioned through his ear, as through a funnel, when he spends his whole life humming them and delighting in them, then, at first, whatever spirit he has is softened, just as iron is tempered, and from being hard and useless it is made useful. But if he keeps at it unrelentingly and is beguiled by the

THE PLEASURE OF RESONANCE 29

music, after a time his spirit is melted and dissolved until it vanishes, and the very sinews of his soul are cut out and he becomes "a feeble warrior."[41]

More than two millennia later, Wilhelm Heinrich Wackenroder was describing the same phenomenon in much the same terms. His fictional musician, Joseph Berglinger, writes this in a letter to a friend:

> Art is a seductive, forbidden fruit. Anyone who has ever tasted its innermost, sweetest juice is irredeemably lost for the active, living world. He crawls ever more constrictedly into his own personal, private pleasure, and his hand loses altogether the power to extend itself in an effective manner toward a fellow human. Art is a deceptive, delusional superstition; we fancy to have in her before us the deepest, innermost humanity, and yet it always foists on us only a beautiful *work* of mankind in which are deposited all the selfish, self-serving thoughts and feelings that in the active world are unfruitful and ineffective. And I, idiot, regard this work as higher than humankind itself, which God has made.[42]

The challenge for Enlightenment critics, then, was to reconcile the pleasure of music with the preservation of personal autonomy. They pursued two different but complementary directions in their efforts. The first was metaphysical. Idealists like Wackenroder, Friedrich Wilhelm Schelling, and Friedrich Schlegel embraced resonant listening as a means of transcendence, a source of metaphysical insight. For them, music's value lay in its ability to disclose a higher realm of being. By this line of thought, listeners were transported not simply to an alternative state but to an altogether higher plane of existence, with the possibility of experiencing at least a faint sense of what E. T. A. Hoffmann, in his 1810 review of Beethoven's Fifth Symphony, would famously call the "wondrous realm of the infinite"[43]

These Idealists valued escape and insight more than pleasure but for this reason could not avoid the charge of *Schwärmerei*, a disparaging term for the kind of metaphysical rapture especially evident in the prose of Wackenroder, the quintessential Idealist. In an essay entitled "The Wonders of Music," Wackenroder praises the art's ability to lift him above and beyond the earthly realm. Whenever oppressed by the "warfare of the world," he closes his eyes and withdraws "quietly" into "the land of music, where we forget all the croaking of humans, where there is no chattering of words and languages, no jumble of letters and monstrous hieroglyphic characters to make us dizzy, but where instead all the anxiousness of our heart is suddenly healed through a gentle touch."

> And how? Are questions answered for us here? Are secrets revealed to us? Ah, no! Rather than all sorts of answers and revelations, we are shown airy, beautiful cloud-forms whose sight calms us, we know not how. With bold certainty we make our way through the unknown land. We greet and embrace as friends strange spirits unknown to us, and all those incomprehensibilities that assail our minds and are the sickness of the human race disappear from our thoughts, and our spirit becomes healthy through the vision of miracles that are yet even more *incomprehensible* and sublime.[44]

This rhapsodic fantasizing represents one means by which to elevate the act of listening beyond sensory pleasure. Art became a religion of sorts in its own right—*Kunstreligion*—but in the end, insight by this path remained accessible only to the faithful.

The second major path toward a reconciliation of pleasure and personal autonomy lay in the pursuit of what we can now recognize as reflective listening, which offered a very different and more musically grounded alternative against the charge of self-destructive hedonism. As we shall see in Chapter 3, it shifted the locus of music's pleasure from the sensory to the intellectual. For if resonant listening encourages sensations of possession and transport, reflective listening encourages precisely the opposite: it distances us from the object of our attention and tempers aroused passions by subjecting them to judgment. And as we shall see in Chapter 2, it was repeated violations of music's fourth wall in the instrumental repertories of the late eighteenth and early nineteenth centuries that began to compel audiences, whether they realized it or not, to listen reflectively.

2

Resonance Subverted

Sterne, for example, speaks repeatedly at length and deliberatively about certain incidents before finally concluding that not a single word of it all has in any case been true. One can sense something similar to the audacity of annihilating humor—an expression of disdain for the world, as it were—in certain music, e.g., Haydn's, which annihilates entire key-areas through one that is foreign, and which storms along between pianissimo and fortissimo, presto and andante.

—Jean Paul (1813)[1]

Music was the last of the arts to openly acknowledge its artificiality. By the end of the eighteenth century, the dramatic, visual, and literary arts could all look back on rich traditions of self-referentiality. Playwrights, after all, had been openly calling their audiences' attention to the craft of drama as early as Greek antiquity. "Old comedy," as the noted classicist Oliver Taplin has observed, "is ubiquitously self-referential."[2] In *The Acharnians*, to cite but one example, Aristophanes has Dikaiopolis, the comedy's central character, go in search of a playwright, anticipating Pirandello by some twenty-five centuries. Ancient drama's very institution of the chorus helped reinforce a certain sense of distance between spectators and the action on the stage.[3] Eighteenth-century German audiences, in turn, seem to have been unable to get enough of the gluttonous and farcical character of Hanswurst ("Jack Sausage"), who consistently subverted whatever degree of theatrical illusion a play's other characters might have created.[4]

Music's Fourth Wall and the Rise of Reflective Listening. Mark Evan Bonds, Oxford University Press.
© Oxford University Press 2025. DOI: 10.1093/9780197806401.003.0003

32   MUSIC'S FOURTH WALL

Painters, for their part, had long cultivated the genre of *trompe l'oeil*, a type of art whose very goal was to be recognized (and admired) as deceptive; such images project an open awareness that they are in fact images.[5] One particularly striking example of the genre is Cornelius Norbertus Gijsbrechts' *Trompe l'oeil: Bagsiden af et indrammet maleri*, an unframed painting depicting the reverse side of a canvas mounted on a stretcher, with painted nails holding the "back" of the "image" in place.[6] Countless other examples have come to be categorized under the rubric of "metapainting," which the art historian Lorenzo Pericolo defines as "the self-staging of painting in painting," in which artists call attention to the inherently fictional nature of the objects they have created.[7]

In the second half of the eighteenth century, it was novelists, however, who employed self-consciously reflective techniques as never before.[8] This was in large measure a reaction against what one historian of emotions has called the era's "cult of emotional authenticity."[9] Critics of the time—and to judge by sales, the reading public as well—placed value on any work of art that could elicit an emotional response, and the more extreme that response, the better. Three epistolary novels exemplify this phenomenon: Samuel Richardson's *Pamela* (1740), Jean Jacques Rousseau's *Julie; ou La nouvelle Heloïse* (1761), and Johann Wolfgang Goethe's *Die Leiden des jungen Werthers* (1774). Richardson's novel spawned countless imitators (and parodies), while *Julie* unleashed what the historian Robert Darnton has called an "epidemic of emotion," all the more surprisingly, as Darnton points out, in that it came in response to "six volumes of sentiment unrelieved by any episodes of violence, explicit sex, or anything much in the way of plot."[10] Goethe's novel, in turn, evoked personal responses so powerful that it acquired a reputation for encouraging suicide in the wake of unhappy love affairs.

It was this blurring of boundaries between real and fictional worlds that encouraged a new counter-reaction of literary and dramatic reflectivity. The extreme emphasis on the immediacy of feeling all but

RESONANCE SUBVERTED

invited a response in the form of novels that did not take themselves quite so seriously, at least on the surface. No one carried out this program more brilliantly than Laurence Sterne, first in *The Life and Opinions of Tristram Shandy, Gentleman* (1759–67) and then in an entirely different manner in *A Sentimental Journey through France and Italy* (1768). Like so many books of its time, *Tristram Shandy* has its marbled end-pages, dedication, and preface, but unlike any other, these are scattered throughout the body of the text. Two consecutive chapters each consist of nothing more than a blank page, and Sterne elsewhere offers yet another blank page upon which readers are invited to draw their own illustration of one of the work's characters. Ostensibly the memoirs of a fictional character (Tristram Shandy), the author (Laurence Sterne) is never very distant. It is impossible to lose oneself in this book because it constantly reminds us that we are reading a book.[11]

A Sentimental Journey, in turn, was widely hailed as *the* sentimental novel of its day, even as a growing number of critics came to recognize it as a parody of that genre. In one of many episodes, Parson Yorick, the narrator of the tale, congratulates himself on his sensitivity to his surroundings yet becomes so engrossed in the moment that he loses all sight of what lies just beyond it. In a lengthy inner dialogue, he resolves to carry out charitable acts while on his journey but is interrupted by a mendicant monk to whom he refuses to give a single *sou*. Yorick proceeds to justify his niggardly response with yet another inner dialogue that utterly contradicts his thoughts of only a moment before. In this novel's world of extreme self-awareness, everything else—logic, continuity, and consistency—takes a backseat to the overwhelming sentiment of the moment. We, as readers, recognize the comedy of the actions even if the novel's narrator does not.

Music's turn to self-reflectivity, then, while long in coming, was very much a product of its time, part of a broader series of reactions against the extreme emotionalism of what has since come to be called the Age of Sensibility.[12]

The Framework of Oratory

The subversion of resonant listening is ultimately a subversion of oratory, the conceptual framework that had for so long governed both the production and reception of music. The goal of the orator or composer is to move listeners in a desired direction. For an orator or composer to remind those listeners that they are being manipulated runs counter to that goal. The long-assumed parallel between music and oratory helps explain why composers were for so long reluctant to call attention to the artificiality of their art. Self-reflective music undermines the art's very purpose: to move listeners' emotions.

Rhetoric is the still broader overarching concept here. It consists of two types: primary rhetoric is the art of oral persuasion as exemplified by oratory, while secondary rhetoric is the arsenal of techniques in which the act of speech cedes priority to the text.[13] The parallel between primary rhetoric and vocal music is particularly close: both move through time and through the vehicle of language, and both are able to fulfill the three principal obligations of orators toward their listeners: to educate (*docere*), delight (*delectare*), and move (*movere*). Composers, as the seventeenth-century French polymath Marin Mersenne observed, were in effect "harmonic orators," for it was their duty to consider the design and intention of the text to be sung so that in performance the words would have "at least as much power over listeners as if it were recited by an excellent orator."[14]

Without words, instrumental music could not educate, but it could certainly delight and move, and by the middle third of the eighteenth century, commentators were routinely applying the principles of oratory to explain its power. Theorists of the time appropriated the principles, vocabulary, conventions, and strategies of primary rhetoric to music to rationalize an otherwise abstract art. The image of untexted music as a language in its own right, the "language of the heart," proved irresistible. Even without words, instrumental music could boast its own grammar and syntax: melodies were said to consist of antecedent and consequent phrases organized into larger sentences ("periods") and paragraphs. Movement-length structures began with a theme or subject (two more terms drawn from rhetoric) and developed it in a manner that was coherent and intelligible to listeners. Compositional treatises urged composers to provide sufficient variety within an overall structure of unity through skillful combinations of repetition and variation, and through contrasting themes, tonalities, and timbres. Some critics of the time developed a theory of so-called "figures" analogous to those of oratory; like all other elements of music, these figures served as means to the end of moving listeners emotionally.[15]

Oratory entailed a corresponding set of assumptions for listeners. Anyone listening to a speech considered it self-evident that the burden of persuasion rested entirely on those who created and delivered a text. The premise was really quite simple: an orator who failed to delight and move an audience was, by definition, a bad orator; composers and performers were judged by the same standard. Listeners, in other words, perceived no need to prepare themselves in any way for the experience of what they were about to hear, be it a speech or a musical performance, for they did not consider listening a skill. The idea that they might be expected to possess prior knowledge of some kind in order to be delighted or moved by what they were about to hear would have struck them as absurd. "What would one think," the Abbé Dubos asked (rhetorically) in his *Réflexions critiques* of 1719, "of a musician who maintained that those who know nothing of music are incapable of deciding if the minuet he has composed pleases them or not? When an orator makes his listeners yawn and fall asleep, is it not agreed that he has made a bad speech, even without asking the listeners his discourse has tossed aside whether or not they have an understanding of rhetoric?"[16]

Indeed, one of the long-standing principles of rhetoric was the imperative to appeal to as broad an audience as necessary. Quintilian, for example, urged orators to speak in a way that would "be approved by the learned and clear to the uneducated."[17] Writers on music embraced this principle with ease. In his epochal treatise on counterpoint, *Gradus ad Parnassum* (1725), the Austrian composer Johann Joseph Fux quoted

Cicero's *Rhetorica ad Herennium* on this point: "Laymen, reading good orations and poems, approve the orators and poets, but without comprehending what has called forth their approval, because they cannot know where that which especially delights them resides, or what it is, or how it was produced."[18] Fux added to this his own opinion that a composition in good taste is one that "avoids the common or extravagant, incorporates the sublime even while proceeding in a natural manner, and is also capable of giving pleasure to those who understand the art of music."[19] The "also" (*etiam*) in the closing phrase is telling: music must in the first instance be pleasing to those who are *not* in a position to grasp its inner workings. The composer Johann Joachim Quantz put the matter this way in 1752:

> Reason teaches us that if in ordinary speech one demands something from someone else that we must make use of such expressions as are understood by the other person. Now, music is nothing other than an artificial language by which one should make one's musical ideas known to the listener. If one did this in a dark or bizarre manner which would be incomprehensible to the listener and convey no sentiment, of what use would be the toil one had made for so long in order to be regarded as learned? If one were to demand that listeners consist entirely of connoisseurs and learned musicians, the number of listeners would not be very large. One would have to look for them only among professional musicians, and among those, only a few at that.[20]

Johann Adam Hiller made much the same point a few years later. If an instrumental work's melody "artfully expresses the sentiments of the heart," it will "infallibly attract the applause of all listeners, including those who understand the art as well as those who do not."[21] A Parisian review of a collection of works for harp by Johann Baptist Hochbrucker similarly observed that "this music has the double merit of pleasing true connoisseurs as well as those who judge only by sentiment."[22]

It was within this tradition that Leopold Mozart famously urged his son to think about writing for the "unmusical public" as well as the musically learned. "You know that there are a hundred ignoramuses for every ten true connoisseurs," he wrote in 1780, "so do not forget the so-called popular, which tickles the long-eared as well."[23] Wolfgang

RESONANCE SUBVERTED

assured his father a few years later that the new concertos he had composed (K. 413, 414, and 415) were "precisely halfway between being too difficult and too easy. They are quite brilliant and fall into the ears in a pleasing manner, though of course without falling into emptiness. Here and there connoisseurs alone will be satisfied, yet in such a way that even amateurs would have to be pleased without knowing why."[24] Without invoking the categories themselves, Mozart here in effect identifies the difference between reflective and resonant listening.

The conceptual model of music as a form of oratory also meant that listeners expected to be able to judge a speech or musical performance on a single hearing. Listening, in other words, was a one-and-done affair. Unlike the visual arts or the printed word, speech and music were transitory and ephemeral. Hence the presence of a violin or some other musical instrument in so many *memento mori* paintings: sound, like life, is fleeting. Without a physical focus of attention—a painted canvas or a printed page—an oration or musical performance had to make its impact immediately and decisively. If on first hearing that performance did not succeed—which is to say, did not delight and move its audience—then the fault lay with the composer, the performers, or both, but not with listeners. The very idea of giving composers the benefit of the doubt and withholding judgment until there had been an opportunity for subsequent hearings was all but unknown in the eighteenth century. It did not begin to surface until the early nineteenth, and even then only sporadically, as we shall see below.

To what extent did eighteenth-century audiences actually listen to musical performances? The available evidence suggests that concert audiences of the time typically consisted of a mix of attentive and inattentive listeners, and in this respect they were no different from audiences of today.[25] There is not much to say in the present context about those who attended musical gatherings strictly for social purposes or against their will, and who paid no attention to the music being performed. But others seem to have been willing to engage and remain engaged with what they were hearing if it seemed to hold out the possibility of rewarding their attention. Even Fontenelle, after all, had been trying to follow what he was listening to before making his celebrated outburst ("Sonata, what do you want of me?"). Had he not been attending to the music, it would not have annoyed him.

The unnamed composer of the sonata that sparked Fontenelle's outrage had, at any rate, violated one of the cardinal rules of oratory: to hold the attention of listeners by avoiding the extreme of tedium, on the one hand, and incomprehensibility on the other. Composers had to walk a fine line here, for listeners' minds could wander if the music was too predictable, and they could wander just as easily if it was too unpredictable and for that reason too difficult to follow. "The greatest secret of eloquence," the priest and orator Bernard Lamy declared in his *La rhétorique ou l'art de parler*, a treatise that went through some twenty editions after its first publication in 1675, "is to maintain the attentiveness of listeners' minds and prevent them from losing sight of the goal to which they must be led."[26] Orators since the age of antiquity had repeatedly emphasized the importance of this balancing act, and it remained a fixture of subsequent how-to books aimed at orators and composers alike. On the one hand, a speech that included no striking turns of phrase or surprises might easily cause listeners to lose interest in what they were hearing because it was not unusual enough. As Aristotle had argued in his *Rhetoric*, "clearness is secured by using the words (nouns and verbs alike) that are current and ordinary," but "variation from what is usual makes the language appear more stately . . . It is therefore well to give to everyday speech an unfamiliar air: people like what strikes them, and are struck by what is out of the way."[27] Quintilian likewise observed that while obscurity was to be avoided, an excess of clarity could be banal and insulting to listeners.[28] And in his widely read *Anfangsgründe aller schönen Wissenschaften* (1748–50), Georg Friedrich Meier pointed out that the unexpected encouraged attention in all the arts, whereas an absence of the unexpected caused the mind to wander. "Anyone who wants to think beautifully must take pains to ensure that readers or listeners encounter something new in those beautiful thoughts. Should we read a poem and sense that there is nothing new in it, then we will set our reading aside."[29]

Advice along these lines permeates compositional manuals of the eighteenth century. Mattheson, in his *Der vollkommene Capellmeister* of 1739, recommended "pleasing" and "artful" surprises in a melodic line, provided they did not disrupt the coherence of the whole. Heinrich Christoph Koch, much later in the century, advocated a similarly careful combination of the expected and unexpected.[30]

Bad playing was another source of potential distraction and could include even the visual aspects of performance. "For how can an attentive listener be moved to pleasure," Mattheson asked, "if that person is constantly irritated by a noise" made by someone who is "beating time, either with their feet or arms? If that listener sees a dozen violinists who make bodily contortions as if they were suffering from a malevolent illness? If the keyboard player contorts his mouth, moves the forehead up and down and distorts his visage in a way that would frighten children?"[31] Opinions differed on this point, however: when Burney witnessed C. P. E. Bach's fantasizing at the keyboard, he clearly felt that Bach's physical gestures enhanced the emotional power of the whole.[32] Then as now, it would seem, listeners are divided on the merits of performers giving "voice" through physical as well as audible expression.

Virtuosity was another potential cause of distraction, though here again, opinion was divided. Some critics found it empty and mechanical, while others regarded it as the source of a different kind of pleasure. Given its prominence in certain genres (most notably operas and concertos), virtuosity clearly had its proponents. As Mattheson acknowledged, "awe at an unusual degree of proficiency is also a way of moving the emotions."[33] Excessive virtuosity nevertheless remained suspect in many quarters. The Scottish philosopher James Beattie asked if "flourished cadences, whether by a voice or instrument, serve any other purpose, than to take off our attention from the subject, and set us a staring at the flexibility of the performer's voice, the swiftness of his fingers, or the sound of his fiddle? And if this be their only use, do they not counteract, instead of promoting, the chief end of music?"[34] The "chief end of music" was to move the passions, and in this sense, virtuosity operated outside the framework of rhetoric. By calling attention to their art, virtuosos necessarily inhibited listeners' ability to "lose" themselves in the music, for as Annette Richards has observed, "the virtuoso, like the narrator, flirts with the undoing of aesthetic illusion."[35]

Orators and artists of all kinds were in fact repeatedly urged to avoid calling attention to the technical means they used to move their audiences. This, too, was standard advice from antiquity onward. Quintilian had maintained that "everything" in an oration "must seem to spring from the case itself rather than the art of the orator. But our modern orators cannot endure this and imagine that their art is wasted unless it obtrudes itself, whereas as a matter of fact the moment it is detected it ceases to be art."[36] Meier, in his *Anfangsgründe aller schönen Wissenschaften*, encouraged artists to "avoid everything that might divert attention from the thing itself," particularly the "contemplation of the signs and images in which the object is clad."[37] Sulzer similarly observed that an object has "aesthetic power" only to the extent that it "is capable of diverting our attention from its nature"—its *Beschaffenheit*, its mechanical constitution—and directs our notice "to the effect the object makes on us, particularly our inner state."[38] If applied to music, this amounts to a prescription for composing in a manner that would preclude an awareness of the composer's or performer's agency, which is to say, in a manner that encourages resonant listening.

Ars est celare artem goes the age-old dictum, variously attributed to Ovid, Quintilian, and Longinus: art is the concealment of art, or as it might also be read, there is art to concealing art.[39] "To avoid all display or art," as Quintilian put it, "in itself requires consummate art: this admirable canon has been insisted on by all writers."[40] The best actors, after all, are commonly thought to be those who make us forget they are acting, and the same might be said of musicians who can make us forget they are performing or—more to the point here—composers who can make us forget they have crafted the music we are hearing. Naturalness was a touchstone of all the arts, including music. For the composer-theorist Joseph Riepel, "art should be concealed, in order that nature maintain the upper hand at all times."[41]

This perspective helps explain the repeated aspersions Enlightenment critics so frequently cast upon counterpoint, the compositional equivalent of virtuosity. In an era that espoused "naturalness" in art, counterpoint proved especially problematic for listeners. Connoisseurs might delight in it, but lay listeners, for the most part, apparently did not. Quantz, for example, urged composers to avoid pedantry on the grounds that listeners should perceive "nature shining forth everywhere" as opposed to "meticulous industriousness."[42] Sulzer maintained along the same lines that while connoisseurs might welcome the artfulness of a strict fugue in a chamber music trio, this kind of writing produced no effect on "the amateur of feeling" because it did not convey anything that would lead to "great feelings." As a genre, then, the chamber trio "requires of the composer the ability to hide art behind expression."[43] An anonymous Parisian critic, responding in 1778 to an unidentified symphony by Mozart (probably the Symphony in D Major, K. 297/300a), praised the richness of ideas and motifs in the first two movements and noted that "the science of counterpoint shined forth" in the finale and "won the approval of amateurs" in spite of this being "the kind of music that can engage the mind without ever touching the heart."[44]

These and other similar injunctions are consistent with the means by which to both evoke and liquidate what Kames, as we have seen, called "ideal presence" in art. One means of disrupting a reader's "waking dream," as Kames argued, was an "improbable incident" that disturbed by virtue of its improbability. Temporal interruptions could also break the spell: something as simple as a change of scenery on the stage, even if "done in a trice," could cause spectators to be reminded that what they are seeing is "imaginary, and that the whole is a fiction."[45] Later in the century, the Scottish essayist Archibald Alison lauded those works in which "the hand of the artist disappears, and the embellishments of his fancy press themselves upon our belief . . . We immediately pronounce that the composition is perfect, we acknowledge that he has attained the end of his art; and in yielding ourselves up to the emotion which his composition demands, we afford him the most convincing mark of our applause."[46]

The key point here is the beholder's willing immersion in the aesthetic experience. Under optimal circumstances, this meant a lack of awareness of the hand behind the art. As Gotthold Ephraim Lessing put it in 1767:

> And how weak must be the impression made by the work if in that very moment [of beholding it] one is more eager than anything else to raise an objection against the figure of the author? The true masterpiece, it seems to me, fills us with itself so entirely that we forget about its creator and perceive it not as the product of a particular individual, but rather of nature as a whole. . . . If one is so curious about the artist, then the illusion must be very weak, one must sense little that is natural and yet be all the more aware of artificiality.[47]

Such assertions make contemporaneous transgressions of music's fourth wall all the more remarkable, for they violate one of the core principles of primary rhetoric in that they compel listeners to reflect on the agency of the composer, thereby engaging their minds at the expense of their hearts.

Breaking the Fourth Wall

The threshold of what might draw attention to the hand of the composer will necessarily vary from listener to listener. The violations of music's fourth wall to be discussed in what follows are limited to obvious moments of rupture, instances that could plausibly have been perceived as particularly striking to lay listeners of the eighteenth century, as opposed to professional musicians. More subtle techniques admired by *cognoscenti*—monothematic expositions, false recapitulations, invertible counterpoint, unusually chromatic harmonies, and the like—are not to be confused with moments that require little more than attentiveness as opposed to technical knowledge of the art of music.

The focus of what follows here will be the music of Joseph Haydn, the most celebrated composer of instrumental music of his time. He was also, as Daniel Chua rightly observes, the first composer "to glory in the sheer artificiality of instrumental music."[48] Haydn was by no means the only composer of his time to break music's fourth wall, yet he did so with far greater frequency and intensity than anyone else. And a good number of his contemporaries, as we shall see, recognized this tendency and did not always welcome it.

Context is vital. The overwhelming majority of Haydn's instrumental music operates within the framework of primary rhetoric, which is to say, within a framework that allows us to be persuaded and to lose ourselves, if we so choose, in the experience of listening. Moments that remind us of the artificiality of what we are hearing achieve their effect precisely because they are infrequent enough to stand out as different in kind. Yet they are also common enough, at least in Haydn's output, to have helped encourage a gradual shift from resonant to reflective listening among lay listeners in general.

Almost all of the examples that follow here have been interpreted by other writers, often quite insightfully, as instances of musical humor, which indeed they are.[49] But humor, as noted earlier, has consequences that go far beyond laughter. By its very nature, humor encourages us to consider things from a distance. Puns, for example, highlight the utterly arbitrary nature of language by calling attention to just how distant two homonyms can be in their meanings. The ending of Haydn's String Quartet op. 33, no. 2, as more than one critic has pointed out, amounts to something like a musical pun: the finale's opening phrase also serves as its closing phrase, exposing two very different syntactic functions. Passages like this tend to draw attention away from music as an experience and toward music as an object. Indeed, the "joke" itself has been dissected and explained so often that it would be possible to write a small book surveying the various ways in which the music creates this effect.[50]

The finale of the "Joke" Quartet is an admittedly extreme but by no means isolated example of a work that makes us aware of music's inherently artificial nature. For present purposes, the broader and more important point is that this finale is music about music, music that steps outside of itself and foregrounds the signs of its own production. In so doing, it diverts our attention away from its effect on us and toward its structure as an artifice: it compels us to listen reflectively.

Similar "false endings" occur in the finale of the String Quartet in B♭, op. 50, no. 1 (1787, m. 222), in the first movement of the String Quartet in E♭, op. 50, no. 3 (m. 111), and in the finale of the Symphony no. 90 in C Major (1788), where there is a rest of four-and-a-half measures after the clear and decisive cadential figure that ends on the downbeat of m. 167. In Sir Simon Rattle's live recording of the symphony with the Berlin Philharmonic at the Philharmonie in February 2007, the audience bursts into applause shortly after m. 167 and chuckles when it realizes its mistake the moment the music resumes. Granted, Rattle's decision to broaden the tempo moving into the cadence at m. 167 amounts to a form of musical entrapment. This false ending is nevertheless so seductive that on the repeat of the finale's second reprise, applause erupts once again after the same cadence, only to be cut off when the music resumes. By this point, listeners cannot help but realize that they have been manipulated.[51]

Examples like these illustrate the paradox that silence—the absence of sound—is a highly effective means by which composers can assert their presence in the minds of listeners. Almost every piece of music has its rests and pauses, but these typically appear at moments of demarcation between phrases of a melody or between sections of a larger movement or work, or at the conclusion of the whole; as such, they help us recognize the articulation of musical units both large and small. They serve much the same function as commas, periods, and paragraphs in a written text. But when musical silences last longer than might be expected within a particular context, or when they occur at moments when they normally would not, they draw attention to the construction of the music: any emotional response we might be experiencing at that moment is effectively interrupted by these interruptions of silence.[52] Rather than losing ourselves in the flow of the music, we are reminded of the structure of things and the hand of the unseen composer. The music has broken through the imaginary fourth wall.

Even relatively brief silences can be disorienting if they appear unexpectedly. The finale of Haydn's Keyboard Sonata in C Major, Hob. XVI:50 (ca. 1794) is full of such moments. The music comes to a screeching halt on a dissonance early on (m. 10), followed by a rest marked with a fermata. Where are we? Why has the music stopped so soon after it has just started? Even listeners with only a modest familiarity with the idiom will likely find the moment odd. It is almost as if the composer himself is not sure where the music is going. The net effect is to remind us that it is he who is ultimately in control of what we hear: the performer, after all, is playing from a score or the memory of a score. And if we should imagine that the performer is, in fact, improvising, this would have the effect of sounding like a failure to launch, which in turn would similarly call attention to the mechanics of the entire enterprise.

A similar moment of unexpected silence occurs in the first reprise of the third-movement scherzo of the String Quartet in G Major, op. 33, no. 5 (1782). Here, the forward momentum of the music is clearly (and conventionally) driving toward a cadence, but everything suddenly breaks off with a full measure of silence (m. 8) precisely at the moment when we would expect a cadence on the tonic. Instead, we get nothing. The resulting dominant-tonic resolution (m. 9–10) contrasts dynamically as well: what we would have reasonably expected to end loudly instead ends softly.

Large-scale formal anomalies abound in Haydn's instrumental music, but some are so obvious they cannot help but create a distancing effect on listeners. The Symphony no. 60 in C Major (1774), known as "Il distratto" because it employs the incidental music Haydn had written for a German-language production of Jean-François Regnard's comedy *Le Distrait*, is full of strange moments. With or without knowledge of the play, listeners would have been struck by any number of highly unusual turns in the music: after a portentous (and conventional) slow introduction, the exposition begins with an energetic theme that moves to the expected dominant but then seems to lose its train of thought: the players keep repeating the same note over and over, ever more slowly, before finally pulling themselves together to get things back on track. The depiction of distraction is itself distracting. In the presto fourth movement, the development begins (at m. 61) with wholly unrelated thematic material: the folk tune known as "The Night-Watchman's Song." This would have raised any number of questions in listeners' minds regardless of their familiarity with the tune, for in terms of its musical character, this theme is completely out of joint with anything heard up to this point in the movement. Listeners would have had similar questions about the allusion to the plainchant "Lamentations of Jeremiah" (beginning at m. 13), interrupted by an enormously loud and unexpected fanfare (m. 29) that gives way, just as unexpectedly, to a return of the movement's opening theme. And any listener who, in spite of all this, might somehow have been lulled into the flow of this serene sound will be jolted by the comically repeated figure that keeps getting faster and faster to close out the movement. Haydn saves the biggest disruption of all for the sixth-movement finale, whose presto opening comes to an early halt (m. 16) with silence and then twelve measures of the first and second violins retuning their instruments. Haydn even goes so far as to write the pitch F below middle C—a pitch not otherwise available on a normally tuned instrument—to create yet another layer of dissonance. The "Night-Watchman's Song" returns unexpectedly (m. 61). Or can anything in this symphony truly be called unexpected?[53]

Not everyone in Haydn's time took delight in such wit. Like many of his contemporaries, the composer and theorist Heinrich Christoph Koch deplored the mixture of the serious and comic in music, and in his *Versuch einer Anleitung zur Composition*, the most comprehensive compositional treatise of its day, he took Haydn and "Il distratto" to task without citing either by name. The reasoning behind Koch's objections is striking. "Characteristic" music—roughly comparable to what would later come to be known as program music—is not a vehicle for sentiment (*Empfindung*) but rather a "plaything for understanding" (*Spielwerk für den Verstand*). This is "inimical" (*schädlich*") to the "one sole purpose" of the art of music. Koch urges aspiring composers to remember that their "exclusive goal" should be "to delight your listeners through beautiful sentiments alone."[54] The problem with a symphony like "Il distratto," as he sees it, is that the emotional engagement of listeners is compromised by their simultaneous need to understand the motivations behind the many bizarre turns in what they are hearing. "Instead of affecting the

RESONANCE SUBVERTED   47

heart through art, one tries to occupy the listener's understanding with wit."[55] Reflection compromises resonance.

Haydn flouts convention more radically still in the Symphony no. 45 in F♯ minor ("Farewell," 1772), in which the musicians famously fall silent section by section over the course of the finale, leaving only two violinists at the end. The motivations behind this bizarre finale remain contested: many stories were circulating even in Haydn's day, but the music seems intended to have carried a message of some kind, which is to say, to be perceived reflectively. For whatever reason, Haydn wanted his original audience—Prince Nicholas Esterházy, for all practical purposes—to understand (or at the very least to wonder) why the music unfolds in the way it does. In an apparent preview of oddities-to-come, the first movement violates music's fourth wall when the otherwise stormy development section is interrupted by a lyrical and decidedly lightweight interlude in D Major (m. 108–40) that is thematically unrelated to anything we have heard before. It never returns.[56]

The finale of the Symphony no. 46 in B Major (1772) features its own head-scratching moment when the beginning of the third-movement minuet returns without warning and more or less intact at m. 153. The change could scarcely be more abrupt or unexpected: quite aside from the unusual recall of material from an earlier movement, the tempo shifts from presto to allegretto and the meter from duple to triple. But in the end, after a long moment of silence, the music returns to the finale's opening idea to close things out. It is as if the recall of the minuet—all thirty-four measures of it—had never happened.[57] Again, the attentive listener would almost certainly wonder what this unusual interpolation might signify. That remains a mystery, but by suggesting a mystery of any kind, the composer has all but forced us to listen reflectively.

Comparable formal anomalies confront us in many other works as well. The finale of the String Quartet in C Major, op. 54, no. 2 (1788), opens with what would appear to be a slow introduction: unusual in a finale but not in itself attention-grabbing. But the slow tempo goes on far too long for it to be merely an introduction. The music finally turns fast (presto) at m. 56, only to return to the original adagio tempo at m.

123.[58] The finale of the Symphony no. 67 in F Major (1778), by contrast, opens conventionally enough in a fast tempo (Allegro di molto) and follows the standard pattern of a sonata-form exposition, only to shift to a slow tempo (Adagio e cantabile) with new thematic material and a wholly new sonority quite unusual within a symphony: the first twenty-four measures of this new section are given to two solo violins and a solo cello; winds and the other strings eventually join in, but the thematic and timbral contrast with the finale's opening could scarcely be greater. Finally, at m. 146, the movement's original theme returns at the beginning of what turns out to be a recapitulation. Again, the divergence from the structural norm is so extreme that the music draws attention to itself as an artificial construct.

The lyrical theme-and-variations second movement of the Symphony no. 79 in F Major (1783/84) holds comparable surprises. Just when the movement seems to be coming to a close, the music suddenly speeds up (un poco allegro) with an entirely new theme of a very different and lively character. This new theme gets its own series of variations, and the original theme never returns. It is as if we have been given two movements in one.

The Symphony no. 98 in B♭ Major (1792) includes two prominent moments that would have called the attention of its original London audience to the hand of the composer. The slow movement begins with a near-quotation of the opening to "God Save the King." How many listeners on first hearing would have begun to rise out of their seats around m. m. 4? And sat down in embarrassment soon thereafter? In the finale's coda (beginning at m. 365), Haydn wrote out an elaborate accompanimental passage for solo keyboard ("cembalo"), which he presumably would have performed himself, calling visible attention to his agency as composer.

Unexpected changes in dynamics can also wake us out of any dreams a work of music might have induced. The drum stroke early in the slow movement of the Symphony no. 94 in G Major ("Surprise," 1791) is the best-known example. After a rhythmically and harmonically conventional—indeed overly conventional—eight-measure statement

RESONANCE SUBVERTED 49

in the strings alone, marked *piano*, Haydn repeats the same phrase, this time *pianissimo* and with pizzicato accompaniment. But then he drops the hammer on the final beat of this second statement, with a *fortissimo* sudden chord from the entire orchestra, including the timpani. Haydn himself acknowledged that with this stroke, he wanted to make an effect, and there can be no question of his success. Albert Christoph Dies, one of the composer's early biographers, was not present at the premiere, but the veracity of his second- if not third-hand account of the event is, for present purposes, less important than the assumptions it reflects. This sudden "thunder" of sound, Dies tells us, "startled those who were asleep; everyone was wide awake and looked at each other with perturbed and astonished expressions." One "sensitive young woman" was so overwhelmed by the surprising effect of the music that she fainted and had to be taken outside into the fresh air. Some of those present used the incident as grounds for reproaching Haydn, saying that up until this point, he had "always surprised in a gallant manner, but this time he was too coarse."[59] What is significant in this account and many others from Haydn's time about this moment in the "Surprise" Symphony is that the emphasis is on shock and not on humor.[60]

Sudden contrasts between soft and loud also feature prominently in the Adagio cantabile of the Symphony no. 68 in B♭ (ca. 1778). An unobtrusive repeated two-note bass figure of sixteenth notes accompanies the lyrical melody, rather like the better-known accompanimental figure of the "Clock" Symphony's slow movement (Symphony no. 101). But between phrases of the earlier work's melody, this two-note figure, exposed on its own, erupts from time to time into *forte* for just a single beat before immediately resuming its previous quiet progression. The contrast between the grace of the melody and the accompanimental figure's unpredictable alternation of lightness and cloddishness is striking. A similar dynamic outburst in a repeated accompanimental figure occurs in the second movement of the Symphony no. 83 in G minor ("La Poule," 1785, m. 57, 59, etc.).

The Largo cantabile second movement of the Symphony no. 93 in D Major (1791) makes similar use of dynamic contrasts, alternating between a quiet, lyrical theme in the strings and loud trumpet-and-drum outbursts from the orchestra. But the momentum eventually begins to flag, and the harmonic rhythm becomes slower and slower, signaling the approaching end of the movement. The inevitable closing cadence is over-prepared and repeatedly delayed: everything slows to a crawl, and time seems suspended. But anyone who has lost themselves in this dream-like music will be rudely awakened by the bassoons' low *fortissimo* blast in m. 80, the sound of which commentators have since repeatedly likened to a fart.[61]

Instrumental recitative is another device which, by its very nature, provokes reflective listening, for it raises the question in listeners' minds about exactly what the instruments are trying to "say." Such a passage occurs in the G-minor third movement of the String Quartet in G Major, op. 17, no. 5 (1771), in which the first violin assumes the persona of a tragic heroine, at times in dialogue with the other instruments but always controlling the pace through a series of carefully placed fermatas.[62]

The unmediated juxtaposition of starkly contrasting and seemingly incongruous thematic ideas also has a tendency to draw attention toward the structure of a thing as opposed to its effect. One example that can serve in place of many occurs in the first movement of the Symphony no. 80 in D minor (1783/84). The opening is stormy and rhythmically turbulent, and the driving energy of the music continues even after the conventional modulation to F Major. But then, after the music has cadenced in the new key of F major at m. 57—a point at which one would expect a return to the beginning of the exposition, in D minor— everything changes. We hear a Ländler-like theme with pizzicato accompaniment, a theme recent scholars have variously described as a melody of "waltz-like frivolity," a "cheap tune," and most tellingly of all, a "little oompah dance."[63] The contrast with everything that has come before is all the more striking because the harmonic rhythm has suddenly slowed from every beat to only once each measure, creating the impression of a tempo change even though there is none: the headlong momentum of the music has suddenly disappeared. The brevity of the new theme—a mere eight measures—also surprises. It is as if the eight-measure tag-end of a completely different theme had wandered in from some altogether different movement. Nor do the surprises stop there: after two full measures of silence—what happens next?—this tag-end of a theme picks up again in the unlikely key of D♭, the flat submediant of F Major. Even listeners without knowledge of harmony or the conventions of sonata form are likely to be struck by the extreme contrasts of themes, moods, and keys.

Quasi-improvisatory elements—the speeding up and slowing down of the music's pace, the fragmentation of melodic ideas, unusual repetitions—can also create the sense of a composer having "lost the thread" of a thematic argument. As James Webster says of the second movement of the Piano Trio in E♭, Hob. XV:29 (ca. 1795–97), "it is as if we could 'overhear' Haydn, the performing composer, in the act of changing his mind and steering the Andantino in an unforeseen direction," noting that in passages like this, "the composer, who is usually at most a latent or potential presence, moves into the foreground of consciousness."[64]

We need not imagine that these moments and many others like them created a sense of distance between Haydn's listeners and his music, for his contemporaries provided ample witness to precisely this reaction.[65] Charles Burney noted in 1789 that Haydn's "compositions are in general so new to the player and hearer, that they are equally unable, at first, to keep pace with his inspiration . . . The first exclamation of an embarrassed performer and a bewildered hearer is, that the Music is very *odd*, or very *comical*; but the queerness and comicality cease, when, by frequent repetition, the performer and hearer are at their ease."[66] Burney recognized Haydn's contrasting approaches to his art when he summed up the composer's instrumental output in this way:

> Haydn's allegros . . . exhilarate every hearer. But his adagios are often so sublime in ideas and the harmony in which they are clad, that though played by inarticulate instruments, they have a more pathetic effect on my feelings, than the finest opera air united with the most exquisite poetry. He has likewise movements that are sportive, *folatres*, and even grotesque,

for the sake of variety; but they are only the *entre-mets*, or rather *inter-mezzi*, between the serious business of his other movements.[67]

The "serious business" of music was, of course, the principal goal of every composer of the time: to move the passions of listeners. But some of Haydn's movements, as Burney recognized, run counter to this goal: they are playful moments that serve as "intermezzos" between music's main courses. Why, then, the mixture of serious and unserious? Burney is certainly correct in pointing out that these "other" movements create variety, but he makes no attempt to justify or explain Haydn's two very different approaches to his art.

Unlike many of his contemporaries, Burney did not reproach Haydn for his contrasting styles. Plenty of other critics did, though, and they directed their ire at composers beyond Haydn as well.[68] At least some of these objections can be read as a reaction against broader style changes of the time. From mid-century onward, younger composers (including Haydn) were moving toward a style that featured periodic phrase structure, even in movements not based on dance rhythms. This in turn facilitated a juxtaposition of contrasting themes, which could entail striking contrasts of mood. This manner of writing was a departure from the style of an earlier generation, exemplified by the music of J. S. Bach and Handel, composers who favored the elaboration of a single affect within any given movement. One important exception among this earlier generation of composers was Domenico Scarlatti, whose keyboard music often features irregular rhythms and striking contrasts of theme and affect. Not surprisingly, even his admirers found his works strange. Burney, for his part, called Scarlatti's keyboard sonatas "original and happy freaks."[69] And in the prefatory note to his *Essercizi per gravicembalo* (1738), Scarlatti himself advised his public that "Whether you be amateur or professional, do not expect in these compositions any intention of profundity but rather an ingenious toying with art in order for you to become skilled upon the harpsichord."[70]

But it was the generation of composers born in the 1730s that cultivated this new style of surprising contrasts with special intensity. In addition to Haydn (1732–1809), the composer-critic Johann Adam Hiller singled out three others for their inclination toward the "comic and trifling" in spite of their obvious talents: Leopold Hofmann (1738–93), Johann Anton Fils (or Filtz, 1733–60), and Carl Ditters (later von Dittersdorf, 1739–99). "Granted, one finds among their works that which is well wrought, splendid, and moving . . . but the strange mix of styles—the serious and the comic, the sublime and the lowly, which are so often found juxtaposed in one and the same movement—does this not at times create a repugnant effect?"[71] It is not the comic per se that Hiller regarded as the problem, but rather its juxtaposition with the serious. The comic taste, as he conceded on another occasion, was entirely appropriate in its proper place, as, for example, in comic opera.

> We nevertheless do wish that it would not try so much to insinuate itself into other places where it does not belong; and that composers would not mix the comic and the serious at every moment in one and the same work. Nowadays we hear so many concertos, symphonies, and the like, that in their measured and magnificent tones allow us to sense the dignity of music; but just when you least expect it, in springs Hanswurst, right into the middle of things, and the more serious the emotion that had immediately preceded his arrival, the more he arouses our compassion with his vulgar tricks.[72]

The evocation of Hanswurst is revealing: a disruptive, slapstick figure, he is the German counterpart to Harlequin of the *commedia dell'arte*, an irreverent jokester who consistently undermines theatrical illusion and reminds audiences that what they are seeing on the stage is just that: staged. He is a figure whose very presence breaks the theater's fourth wall, and he was very much in the minds of German critics of the day, for this was the time of the so-called *Hanswurst-Streit*, a campaign led by moralists like Johann Christoph Gottsched and Joseph von Sonnenfels to banish the character of Hanswurst from the stage.[73]

Hiller was not alone in rejecting such a mixture of tones. The theologian Johann Christoph Stockhausen lodged the same complaint about Haydn and others: Carlo (Carl Joseph) Toeschi (1731–88), Christian Cannabich (1731–98), Filtz (again), Gaetano Pugnani (1731–98),

54   MUSIC'S FOURTH WALL

and Carlo Antonio Campioni (1720–88). "One need be only a half-connoisseur in order to recognize the strange mixture of the comic and the serious, the trifling and the moving, which dominates everywhere."[74] Even as late as 1791, the noted critic Carl Spazier was criticizing the minuets of Haydn and Ignaz Pleyel for eliciting laughter at times. The problem, once again, was not the comic in and of itself but the fact that it detracted from the unity of feeling. Spazier insisted that what he wanted a composer of instrumental music to do was to "transport" him "into a particular state of mind." In this respect, he concluded, "I can therefore demand that all the essential and incidental elements in the music agree with this requisite goal, and that nothing should occur that might disturb this principal goal."[75]

It is tempting but too easy to dismiss Hiller, Stockhausen, and Spazier as dour and humorless souls. Perhaps they were, but that is beside the point. Their position on the mixture of the serious and the comic reflects a deeply held conviction shared by many of their time: that the purpose of instrumental music was to move listeners emotionally. To call attention to the artificiality of the art, which inhibited what they considered to be music's true goal.

A composer's personal disposition was no excuse. Many contemporaneous critics regarded the excessive mutability of Haydn's music as manifestations of the composer's *Laune*. The word is often translated into English as "humor," but the term is best understood not in the sense of comedy but rather in the sense of Galenic medicine, which postulated that an individual's health and outlook on life was governed by the balance or imbalance of the four bodily humors: blood, phlegm, black bile, and yellow bile. *Laune* was an overly sensitive susceptibility to these humors, meaning that one's mood could change suddenly and unpredictably. In his 1776 survey of twenty active composers, Carl Ludwig Junker went to considerable lengths in ascribing (but not justifying) Haydn's inappropriate mixture of the serious and comic to his *Laune*:

> No one will deny that Haydn's singularly predominant attitude or (because we are talking about music) singularly predominant sentiment is cutting, bizarre, and that it manifests itself without reservation. . . . *Laune*

RESONANCE SUBVERTED 55

has to be the sole predominant sentiment. But what if we were to find that this is not the only striking character in all of Haydn's works? That would not be proof that I have falsely identified the distinguishing character of his music, but rather, that this sentiment does not predominate at all times and to the same degree. In the same manner, it must be understood that humor has its ebb and flow. Ebb and flow can be determined and modified by the situation, by physical and moral influences, and in general through the circumstances of life. But it cannot be suppressed . . .

Laune, in other words, even in small doses, colors everything around and changes the fundamental character of anything it touches. It is a trap that can be sprung at any moment.

And no capacity, no quality, no power tolerates more modification, more haphazard determination than sentiment, for none of these depends more on the determination of sensory emotion. But name me even one work by Haydn in which *Laune* is not a consistently perceptible feature. You will not find one.

Even if a symphony can never be reproached for featuring a single, solitary sentiment, *Laune* nevertheless cannot be its true imprint, and because Haydn's sentiment is too one-sided, his symphonies are something less than symphonies.[76]

For all its obscurity, the last paragraph here is revealing. We might paraphrase its central point thus: "There is nothing wrong with a symphony that conveys a single mood; but that mood cannot be one that is born of *Laune*, which is itself inherently mutable and thus not really a mood at all."

Over time, however, critics began to accept this mixture of the serious and comic as an attractive feature of Haydn's music and of music in general. This is, in part, a product of the growing acceptance and even prestige of reflective listening. Georg August Griesinger, an agent for Breitkopf & Härtel who interviewed Haydn on many occasions during the composer's last years, lauded what he called Haydn's "*guileless waggishness*, or what the British call *Humour*."

He liked to discover the comical side of an object, and anyone who has spent even just a single hour with him would have to notice that what breathed in him was the spirit of Austrian national merriment. This humor [*Laune*] reveals itself quite conspicuously in his compositions, and his Allegros and Rondos in particular are often designed to tease listeners through deft turns from apparent seriousness to the highest degree of the comic and to attune them to exuberant mirth. In just this manner, the aforementioned "Farewell" Symphony is the realization of a musical joke.[77]

The comment at the end should give us a pause. The ending of the "Farewell" Symphony is certainly unconventional, but there is nothing particularly funny about it. It is humorous only in the sense that it reveals Haydn's humor, or to use Griesinger's term, his *Laune*.

Dittersdorf, too, came to Haydn's defense. When asked by Emperor Joseph II if Haydn did not "at times trifle altogether too much," Dittersdorf responded that Haydn had "the gift to trifle without at the same time debasing the nobility of art."[78] And a 1791 publicity announcement for Haydn's String Quartets op. 64 turned the composer's oft-criticized mixture of high and low into a selling point. In these works, the publisher assured potential buyers, Haydn had "increased his fame" by demonstrating his ability to "unite the trifling and tasteful with the lightest execution, and in such a way that the artist as well as the mere amateur will be completely satisfied."[79] And indeed, over time the distinctiveness of Haydn's music became an asset in the marketplace.[80]

The anonymous author of the entry on Haydn in the *Musikalischer Almanach auf das Jahr 1782*—possibly Johann Friedrich Reichardt—similarly recognized a justification for Haydn's eccentricities, even if the entry places the composer in Salzburg (the residence of his brother Johann Michael) rather than Vienna, Eisenach, or Esterháza. This writer was the first of many to compare Haydn to Laurence Sterne, widely known by the pseudonym of "Yorick," one of the characters in Sterne's *Tristram Shandy* and the principal character of *A Sentimental Journey*, a character whose name evokes the deceased jester in Shakespeare's *Hamlet*. Haydn is

a musical jokester, but, like Yorick, not of bathos but rather of the high comic; and this is dreadfully difficult in music. It is for this reason that so few people sense that Haydn is making a joke even when he is making one

. . . Even his Adagios, where one should actually weep, often have the imprint of the high comic.[81]

The novelist and critic Jean Paul (Jean Paul Friedrich Richter) similarly welcomed the "annihilating humor" of Haydn's music and drew a direct parallel to the works of Laurence Sterne.[82] What is technically "annihilated" is another key area; what is aesthetically "annihilated" is music's fourth wall, for as in Sterne's fiction, the artist repeatedly calls attention to his agency and thus the artificiality of his art.

Another anonymous critic, writing in 1802, pointed out that while "there is of course a very agreeable way in which to develop contrapuntally and artfully ideas that are in and of themselves insignificant," it is "the humoristic manner that is so distinctive" to Haydn. Thus, "even within the most serious appearance we remain conscious that it is all done merely in a joking manner."

> Anyone who wants examples of this readily available to hand should consider any number of finales or most of the so-called minuets in Haydn's more recent symphonies or precisely in this regard the most beloved movement for piano (Haydn's *Oeuvres complettes*, Breitkopf & Härtel, Cahier IV, p. 25f.) There the intent and effect of seriousness corresponds to the tragic appearance of various passages in the comedies of the Spaniards or in Gozzi's fairy tales. This kind of thing does not allow itself to be done successfully, however, without the author having been armed by nature with the gift of humor.[83]

The finale of the sonata in question (the Keyboard Sonata in D Major, Hob. XVI:42) is indeed light-hearted and yet contrapuntally intricate; the counterpoint is non-imitative and, as such, does not call attention to itself in the way that a fugue or canon does. "The Spaniards" the reviewer had in mind probably include such playwrights as Pedro Calderón de la Barca, Tirso di Molina, and Félix Lope de Vega, many of whose dramas employ techniques of metatheater from time to time. Carlo Gozzi's "fairy tales," in turn, frequently drew on elements of the *commedia dell'arte*, a type of comedy that routinely violated the theater's fourth wall. His *fiabe teatrali* are known to have influenced E. T. A. Hoffmann.[84]

58   MUSIC'S FOURTH WALL

Finally, as regards Haydn's propensity to break the fourth wall in his instrumental music, we cannot ignore the possibility that he may have had personal motivations for openly calling attention to his agency. He wrote the great majority of his symphonies for the Esterházy court and even more specifically for Prince Nicholas Esterházy himself. Haydn was known—and routinely identified on the title pages of his published music—as Prince Nicholas' *Kapellmeister*. This relationship was in one sense liberating for Haydn, in that it provided him with a steady income and put at his disposal an outstanding orchestra. But it was also limiting, in that he was very much a servant of the Prince, who controlled his comings and goings to no small degree. As late as 1790, Haydn was complaining to Marianne von Genzinger that he had "once again been compelled to remain at home" in Esterháza, forbidden from making the relatively short journey to the imperial capital, even though the Prince himself was away from Esterháza. "Your Grace can imagine what I thereby lose. It is indeed sad always to be a slave; yet Providence wills it."[85] In this respect, Haydn's music represented a means by which to establish his own identity apart from that of his patron. Indeed, the relationship between Haydn and Prince Nicholas can be read as an enactment of the master-slave dialectic in Hegel's *Phänomenologie des Geistes* (1807). Other composers of his time also called attention to their agency, but none so forcefully and consistently as Haydn, perhaps because no other sensed so acutely the contrast between servitude and fame.

Beyond Haydn

Haydn acknowledged to his early biographer Griesinger that he had been profoundly impressed by Carl Philipp Emanuel Bach's keyboard sonatas at a young age, adding that "anyone who knows me well must recognize that I owe a great deal to Emanuel Bach, and that I have diligently studied and understood him."[86] This debt presumably included the elder composer's penchant for surprising turns of phrase and frequent stops and starts, tendencies that at the time led to repeated charges of *Bizarrerie*.[87] Burney, for one, noted that "complaints have been made against [Bach's] pieces, for being *long, difficult, fantastic,* and *far-fetched*."[88] The question of influence, moreover, seems to have been reciprocal: Dean Sutcliffe has suggested that the finale of the Sonata in E minor, H. 281, and the Rondo in C minor, H. 283, both published in 1785, may "show the composer trying his hand at something that Haydn had done so memorably at the end of his Op. 33 No. 2 of 1781"—that is, to play with and against expectations of how works end.[89] C. P. E. Bach's symphonies, too, are full of the unexpected.[90]

Sutcliffe has further identified any number of moments in instrumental works of the time in which composers explored various means by which to draw the attention of listeners to the formal structure of what they were hearing. His survey includes works by Johann Baptist Vanhal, Luigi Boccherini, Pleyel, and Dittersdorf, whose String Quartet in G Major, K. 193, closes its first movement in a way that "exposes . . . the arbitrary nature of our symmetrical syntactical expectations," and in a manner that is "truly disconcerting . . . After the sound has stopped the listener must think about what has just happened, and in that sense it is the listener who completes 'the music'."[91]

Mozart's music offers a curious counterexample to Haydn's. While Mozart's critics found his music at times overly complex, they rarely called it odd or comical: words like *Laune* or *humoristisch* almost never figure in accounts from his time. Emperor Joseph II's pronouncement that *Die Entführung aus dem Serail* contained "too many notes," even if apocryphal, is consistent with those critical responses of the day that found Mozart's music overwhelming—too much of a good thing, in effect—but not alienating. An anonymous Viennese critic opined that in his "artful and truly beautiful writing," Mozart went "too far in an attempt to be a new creator" and in the process shortchanged "sentiment and the heart." The six string quartets dedicated to Haydn ("Opus 10," 1785) were "too heavily seasoned—and what palate can tolerate that for very long?"[92] And while *Der musikalische Spaß*, K. 522, offers a rare example of obvious humor in Mozart's instrumental music, its title announces the work as a joke (*Spaß*) before even a single note of it has sounded.[93] The humor of the first minuet of the "Haffner" Serenade, K. 250, in turn, depends on prior knowledge of the folksong being quoted and transformed from major to minor.[94] In the end, much as we may admire Mozart's artistry today, he rarely called attention to his agency in any overt way. There are occasional such moments in the operas (e.g., a quotation of his own "Non più andrai" from *Le nozze di Figaro* in the finale of *Don Giovanni*) but not to any comparable degree in the instrumental works.

Beethoven, on the other hand, imposed himself on listeners from the start, as has long been recognized. "Bizarre" is a word that figures prominently in contemporaneous responses to his music: critics repeatedly noted its difficulty for performers and listeners alike. One Viennese reviewer, having taken in an early performance of the Third Symphony (*Eroica*) in 1805, complained that music could soon "come to such a point that everyone who is not precisely familiar with the rules and difficulties of the art would find absolutely no enjoyment in it, but, oppressed instead by a multitude of unrelated and overabundant ideas and a continuous tumult of the combined instruments, would leave the concert hall with only an unpleasant feeling of exhaustion."[95] Another reviewer who attended a different performance of the *Eroica* around the same time allowed that even the most impartial connoisseur who listened intensely across repeated performances of the work would likely fail to grasp the coherence of the whole.[96]

Granted, the *Eroica* is an exceptionally demanding work, even by Beethovenian standards. Yet even the Violin Sonatas, op. 12—not generally considered to rank among the composer's more forward-looking compositions—struck one critic of the time as a set of works that pursued a "bizarre, arduous path" in "a search for unusual modulations, a loathing of conventional connections, a piling-up of difficulty upon difficulty." The end result, this writer claimed, is "that one thereby loses all patience and joy."[97] Even as late as 1825, one British reviewer had nothing good to say about the Seventh Symphony, save its almost universally popular Andante. Beyond this, Beethoven had "indulged a great deal of disagreeable eccentricity." Repeated hearings had not helped. "Often as we now have heard it performed, we cannot yet discover any design in it, neither can we trace any connexion in its parts. Altogether it seems to have been intended as a kind of enigma—we had almost said a hoax."[98]

Such judgments from Beethoven's lifetime are too common to be dismissed as products of collectively dim minds. We can better understand the initial resistance to many of his works if we remind ourselves that they demanded a kind of listening that was new for most of his contemporaries. The paradox, of course, is that it is precisely his music's artfulness, its capacity to surprise and provoke interpretation, that has since come to be valued in his art.[99] A great many of his works compelled his audiences to listen reflectively and beyond that, to take note of his agency. The later works offer especially rich and frequent examples. The minor-mode finale of the String Quartet in F minor, op. 95 (1810), ends with a brief and lighthearted F-major Allegro that runs counter to the consistently somber mood of the movement and indeed the entire work up to that point. A. B. Marx, for one, confessed in 1863 that he could gain no "clear idea of the whole, or even merely a sense of unified psychological development," and he declared that these closing forty-three measures were not a coda at all but rather a separate fifth movement, for to his mind they bore no relationship to anything that had come before, either thematically or in terms of mood. Beethoven's label for this quartet—"Serioso"—in fact plays on the double meaning of the word, conveying either a sense of extreme seriousness or a seriousness so extreme as to be insincere, and the elfin close seems to question the ponderous sincerity of all that has preceded it.[100] The seemingly premature entry of the cello at the beginning of the fifth-movement Presto of the String Quartet in C$\sharp$ minor, op. 131 (1826), to cite but one further example, is confirmed as "correct" through its repetition at various subsequent points in the movement, but each of these returns is odd enough to make us wonder if what we are hearing is really what we are supposed to be hearing. The net effect is to make us pointedly aware of the presence of the composer and his ability to dictate the course of events.

If we are to believe the much later (1852) account from his pupil Carl Czerny, Beethoven would at times break the fourth wall in his own keyboard improvisations:

> His improvisation was most brilliant and striking: in whatever company he might chance to be, he knew how to produce such an effect upon every hearer, that frequently not an eye remained dry, while many would break out into loud sobs; for there was something wonderful in his expression, in addition to the beauty and originality of his ideas, and his spirited style of rendering them. After ending an improvisation of this kind, he would burst into loud laughter, and banter his hearers on the emotion he had caused in them. "You are fools!" he would say. Sometimes, however, he would feel himself insulted by these indications of sympathy. "Who can live among such spoiled children," he would cry . . .[101]

It would be easy to dismiss this as yet one more entertaining if possibly apocryphal anecdote, were it not supported by so many passages of music Beethoven committed to paper, as in the examples cited above.

With Beethoven, then, we are worlds removed from the framework of oratory. It is all the more telling, then, that he liked to refer to himself not as a composer—someone who literally "puts things together"—but rather as a *Tondichter*, a tone poet. This marks a conceptual shift from rhetoric to poetry, a shift to be examined in detail in Chapter 4. Poetry is an openly self-conscious art, and that is how an increasing number of the composer's contemporaries perceived Beethoven's music. Many critics struggled with this, especially at first, but over time, the idea of music as something to be understood and not simply experienced became the norm.

Listeners of the time were also increasingly inclined to hear Beethoven's works as a form of musical autobiography, and so they welcomed any information that might help them better understand his music. These ranged from the general (deafness as an explanation for the difficulty of the late style) to the specific, the latter often wholly speculative.[102] The broader idea of works-as-life took hold rapidly in the second half of the 1820s, and it came to be assumed that understanding a given work of music entailed understanding the composer. As the novelist and critic

Ludwig Rellstab noted of an early performance of Beethoven's String Quartet in E♭, op. 127:

> A feeling of solemnity permeated all who were present. Only those had gathered who were in a position to grasp the immortal works of the great man with a sense of true elevation and reverence . . . Even though it may have seemed strange, dark, and nebulous to us, it has its clarity and necessity in the soul of its creator, and it is there that we must seek edification.[103]

Composers writing instrumental music in the wake of Beethoven would sometimes provide their own hints about how their lives shaped what they had written, for example, in the case of Hector Berlioz's *Symphonie fantastique*, Robert Schumann's *Carnaval*, Franz Liszt's *Années de pèlerinage*, and Bedřich Smetana's String Quartet in E minor, subtitled "From My Life." This further strengthened the conviction that music was an object to be interpreted. Schubert, though he never conveyed such clues, would almost certainly have continued to cultivate the self-reflectivity evident in some of his later works had he lived longer. Toward the end of the finale of the Piano Sonata in A Major, D. 959 (1828), the music keeps stopping and re-starting in a way that draws attention to its apparent uncertainty over how best to proceed. The return of the slow movement's main theme in the course of the finale of the Piano Trio in E♭, D. 929 (also 1828) similarly compels listeners to consider the implications of its unexpected return and the reasons behind it. Schumann incorporated these and other similar devices into his early piano works, which are full of rapid and seemingly unmediated changes of theme, tempo, texture, and dynamics, not to mention self-quotations. Scholars have since come to recognize important parallels between the aesthetics of these works and the fiction of E. T. A. Hoffmann and Jean Paul.[104]

In retrospect, the decades around 1800 stand out as a high point of aesthetic self-reflectivity in literature and drama as well as in music. Sterne inspired a host of writers who drew attention to the fictional nature of fiction. The narrator of Denis Diderot's *Jacques le fataliste* (1771, published 1778) denies that he is writing a novel, thus reminding readers that they are reading a novel. The novels of Theodor Gottlieb von Hippel, Jean Paul, and E. T. A. Hoffmann make it similarly difficult for readers to forget they are reading, and more than one critic of the time compared Jean Paul's prose to Beethoven's music.[105] On the stage, the fourth-wall-violating dramas of Ludwig Tieck, a personal acquaintance of Beethoven, repeatedly mocked the conventions of the theater. In an early scene from Tieck's *Der gestiefelte Kater* (1797), for example, Prince Nathanael, having arrived from a distant land, has an audience with the king:

> KING: But one more thing, tell me: Given that you live so far away,
>   how is it that you can speak our language so fluently?
> NATHANAEL: Quiet!
> KING: What?
> NATHANAEL: Quiet! Quiet!
> KING: I don't understand.
> NATHANAEL (*softly to him*): Calm yourself about this, otherwise the
>   public down there will notice that this is in fact very unnatural.

And before long, a "member" of the audience in fact cries out in frustration against the play's contradictions and artificialities. "Why can't the prince just talk a little in a foreign language and have his interpreter translate it into German?"[106] In Tieck's *Die verkehrte Welt* (1798), the character Scaramuz (Scaramouche) is caught in a thunderstorm while riding through a forest on his donkey, only to shout out

> Where in blazes does this thunderstorm come from? There's not a single
> word about it in my role. What sort of funny business is this? My donkey
> and I are getting soaked to the skin . . . Machinist! Machinist! In the devil's
> name stop this at once![107]

The machinist comes on stage and responds that his hands are tied because "the public wanted it to be this way." Scaramuz asks the audience if this is indeed the case, and planted cast members respond in the affirmative. Later on in the scene, the machinist describes to Scaramuz how he makes thunder (an iron ball rolled above the theater's ceiling) and lighting (powdered colophony through a flame). Any sense of theatrical illusion has by this point long since vanished.[108]

Similar devices occur throughout other dramas of the time. In Hoffmann's *Prinzessin Blandina* (published in 1815 as part of the *Fantasiestücke*), the stage manager and director discuss the play as it unfolds. In Joseph von Eichendorff's *Krieg den Philistern* (1824), the Author is a character who comments on the whole and engages in dialogue with "The Public," another "character" in this "dramatic fairytale."

Over time, however, the appeal of self-reflectivity began to fade. The reputations of Sterne, Hippel, and Jean Paul declined, and even Tieck eventually turned away from its principles and techniques after about 1810.[109] Composers in general, including even Schumann, became more "serious" in their works, avoiding, for the most part, devices that openly called attention to their agency, in part because the practice of listeners attending to their agency had by now become a given in the concert hall. Once concertgoers began to perceive instrumental music as essentially autobiographical, they had all the more reason to hear it as serious and sincere. Musical listening, as the philosopher Peter Szendy puts it, had become "*listening-to-a-work* . . . that is to say also to its composer."[110] By its very nature, autobiographical music was assumed to be sincere, which is why, self-reflective music went largely underground throughout the middle decades of the nineteenth century.

Self-reflective music began to make a comeback in the closing decades of the century when belief in the integrated self began to erode. Gustav Mahler led the charge. As has long been recognized, his works are replete with irony, which is to say, juxtapositions of contrasting "voices," none of which can claim priority over any other. True irony, as opposed to sarcasm (whose intended meaning is obvious), presents opposing perspectives that are equally plausible. The third movement of Mahler's First Symphony exemplifies the composer's cultivation of multiple and utterly contrasting musical perspectives. It opens with a minor-mode version of the children's song "Bruder Martin" ("Frère Jacques"), then moves to a hauntingly beautiful melody from one of Mahler's own earlier songs, which in turn is interrupted by outbursts of klezmer-like music. Not surprisingly, many of Mahler's contemporaries found his music insincere.[111] But a generation of younger composers—most notably Erik Satie, Charles Ives, Igor Stravinsky, Sergei Prokofiev, Kurt Weill, and later John Cage—followed Mahler's lead, undermining at times the long-unassailable unity of the self and the corresponding seriousness of "serious" music. They went to great lengths at various points in their careers to call attention to the artificial nature of their art.

This later turn to self-reflectivity nevertheless took place within a culture whose listeners had long since accepted an obligation (at least in principle) to come to terms with what they were hearing. The more fundamental change in the public's assumptions about how to listen in the concert hall had begun to take root at least a century before. Changing conceptions about the nature of instrumental music around that time, as we shall see in the next chapter, had further encouraged the shift to reflective listening.

3

The Pleasure of Reflection

The critic of art, if he wishes to judge fairly, must sympathize with the artist about the idea he has carried out and must think in the same way. He must also judge from the perspective of the artist and must at the very least intuit what the artist wanted and what inspired him.

—Christian Friedrich Michaelis (1806)[1]

The rise of reflective listening, encouraged by works in which composers openly called attention to the inherently artificial nature of their art, played a key role in instrumental music's elevated status at the turn of the nineteenth century. Movements like the finale of Haydn's "Joke" Quartet stimulated a cognitive as well as a sensory response. Over time, more subtle but repeated instances of music that violated music's fourth wall helped change the most basic assumptions about the protocols of listening in the concert hall.

Simultaneous developments in broader aesthetic thought reinforced these changes, for it was during the second half of the eighteenth century that judgment—an act of reflection—became central not only to discourse about aesthetic experience but to aesthetic experience itself. Beauty was the object of this judgment, so much so that the highest realm of the arts gradually coalesced into what came to be known in French and German as the arts of beauty (*les beaux-arts*, *die schönen Künste*) or in English, the fine arts.[2]

Instrumental music's place within the fine arts remained muddled throughout most of the eighteenth century, however, for it was an art

Music's Fourth Wall and the Rise of Reflective Listening. Mark Evan Bonds, Oxford University Press.
© Oxford University Press 2025. DOI: 10.1093/9780197806401.003.0004

fundamentally different from all others: invisible, ephemeral, and essentially non-representational. Beauty, moreover, had played a fairly marginal role in the aesthetics of music up to this point. Critics had used the word quite freely and often, to be sure: they were quick to praise melodies, harmonies, or entire works as beautiful, but they consistently regarded beauty as a source of sensory pleasure, not as the basis on which to judge exemplars of the art. A few observers of the time insisted that instrumental music could provoke more than just sensory pleasure, but they failed to explain the nature of that pleasure in any detail and, as we shall see, they would in any case remain very much in the minority.

Immanuel Kant's *Kritik der Urteilskraft* of 1790 changed everything. This may seem paradoxical, given his oft-quoted dismissal of instrumental music as more a matter of "pleasure" than "culture" and his ambivalence about whether instrumental music even rose to the level of the fine arts at all. He accorded vocal music a secure place in the hierarchy of the arts on the grounds that it projected and enhanced a text, thereby putting this kind of music on a par with the verbal arts of poetry, drama, and the like. But when it came to instrumental music, Kant seems to have been incapable of imagining anything other than resonant listening. He held that the pleasure of any fine art was "not a pleasure of enjoyment, from mere sensation, but one of reflection; and thus aesthetic art, as beautiful art, is one that has the reflecting power of judgment and not mere sensation as its standard."[3] By these terms, Kant could not possibly have accorded instrumental music a place within the fine arts. With the growing acceptance of reflective listening, however, post-Kantian philosophers and critics were able to apply Kant's own criteria to make room for instrumental music as a fine art by regarding it not solely as an experience but also as an object for reflection.

Before Kant

For all their differences, eighteenth-century writers on the arts agreed that pleasure was essential to any aesthetic experience. Judgment was, by

THE PLEASURE OF REFLECTION 69

and large, an afterthought. The Abbé Du Bos, for example, writing in 1719, considered judgment an action to be applied only if one desired to understand in retrospect the sources of one's pleasure. And sentiment— feeling, not reason—took priority over judgment. "Does the work please, or does it not? Is the work generally good or bad? It is the same thing. Reason should intervene only in the general judgment we make of a poem or a painting to support a decision of sentiment, and to explain which faults prevent it from pleasing, and which are the pleasing aspects that make it attractive."[4]

Elsewhere in the same treatise, Du Bos emphasized that in responding to an affecting object, "the heart is agitated of itself, by a motion previous to all deliberation . . . Our heart is made and organized for this very purpose: its operation therefore runs before our reasoning, as the action of the eye and ear precedes it in their sensations . . . But the principal value of poems and pictures is to please us . . . We are therefore able to judge whether they have succeeded, when we know whether their performance is affecting or no."[5]

Philosophers and critics of the time also generally agreed that sentiments are compulsive, not free. On this basis, Jean-Pierre Crousaz, for one, distinguished them quite clearly from ideas, noting in 1715 that:

> ideas occupy the intellect, sentiments interest the heart; ideas amuse us, they exercise our attention and sometimes fatigue it, depending on whether they are more or less composed and combined. But sentiments dominate us, they seize us, they take us over and make us happy or sad according to whether they are sweet or annoying, agreeable or disagreeable. One's ideas are easily expressed, but it is very difficult to describe one's sentiments; it is impossible, even through language, to give an exact understanding of them to those who have not had similar experiences.[6]

The relationship between the senses (experience) and the mind (judgment) became the central question for eighteenth-century aestheticians. Some writers placed greater weight on one than the other, but all acknowledged that taste is what mediated the two. "Taste," as Johann Mattheson observed in 1744, is "the inner sensation, selection, and judgment that in matters of the senses make us aware of our mind. If the tongue has its own mind, as Plinius would have it, then the mind itself has as it were its own tongue with which it tastes and assays its objects."[7] Johann Adolph Scheibe would make a similar claim a year later, noting that taste is "the capacity of the mind to judge what the senses perceive."[8]

It was not until the 1770s that a small number of commentators began to suggest that the pleasure from instrumental music could be intellectual as well as sensory. The key figures here are the composer-critics Johann Nikolaus Forkel and Johann Friedrich Reichardt, the historian and critic Charles Burney, and the philosopher Adam Smith. In every instance, judgment is not simply an evaluation carried out after the fact of perception but an element operating alongside perception itself. All four describe key elements of reflective listening.

Forkel went to great lengths to encourage the public to listen in a way that provided "not only a *sensory* but also an *intellectual delight*."[9] In 1777, he instituted a series of public lectures in Göttingen and advertised them with a prospectus entitled "On the Theory of Music, insofar as it is Necessary and Useful for Amateurs and Connoisseurs."[10] One senses here and in the surviving texts of later similar lectures an almost evangelical zeal to teach lay audiences how to listen.[11] Two years later, he announced that he would give what amounted to pre-concert lectures on the works he was to conduct with his Collegium Musicum at the University of Göttingen. He promised to parse (*zergliedern*) those works using live musical examples from the orchestra itself so that listeners would be better able to "find the merits and beauties of these pieces." The "true perspective" from which to judge a work, he maintained, is that of the composer, and specifically the composer's "intention and objectives."[12]

This was an extraordinary statement for its time. The very idea that a lay audience should come to a concert armed with a certain degree of knowledge about the art is in itself remarkable, as is the idea of listening from the perspective of the composer—which is to say, to listen to the work as an object.

No less significant is Forkel's description of listening as an act that involves memory, comparison, and anticipation. He was particularly

THE PLEASURE OF REFLECTION 71

keen to apply this perspective to instrumental music, for while the text of a vocal work "translates" the notes, an instrumental work "demands" that listeners—or at least those who possess "sufficient knowledge and experience of the art"—be able to "retain those tones in their memory, compare them with one another, and thereby feel the meaning the composer intended those tones to have."[13] This may seem unremarkable today, and it would have seemed equally unremarkable to professional musicians of Forkel's time, but the idea that lay listeners should actively commit to memory a work's opening theme in order to compare it to its literal or varied re-appearances later on in work is strikingly novel.

> Every musical period of even a moderate length strains the listener's attention if he follows it properly in all its smallest parts and comprehends the coherence of the whole. For this reason the highest possible distinctness and clarity are necessary in the construction of periods, because without them the listener becomes either tired or distracted and is consequently in no condition to follow the course of the whole and receive the pleasure expected from the piece. This general overview of the whole with all its individual parts must be made as easy as possible, all the more so given that music is one of those languages for which only very few listeners possess a complete dictionary . . . .[14]

This amounts to what has since come to be called synoptic or structural listening. Saint Augustine had described it long before in his account of reciting (singing) a psalm by noting the way in which his attention moved seamlessly across present, past, and future.[15] René Descartes characterized it in his *Compendium musicae* of 1618 (published posthumously in 1650) as the ability of our imaginations to recall at the end of a melody (*cantilena*) what we had heard at the beginning and throughout the rest of it.[16] As Karol Berger points out, this kind of listening "involves actively following the whole with a mind stretched between expecting, remembering, and attending . . . Meaning unfolds gradually in time as each event is provisionally interpreted in light of the expectations it engenders and the memories it evokes, and as past events are continuously reinterpreted in the light of later events and remaining expectations."[17] Leon Botstein, in turn, has called this form of listening "philosophical,"

72 MUSIC'S FOURTH WALL

in that it traces the continuity of thought across a relatively wide trajectory of time.[18]

Synoptic listening also figures into Johann Friedrich Reichardt's call for a synthesis of sensory and intellectual powers in listening to music:

> Music is inherently and by itself a delight, without any imitation of feelings and passions. For even if it might not make us sad, happy, or arouse astonishment, it can tickle our ears in so charming a manner and in such a way as to delight us simply through a pleasant mixture of tones. It can moreover pleasantly engage our understanding and thereby delight us in a noble manner through the manifold and artful relationship of the tones among themselves, through their entanglement and resolution. Finally it can combine the two. This is the reason why we find delight in purely instrumental music, even though it expresses no specific feeling or passion. This is also the reason why the mere amateur is pleased above all by the instrumental music of the Mannheim composers, which tickles the ear pleasantly, and why the learned connoisseur is pleased above all by the music of the so-called Berlin style, which engages the understanding. It is also why the judicious combination of the two guarantees the proper and sensitive connoisseur the highest delight when listening to instrumental music.[19]

Reichardt makes a number of important points here. He identifies two kinds of pleasure in listening, one resonant ("ear-tickling"), the other reflective ("engages our understanding"), and he explicitly identifies their combination as the highest form of listening. Reflection, moreover— judgment—constitutes a pleasurable activity in its own right. What "pleasantly engages our understanding," he maintains, is the way in which the "tones" intertwine and become enmeshed and are ultimately resolved. The delight from this sort of listening is more than just "pleasing" (*angenehm*): it is "noble" (*edel*). The "manifold and artful relationship of the tones among themselves through their entanglement and resolution" would seem to suggest something that resembles what we would think of today as thematic manipulation—the way a theme unfolds and develops over the course of a movement—or perhaps something broader still, but it would in any case entail a kind of listening that involves memory, which is to say, the capacity to recognize

THE PLEASURE OF REFLECTION 73

the relationship among events that unfold over time, in short: synoptic listening.

Reichardt illustrates these two kinds of listening by appealing to the repertorial preferences of connoisseurs (*Kenner*) and amateurs (*Liebhaber*). Connoisseurs are attracted to the music of the "so-called Berlin style," a style that in the hands of such composers as Johann Joachim Quantz and C. P. E. Bach features considerable counterpoint, while amateurs prefer the homophonic textures of such Mannheim-based composers as Johann Stamitz, Karl Stamitz, and Christian Cannabich, for this is music that "tickles the ear pleasantly." Counterpoint, by its very nature, calls attention to the "manifold and artful relationships of tones among themselves, through their entanglement and resolution" and thus encourages reflective listening, while the simpler texture of homophony, a single melody and subordinate accompaniment, is more conducive to resonant listening. The "ennoblement" of listening through reflectivity will come to the fore in the wake of Kant, as we shall see; Reichardt's position at this point, though largely undeveloped, anticipates later thought to a considerable degree.

Charles Burney would make a similar case for an integration of the sensuous and intellectual in listening, though he was somewhat more ambivalent about the matter. He asserted in 1789 that "there is a tranquil pleasure, short of rapture, to be acquired from Music, in which intellect and sensation are equally concerned." On the whole, however, he remained committed to the predominant mode of resonant listening, defining music as "the *art of pleasing* by the succession and combination of agreeable sounds." He insisted, as noted earlier, that "every hearer has a right to give way to his feelings, and be pleased or dissatisfied without knowledge, experience, or the fiat of critics." Judgment, to his mind, was an altogether different matter. The listener who has "a right to give way to his feelings" regardless of his musical knowledge or abilities "has *certainly no right to insist* on others being pleased or dissatisfied in the same degree."[20] Judgment in this sense comes after the fact of listening.

74   MUSIC'S FOURTH WALL

And judgment, in Burney's view, could actually inhibit a listener's sense of pleasure if taken too far:

> With respect to all the feuds and contentions lately occasioned by Music in France, they seem to have annihilated the former disposition of the inhabitants to receive delight from such Music as their country afforded. There are at present certainly too many critics, and too few candid hearers in France as well as elsewhere. I have seen French and German *soi-disant connoisseurs* listen to the most exquisite musical performance with the same *sans-froid* [*sic*] as an anatomist attends a dissection. It is all analysis, calculation, and parallel; they are to be wise, not pleased. Happy the people, however imperfect their Music, if it gives them pleasure! But when it is an eternal object of dispute; when each man, like Nebuchadnezzar, sets up his own peculiar *idol*, which every individual is to fall down and worship, or be thrown into the fiery furnace of his hatred and contempt, the blessing is converted into a curse.[21]

Burney nevertheless shared Forkel's belief in the need for musical amateurs to become more educated about the art, if only to help them identify the principles by which they could judge a given work of music if they chose to do so. Those principles include "having a clear and precise idea of the constituent parts of a good composition," which he identified as "melody, harmony, modulation, invention, grandeur, fire, pathos, taste, grace, and expression . . . In this manner, a composition, by a kind of chemical process, may be decompounded as well as any other production of art or nature."[22] Burney even proposed a response to Fontenelle's "famous question," putting these words into the mouth of the interrogated sonata:

> The famous question, therefore, of Fontenelle: *Sonate, que* [*me*] *veux tu?*... would never have been asked by a real lover or judge of Music . . . If a lover and judge of Music had asked the same question as Fontenelle, the Sonata should answer: "I would have you listen with attention and delight to the ingenuity of the composition, the neatness of the execution, sweetness of the melody, and the richness of the harmony, as well as to the charms of refined tones, lengthened and polished into passion."[23]

The order of these criteria is revealing. The "ingenuity" of the work takes pride of place, and "charms" come only toward the end. This "response"

THE PLEASURE OF REFLECTION 75

is framed not in terms of rhetoric but rather in terms of analysis, or to use Burney's own terms, "dissection" or "decompounding." For all his ambivalence about reflective listening, Burney recognized its value. "There have been many treatises published on the art of musical composition and performance," he noted, "but none to instruct ignorant lovers of Music how to listen, or to judge for themselves. So various are musical styles, that it requires not only extensive knowledge, and long experience, but a liberal, enlarged, and candid mind, to discriminate and allow to each its due praise."[24]

The most extended account of a conjunction of heart and mind in listening to instrumental music appears in Adam Smith's essay "Of the Nature of that Imitation Which Takes Place in What are Called the Imitative Arts," written possibly as early as the 1750s but not published until 1795, five years after his death. There is strong evidence that Smith made revisions of some kind to the text after 1777, but exactly what or when remains unclear.[25] A protégé of Kames, Smith concedes that instrumental music's powers are inferior to those of vocal music, yet he insists that even "without any imitation, instrumental Music can produce very considerable effects . . . Whatever we feel from instrumental Music is an original, and not a sympathetic feeling: it is our own gaiety, sedateness, or melancholy; not the reflected disposition of another person." This "sympathetic feeling" aligns with the notion of resonance. Smith at this point changes his perspective, however, to regard music not as an experience but as an object. "A well-composed concerto," he asserts, "presents an object so agreeable, so great, so various, and so interesting, that alone, and without suggesting any other object, either by imitation or otherwise, it can occupy, and as it were fill up, completely the whole capacity of the mind, so as to leave no part of its attention vacant for thinking of any thing else."[26]

Like Forkel and Reichardt, Smith emphasizes the temporal nature of music and the obligation of listeners to attend to the structure of what they are hearing. Once again, recall and anticipation play a key role. The "enjoyment of music," he concludes, "arises partly from memory and partly from foresight."

76   MUSIC'S FOURTH WALL

> In the contemplation of that immense variety of agreeable and melodious sounds, arranged and digested, both in their coincidence and in their succession, into so complete and regular a system, the mind in reality enjoys not only a very great sensual, but a very high intellectual pleasure, not unlike that which it derives from the contemplation of a great system in any other science.
>
> Each foregoing sound seems to introduce, and as it were prepare the mind for the following: by its rhythms, by its time and measure, it disposes that succession of sounds into a certain arrangement, which renders the whole more easy to be comprehended and remembered. Time and measure are to instrumental Music what order and method are to discourse; they break it into proper parts and divisions, by which we are enabled both to remember better what is gone before, and frequently to foresee somewhat of what is to come after: we frequently foresee the return of a period which we know must correspond to another which we remember to have gone before; and, according to the saying of an ancient philosopher and musician, the enjoyment of Music arises partly from memory and partly from foresight.[27]

We can recognize in this account of synoptic listening a description of what we would today call periodic phrase structure, which allows listeners to "foresee the return of a period"—a phrase or some discrete unit of music—"which we know must correspond to another which we remember to have gone before." The synthesis of recollection and expectation occurs in the mind and, in turn, affects the heart. Here, cognition comes to the fore and provides an essential element of the listener's pleasure.

By the time Smith's comments appeared in print in 1795, his position fit neatly into the mainstream of discourse about listening, which by that point was dominated by responses to Kant's *Kritik der Urteilskraft*.

Kant

The aesthetic issues Kant took up in his *Kritik der Urteilskraft* of 1790 had been intensely debated by generations of philosophers before him. For present purposes, the genealogy of his thinking on these matters is less important than their synthesis and elaboration in his treatise, which elicited an outpouring of creative responses from other writers, many of whom appropriated Kant's ideas in ways he could scarcely have imagined. This is especially true as regards the aesthetic status of instrumental music, for his broader views on the nature of aesthetic perception and the fine arts in general provided the means by which subsequent thinkers could argue that instrumental music was not only the highest form of music but the highest form of all the arts.

To understand this unusual development, which unfolded over the two decades after the publication of the *Kritik der Urteilskraft*, we must keep in mind that Kant's primary concern was with acts of perception and judgment, not the objects of perception and judgment. This is a crucial distinction, for when we read between the lines of what he has to say about instrumental music, it becomes clear that he listened resonantly and only resonantly. In this respect, he was thoroughly typical of his time. Had he been able to listen reflectively—or even simply imagine listening in this way—he would likely have come to very different conclusions.

Kant's low estimation of music without a text was completely consistent with his criteria for the fine arts in general. He praised instrumental music's emotional power quite openly (§53) and even went so far as to acknowledge that its ability to move the passions was greater than that of any other art. His misgivings began when it came time to assign instrumental music its place within the hierarchy of the fine arts. Here he wavered, proposing to rank it either as the lowest of the arts of beauty or as the highest of the arts of pleasure. His criteria for differentiating between the two categories did not allow him to concede to instrumental music anything more than he did.

Thanks to the presence of a text, Kant regarded vocal music as an enhanced form of literary art, whereas instrumental music offered no concepts (*Begriffe*) to engage the mind and was thus more a matter of "pleasure" than "culture" (*mehr Genuss als Kultur*). Kant's dictum points to both the interplay and friction between resonant and reflective listening. For if we attend to the words at all in a vocal work, we are necessarily listening reflectively, processing the meaning of the words and "matching" them, as it were, to the music by considering the interaction of the two. (It would, of course, be possible to ignore a sung text while listening, either willfully or through ignorance of the language, though Kant would have no doubt considered that sort of listening also to be more about pleasure than culture.) Sensory pleasure alone—resonant listening—was, in any case, insufficient: Kant regarded reflection as the defining characteristic of aesthetic experience, and instrumental music provided nothing on which to reflect. He therefore deemed responses to untexted music "pathological," a term with decidedly negative overtones.[28] He may well have had instrumental music in mind when he declared that "taste is always still barbaric when it needs the addition of *charms* and *emotions* for satisfaction, let alone if it makes these into the standard for its approval."[29] A feeling of pleasure or displeasure, as he maintained in his later and more generally accessible *Anthropologie in pragmatischer Hinsicht* of 1798, was spontaneous and therefore did not allow the beholding individual to "rise" to the level of "reflection." "To be subject to affects and passions," he noted, "is probably always an illness of the mind, because both affect and passion shut out the sovereignty of reason."[30] Kant distinguished between affects (that is, moods, such as anger, which come and go) and passions (that is, desires of a longer-lasting quality, e.g., hatred), but he regarded both as objects to be overcome. The key question for him centered on personal autonomy. What he called "inner freedom" required two things: "being one's own master in a given case (*animus sui compos*), and ruling oneself (*imperium in semetipsum*), that is, subduing one's affects and governing one's passions."[31]

While Kant was typical of his time in conceiving of instrumental music as a rhetorical art, he was unique in regarding this as a defect rather than an asset. He harbored serious objections to rhetoric, or more specifically to oratory, rhetoric's application through public speech.[32] He considered oratory a "deceitful art" (*hinterlistige Kunst*), one "not worthy of any respect at all" (*gar keiner Achtung würdig*), not simply because it could be

THE PLEASURE OF REFLECTION 79

used to nefarious ends—this was a long-standing objection going all the way back to Plato—but rather because of its inherently coercive nature, regardless of whether for good or ill.[33] Orators seek to move their audiences toward a very specific goal, and they use every tool in the arsenal of rhetoric to achieve that end. The orator's job, to put it bluntly, is to manipulate listeners. Poetry, by contrast (and by extension, vocal music), is a fine art, for it invites contemplation and elicits a response based on reflection, whereas oratory (and, by extension, instrumental music) is a business, a vehicle of persuasion. Oratory can certainly draw on artfully crafted phrases ("Ask not what your country can do for you, ask what you can do for your country"), but the meaning of such phrases is (or should be) at once clear, their impact immediate. We can reflect on such turns of phrases if we wish, but to reflect on them as we continue to listen is to risk the possibility of losing the thread of the speaker's argument. The purpose of verbal eloquence is to sweep listeners along in the flow of the argument and to provoke assent, not reflection, and certainly not puzzlement.

For Kant, the object of aesthetic judgment is beauty, and that true ("pure") aesthetic pleasure lies in the pleasure of that judgment, not in the pleasure of the senses. Sensory pleasure is not essential to beauty, for "pure" judgments of taste are unaffected by charms or emotions. Thus, the pleasure derived from a work of fine art was necessarily mental rather than sensory.[34] Kant distinguished between the "taste of sense," which centers on pleasure, and the "taste of reflection," which centers on judgment. The first is personal and individual; the second teaches us "to find a free satisfaction in the object of the senses even without any sensible charm," and it is (or should be) universal.[35] To experience beauty, then, is to experience freedom in the open-ended play of imagination and understanding. If one's positive response to an object is purely sensory, the object is pleasurable (*angenehm*); if the object stimulates and encourages the free play of the faculties (imagination and understanding), it is beautiful. Only humans enjoy access to beauty, which synthesizes understanding and the senses. "Emotion," Kant declared flatly, "does not belong to beauty at all."[36]

Kant thus changed the governing parameters of pleasure from the senses to the mind, from experience to reflection, from pleasure to judgment. He distinguished between pleasure (*Gefallen*) as a product of judgment, and enjoyment or gratification (*Vergnügen*) as a product of sensation.[37] As Hannah Ginsborg has pointed out, Kant made no essential distinction between aesthetic experience and aesthetic judgment. His judgment of beauty, as she puts it, "is best understood as the pleasurable experience that we might call 'finding' something beautiful, and which might or not be articulated as the explicit thought or statement that the thing is beautiful."[38] Or as Abigail Zitin formulates it even more succinctly, aesthetic pleasure, for Kant, "is how a certain kind of thinking feels."[39]

Imagination was the faculty that mediated between the senses and reason. This was not a new idea with Kant. The concept of "free play" in aesthetic experience goes back at least as far as Joseph Addison's "On the Pleasures of the Imagination" (1712). Alexander Gerard, in turn, had maintained in his *Essay on Taste* (1759) that the mind experiences pleasure when "forced to exert its activity, and put forth its strength, in order to surmount any difficulty: and if its efforts prove successful, consciousness of the success inspires new joy. Hence moderate difficulty, such as exercises the mind, without fatiguing it, is pleasant, and renders the object by which it is produced agreeable."[40] But Kant drew a much sharper distinction between sensory and intellectual pleasure. The former, he insisted, "is either introduced A) through *sense* (enjoyment), or B) through the *power of imagination* (taste); the second (that is, intellectual pleasure) is either introduced a) through representable *concepts* or b) through *ideas* . . . ."[41] Sensory pleasure was a product of the "agreeable" arts, which in turn were decidedly inferior to the intellectual pleasure afforded by the arts of beauty.

Kant further distinguished between "free beauty" (*freie Schönheit*) and "adherent beauty" (*anhängende Schönheit*) on the basis of his implicit assumption that fine arts are by their very nature representational or mimetic.[42] Adherent beauty offers the mind the opportunity to cognize

THE PLEASURE OF REFLECTION   81

and compare the presented object with its intended ideal. Free beauty, by contrast, is non-representational, and Kant cites as examples of it arabesques and "all music without a text."[43] But in an age before abstract art, this amounted to a deficit, in that free beauty posited no object on which the mind could reflect. Free beauty could not expand or enlarge those faculties of the mind that "have to come together in the power of judgment in order for cognition to arise" because it "plays merely with sensations."[44] It is for this reason that Kant wavers between assigning instrumental music to the lowest place among the fine arts or the highest place among the pleasurable arts.[45]

While he never says so explicitly, Kant strongly implies that another failing of instrumental music is its inability to incorporate what he called aesthetic ideas, products of the imagination set in motion by the perception of an object:

> By an aesthetic idea I mean a presentation of the imagination which prompts much thought, but to which no determinate thought whatsoever, i.e., no [determinate] *concept*, can be adequate, so that no language can express it completely and allow us to grasp it. It is easy to see that an aesthetic idea is the counterpart (pendant) of a *rational idea*, which is, conversely, a concept to which no *intuition* (presentation of the imagination) can be adequate.[46]

"As a productive cognitive power," Kant goes on to say, the imagination "is very mighty when it creates, as it were, another nature out of the material that actual nature gives it."[47] An aesthetic idea, then, stimulates the imagination to mediate between the senses and reason. Kant, at several points, hints that a work of purely instrumental music might be able to accommodate aesthetic ideas but in the end remains ambivalent (if not altogether unclear) on this possibility and never pursues it in any detail.[48] An aesthetic idea in music, to the extent that it might be possible at all, would nevertheless be clearly different in kind and of lesser potency than its counterparts in the more openly mimetic arts.[49] In the end, Kant's conception of art remained firmly mimetic, a position which made it all the more difficult for him to justify non-programmatic instrumental music.

82 MUSIC'S FOURTH WALL

Later critics, as we shall see, would in fact equate musical and aesthetic
ideas, for Kant's characterization of an aesthetic idea in fact maps quite
easily onto a musical theme:

> In a word, an aesthetic idea is a presentation of the imagination which is
> conjoined with a given concept and is connected, when we use imagina-
> tion in its freedom, with such a multiplicity of partial presentations that
> no expression that stands for a determinate concept can be found for it.
> Hence it is a presentation that makes us add to a concept the thoughts of
> much that is ineffable, but the feeling of which quickens our cognitive
> powers and connects language, which otherwise would be mere letters,
> with spirit.[50]

What prevented Kant from making this connection himself was his fundamental belief that instrumental music, like oratory, was essentially
coercive. He could not entertain the notion that music's "ideas"—its
themes and their development and manipulation—might be objects
that could occasion "much thought" to which "no determinate thought
whatsoever, i.e., no *concept*, can be adequate, so that no language can
express it completely."[51] Yet this was precisely the connection that later
critics would make, and in doing so, they consistently emphasized the
expressive limitations of language. Kant himself was unable to make
that conceptual leap because he could not imagine instrumental music
as anything other than a form of oratory, which is to say, as a form of
coercion.

This becomes particularly clear when we recognize how Kant posi-
tions his dismissal of instrumental music in the *Kritik der Urteilskraft*:
it comes immediately after his condemnation of oratory. He lays out
his hierarchy of the fine arts in §53 by starting at the top, with poetry
(*Dichtkunst*), a term that embraces the verbal arts in general:

> Among all the arts *poetry* holds the highest rank . . . It expands the
> mind: for it sets the imagination free, and offers us, from among the
> unlimited variety of possible forms that harmonize with a given con-
> cept, though within that concept's limits, that form which links the ex-
> hibition of the concept with a wealth of thought to which no linguistic
> expression is completely adequate, and so poetry rises aesthetically to
> ideas.[52]

THE PLEASURE OF REFLECTION

It is at this point that Kant recognizes the need to single out one particular form of the verbal arts—oratory—as fundamentally different in kind. Unlike poetry, oratory

> insofar as this is taken to mean the art of persuasion (*ars oratoria*), i.e., of deceiving by means of a beautiful illusion, rather than mere excellence of speech (eloquence and style), is a dialectic that borrows from poetry only as much as the speaker needs in order to win over people's minds for his own advantage before they can judge for themselves; it thus deprives them of their freedom . . . Indeed, because the machinery of persuasion can be used equally well to palliate and cloak vice and error, it cannot quite eliminate our lurking suspicion that we are being artfully hoodwinked. In poetry on the other hand everything proceeds with honesty and sincerity. It informs us that it wishes to engage in a purely entertaining play with the imagination, namely, one that harmonizes in form with the laws of understanding; it does not seek to sneak up on the understanding and ensnare it through sensory representation.[53]

This condemnation of oratory sets the stage for its sister art of instrumental music, for the two function in the same way: both rob listeners of their freedom. From this perspective, it is remarkable that Kant even entertained the notion that instrumental music might somehow be considered a fine art. It was left to a subsequent wave of philosophers and critics to align instrumental music with poetry rather than oratory.

After Kant

To acknowledge instrumental music as a fine art, philosophers and critics had to demonstrate exactly how it might be capable of engaging listeners intellectually as well as emotionally. A few observers, as we have seen—Forkel, Reichardt, Burney, and Adam Smith—had made such an attempt, beginning as early as the 1770s, but none had proposed an actual mechanism by which the experience of instrumental music might go beyond the purely sensory.

When a younger generation of critics and philosophers began to listen with an awareness of compositional agency, however—encouraged by

violations of music's fourth wall, both overt and subtle—they discovered
that Kant's concepts of taste, judgment, beauty, and aesthetic ideas
could be readily applied to the act of listening to instrumental music.
The crucial move here was the abandonment of oratory as the conceptual model for the art. After dominating discourse about instrumental
music for almost a century—from around the 1730s until the early
1800s—this way of thinking largely disappeared, surviving only in such
inherently conservative venues as dictionaries and encyclopedias, genres
prone to perpetuate conventional wisdom. Commentators, for the most
part, simply stopped talking about instrumental music in these terms,
and fairly abruptly at that.[54] The decline of rhetorical imagery reflects
the growing acceptance of reflective listening. Listeners now assumed a
degree of responsibility for making sense of what they were hearing, and
this was not a mode of listening relevant to any kind of oratory, verbal
or musical. "To understand music" became a new part of the discourse
around listening.[55]

This new attitude changed the parameters of the listening experience for lay audiences. It was not a paradigm shift: composers, professional musicians, and connoisseurs, as noted, had long been listening
reflectively, and many, if not most, concertgoers would continue to
listen resonantly, that is, within an oratorical framework, even if they
did not conceive of it in this way. By the middle of the nineteenth century, however, reflective listening had become the accepted standard for
the concert hall, even if that standard often remained more aspirational
than real.

Mixed manifestations of both modes of listening around 1800 are
not unusual. Peter Lichtenthal's *Der musikalische Arzt* ("The Musical
Physician"), published in Vienna in 1807, offers a good example of
this. In an appendix titled "A Few Tips on Listening to a Good Work
of Music," he poses two questions: What constitutes a good work of
music? And how should one listen to it? He begins by equating a musical work with an oration:

> A good musical piece and an oration delivered by an orator from the pulpit
> are one and the same thing. The former always consists of a theme that in

THE PLEASURE OF REFLECTION

a well-developed proposition is increasingly expanded, altered, developed, repeated, etc. One finds in it . . . the selfsame parenthetical clauses and transitions, the selfsame figures and cadences as in an oration.[56]

This much is conventional, if not downright old-fashioned. But the image of the oration vanishes when Lichtenthal moves to his second question about *how* to listen:

Nothing extraneous must distract us when we are listening to a good piece of music; instead, we must with clear consciousness grasp everything possible within our power. For example: what is the theme like? what is the tempo? what is the key, how are the harmonies, the figures, the transitions, the embellishments? what is the plan of the composer, that is, how is the theme carried out, how does it correspond to the object that is to be presented here? and above all, what is the instrumentation like? The essence of all these things tells us if the author has said something or not. Once we have recognized the What and the How, then have we also heard the music.[57]

This is reflective listening through and through, perceiving music as an object and attending to its constituent elements. We are well outside Lichtenthal's initial framework of rhetoric here: orators do not want their audiences dissecting the formal structure of their speeches as they unfold; they want those in attendance to be moved to the desired action or state of mind. Thus, while on the one hand, Lichtenthal retains the traditional image of the musical work as an oration, he does not want audiences to listen to it in the way orators would want them to. His recommended method of listening contradicts both the spirit and practice of oratory, for only orators or composers themselves would try to take in an oration or musical work from the perspective of its creator. Lichtenthal nevertheless maintains that even the average concertgoer must adopt precisely this perspective. The musical oration has become an object of reflection, but with this, the parallels to oratory have lost all meaning. Even without words, music is now something to be understood and not merely experienced.

Friedrich Schiller was one of the first to recognize the implications of Kant's aesthetics for instrumental music. Like Kant, he dismissed aesthetic responses that were purely emotional, and he decried the music of recent times, which to his mind seemed to have been "invested primarily in sensuousness alone, thereby flattering the prevailing taste, which desires only to be titillated, not seized, not powerfully moved, not elevated."

> Everything *mellifluous* [*schmelzende*, literally "melting"] is thus preferred, and even if there is great noise in a concert hall, everyone is suddenly all ears when a mellifluous passage is performed. At that point, an expression of sensuousness that approaches the animalistic usually appears on every face; drunken eyes swim, the open mouth is all desire, a voluptuous trembling seizes the entire body, the breath becomes fast and weak, in short, all the symptoms of intoxication present themselves. This is clear proof that the senses are reveling while the spirit or the principle of human freedom has fallen prey to the power of sensuous appeal. All these emotions, I say, are excluded from art through a noble and masculine taste, because they please solely and exclusively through the *senses*, and art has nothing to do with these.[58]

Schiller went beyond Kant, however, in identifying form as the basis for the construction of music's sensuous material. And here he recognized what sets instrumental music apart, pointing out that "although the *content* of emotions cannot be represented" in any work of art, "the *form* certainly can be." In this regard, there is one art "that has no other object than the form of these emotions. This art is *music*."[59]

Schiller further developed his ideas on this point in an exchange with his more musically knowledgeable friend Christian Gottfried Körner, who in 1795 submitted an essay entitled "On the Representation of Character in Music" to Schiller's new journal, *Die Horen*.[60] Schiller's response to the original (now lost) version of Körner's essay is substantial. He applies to music the Kantian dictum that concepts without intuitions are empty, while intuitions without concepts are blind. Schiller concedes that although "the power of music resides in its physical, material component," the art "becomes aesthetic only through form . . . Without form the music would command us blindly; its form rescues our freedom."[61] Kant's aversion to oratorical coercion is plainly evident here, but form—and more specifically, the listener's perception of form—is the element that allows for cognition and reflection.

THE PLEASURE OF REFLECTION 87

Schiller nevertheless encouraged Körner to give more attention to the material side of music, pointing out that the senses and reason must be synthesized in the act of listening. Reason alone, he maintained, could not explain music's power.

> If you take away from music all *form*, it loses all its *aesthetic* power but not, to be sure, all its musical power.
>
> If you take away from music everything *material* and retain only its pure part, it will thereby lose both its aesthetic and musical power and will become merely an object of understanding. This therefore establishes that you must take music's physical side into account more than you have.
>
> Humboldt and Goethe came to precisely this conclusion. I would wish, then, that you would touch on (even if only in passing) the unique power of music, which rests on its material.[62]

The relationship between abstract form and tangible material is a recurring theme throughout Schiller's *Aesthetic Letters*, also from 1795. Both are essential: each makes the other perceptible, but only the perception of form assures an aesthetic response to any work of art, as opposed to one that is purely sensory.

> In a truly beautiful work of art the content should do nothing and the form everything, for it is through form alone that the whole of the human being is affected; content affects only discrete capacities. The content of a work, no matter how sublime or far-reaching, always affects the spirit in a restrictive manner; only through form can we expect true aesthetic freedom. Herein, then, resides the real artistic secret of the master, *that he eradicates the material through form*. And the more imposing, overbearing, and seductive the material is in its own right, the more unilaterally the master asserts himself with *his* effect. Or to put it another way: the more the beholder is inclined to give in to the material directly, the more triumphant is that art which repels it and asserts its mastery over it.[63]

There is, Schiller goes on to say, "a beautiful art of passion" but no "beautiful passionate art." The latter is an oxymoron, "for the inevitable effect of beauty is a freedom from passions."[64]

Beauty thus transcends the passions, at least in theory. In practice, Schiller seems to have doubted the ability of listeners to resist music's material power. In one particularly revealing sentence, he laments that "through its material, even the wittiest [*geistreichste*] music stands in closer affinity to the senses than true aesthetic freedom permits."[65] *Geistreich* is a capacious term, and its many implications go beyond "witty" to include such qualities as "ingenious," "brainy," and "intellectually stimulating." Moments like the ending of Haydn's "Joke" Quartet might well have allowed Schiller to apply the idea of aesthetic freedom to purely instrumental music, for it is the form that strikes us here far more than the sound itself. Yet even music that sets our minds to work, Schiller implies, retains the capacity to captivate, if not overwhelm, our senses. Music's material power inhibits its ability to create a sense of aesthetic distance.

Schiller certainly recognized the importance of a sense of distance in the verbal arts. He went so far as to declare the goal of comedy as higher than that of tragedy on the grounds that comedy's "is identical with the highest goal of human struggle: to be free of passion, to look around and into oneself always with clarity and calmness, to find everywhere more chance than fate, and to laugh at absurdity more than to rage against malice or weep over it."[66] The purpose of true art, he maintained, is not to transport us into a "momentary dream of freedom" but rather "to *make* us actually free in fact" by awakening in us the power to subordinate the world of the senses to the world of ideas.[67] Art achieves this by creating a sense of distance between the beholder and the beheld, and one means for achieving this in the realm of tragedy is through the use of the chorus. By commenting on the actions on the stage, the chorus serves to remind audience members that they are indeed watching a drama and not reality itself. Schiller is, in effect, arguing that becoming "lost" in the spectacle is not a good thing, for it robs viewers of their personal freedom. In its own way, the theater's fourth wall is a barrier to freedom. Schiller's point here is similar to Kant's objection to oratory as coercive, for an audience that loses all sense of objectivity also loses its ability to judge and thus its autonomy. But the chorus "ennobles" the audience's delight by creating a sense of distance between viewers and the stage.

THE PLEASURE OF REFLECTION

> [Drama] should remain a form of play, but a poetic one. All art is dedicated to joy, and there is no higher or more serious duty than to make people happy. True art is that alone which creates the highest pleasure. But the highest pleasure is the freedom of the spirit in the living play of all its powers.[68]

Schiller stops short of making any specific connection to music here, but the broader context of the *Aesthetic Letters* makes it clear that he intended his principles to be applicable to all art forms. Had his knowledge of music been greater, he might conceivably have pointed to distancing effects in instrumental works by Haydn or even the young Beethoven as sonic analogues of the drama's chorus.

August Wilhelm Schlegel took Schiller's notion of the chorus' function a step further by calling it an "idealized spectator" who "ameliorates the impression of a deeply distressing or deeply moving presentation, in that it reciprocates the actual spectator's own feelings in a way that is expressed lyrically, that is, musically, thereby leading the spectator upward into the realm of observation."[69] In his widely discussed lectures on dramatic art and literature given in Vienna in 1808, Schlegel argued that this sense of distance could also be achieved through irony, and he pointed to Shakespeare as the master of this device. Most poets and playwrights, Schlegel observed, are "partisan" in that they "demand blind belief" from readers and audiences. But "the more passionate the rhetoric, the more easily it falls short of its goal," for the perceptive public will recognize that it is being manipulated, and when it sees through the artifice will question its submission to the will of the artist.

> If on the other hand by a dexterous maneuver the poet occasionally turns the coin over onto its less shiny side, he thereby places himself in a secret understanding with a select circle of his readers, those who are most perceptive. He shows them that he has anticipated their objections and that he is not a captive of the objects being presented, but rather hovers freely above them, and that if he wanted to do things differently he could utterly annihilate that which he himself had magically conjured up.[70]

In England, Samuel Taylor Coleridge espoused a similar approach to the arts, one grounded in imagination and distanced contemplation. He, too, placed special value on the function of the Greek chorus. Schlegel and Coleridge together, as the literary historian Frederick Burwick so trenchantly puts it, "taught their generation a new way of looking at the drama, of watching their own watching." They, along with Goethe, Tieck, and Victor Hugo, "endeavored to transform the deliberations of philosophy and critical theory into the very substance and subject matter of their dramatic representation."[71]

Friedrich Schlegel, August Wilhelm's younger brother, went even further in his zeal to undermine the dictum of *ars est celare artem*. He maintained that "we would not accord much value to a transcendental philosophy that is not critical, that did not also portray the producer along with the product." Modern poetry should unite the kind of "artistic reflection and beautiful self-reflection found in the works of Pindar, the lyric fragments of the ancient Greeks, the antique elegy, and among more recent poets, Goethe. It should portray itself with each of its portrayals; it should be at one and the same time poetry and the poetry of poetry."[72]

Some philosophers (and most music critics, as we shall see) were nevertheless reluctant to declare music's emotional power subordinate to the more detached pleasure to be found in the contemplation of beauty, preferring instead to let both kinds of responses co-exist without necessarily being synthesized.[73] By this line of thought, judgment is supplemental, not essential, and not necessarily a goal in and of itself. In his *Handbuch der Ästhetik* of 1797, for example, Johann Heinrich Gottlieb Heusinger, a *Privatlehrer* of philosophy at the University of Jena, devotes considerable space to music and in the process reveals an outlook that is at once both conventional and forward-looking. He opens his text with the standard observation that "music is the art of eliciting specific feelings in listeners" but then goes on to qualify this by noting that "as an artist of *beauty*," the composer "is not satisfied merely to elicit these feelings but rather to elicit them in such a way that their arousal appropriately occupies all the faculties of the human mind, which is to say: the artist's way of arousing feelings is *beautiful*." Yet even within this Kantian framework, Heusinger declares that "the greatest art" in composing music ultimately

THE PLEASURE OF REFLECTION 91

consists of "bringing listeners to the point one wants to bring them."[74] So much for Kant's battle against oratorical coercion. Heusinger adds that it is advantageous but not essential to be a connoisseur (*Kenner*), for if the composer has understood his task, listeners will sense the unity in any given work even if the grounds for that unity remain indistinct in their minds.[75] Mozart's comment to his father about amateurs enjoying his new concertos "without knowing why" continues to resonate.

Kant's shadow loomed large over the many music critics at the turn of the nineteenth century who also took an interest in philosophy, and they played a key role in disseminating and modifying Kant's thoughts on the art. One of the most prominent, Johann Friedrich Reichardt, a native of Königsberg, was in fact a personal acquaintance of Kant, and he worked tirelessly to disseminate the philosopher's ideas about music. In the various (and invariably short-lived) journals he established, Reichardt published extended excerpts from and commentaries on Kant's writings. Less than a year after publication of the *Kritik der Urteilskraft*, he presented a digest of excerpts from it (linked to the relevant page numbers of the treatise), along with an extended passage from the opening of its §60, dealing with the "Methodology of Taste" ("Von der Methodenlehre des Geschmacks"), introducing the text to readers with the comment that "inquisitive artists and connoisseurs cannot study zealously enough this outstanding, illuminating work."[76] Reichardt at one point declared his intention to write a treatise on the aesthetics of music based on Kantian principles, something Kant himself had encouraged Reichardt to do, but the treatise never materialized.[77]

Johann Friedrich Rochlitz was another ardent Kantian. The very first page of the very first issue of his *Allgemeine musikalische Zeitung* evokes Kant, and he published excerpts relevant to music—on hearing, imagination, the arousing and subduing of the senses, and artistic taste—from Kant's *Anthropologie* within a year of the treatise's appearance.[78] We can get some sense of just how widely Kant's views on music were known at the time from an anonymous essay published by Rochlitz in his journal in 1802 under the title "Revelations about Music from the Works of Philosophers." Its author takes a dim view of Kant's thoughts on the matter but in the process notes that he will not spend much time on them, given that the philosopher's teachings on music were "already known to the readers of this journal."[79]

The familiarity of Rochlitz's readers with Kantian thought was due in no small measure to the writings of Christian Friedrich Michaelis, author of the two-volume monograph *Ueber den Geist der Tonkunst, mit Rücksicht auf Kants Kritik der ästhetischen Urtheilskraft* (1795–1800), a treatise which explicitly names the philosopher in its title ("On the Spirit of Music, with Regard to Kant's *Critique of Aesthetic Judgment*"). Michaelis was a frequent contributor to the *Allgemeine musikalische Zeitung* and other journals devoted to the arts, and he was unusually well connected in the philosophical world of his time. Born in Leipzig in 1754, he studied at Jena, where he heard Schiller lecture on aesthetics and formed a strong connection to the philosopher Carl Leonhard Reinhold, an important popularizer of Kantian philosophy. Michaelis was also acquainted with both Schlegel brothers and became especially close to Johann Friedrich Reichardt.[80]

For all his devotion to Kant, Michaelis believed that the philosopher had not gone far enough in his discussion of music.[81] Paradoxically, he extended the reach of Kant's thoughts on the matter by silently ignoring his categorical distinction between instrumental and vocal music. Thus, whereas Kant had allowed that vocal music, by virtue of its text, could provide listeners with an "aesthetic idea" but instrumental music could not, Michaelis tacitly but consistently assumes that all music is capable of doing this, with or without a text. He at one point even goes so far as to say that "aesthetic ideas constitute the spirit of music."[82] He takes issue with Kant's definition of music as "the art of beautiful play with sensations" and maintains that it can be at once both pleasure (*Genuss*) *and* culture (*Kultur*).[83]

> The definition of music as an *audible and beautified representation of human feelings and passions* therefore strikes me as too narrow ... Perhaps one could call it the art which, *through the manifold connection of tones, touches the feelings, enlivens and occupies the imagination, and attunes the mind to ideas of the beautiful and sublime*; or more briefly, as *the art which,*

THE PLEASURE OF REFLECTION

through an association of tones, arouses in unmediated fashion aesthetic feelings and in mediated fashion aesthetic ideas.[84]

More importantly still, Michaelis stresses the importance of imagination (*Einbildungskraft* or *Phantasie*) in the act of listening, thereby absolving instrumental music of its supposedly coercive nature, for imagination is an act of freedom. "The *indeterminacy* of musical representation"—and by this, Michaelis must surely have had music without a text in mind— "is highly favorable toward the *freedom* of our fantasy. In this respect, the musical delineation resembles the *aesthetic idea* of the poet, which allows us to glimpse an infinite realm of thought. In this manner, music has something *ideal* about itself, something that liberates and gives wings to the power of imagination and elevates it above confined reality."[85] Imagination is a marker of personal autonomy: listeners *do* something with their minds to what they hear, thereby transcending the plane of the exclusively sensory. Imagination is the faculty that elevates the experience of listening, and Michaelis emphasizes the joint agency of composer and listener in this process. "Music can be witty [*geistreich*] and beautiful," he maintained, "only to the extent that it expresses aesthetic ideas, that is, to the extent that it sets the power of imagination into a free and harmonious play, by which means an animating fullness of ideas is presented."[86]

> The artist places us in a position of *freedom*: he moves the powers of our disposition in lively and harmonious activity and arouses our delight in response to a presentation that we ourselves have constructed at his instigation. He places us in a world that does not impose itself on us from the outside but rather arises through our imagination in our mind and heart. It is a work of our own self-activity; it elevates us into a higher sphere in which we behold ourselves as free and autonomous, raised to self-reliance ... We discover ourselves in the products of fine art, in the free play of our imagination, which harmonizes with our understanding, thus liberated from the restraints imposed on us by the everyday prospect of reality, elevated above the compulsion of sensory impressions ... [87]

Michaelis places an aesthetic burden on listeners and composers alike: listeners who know little or nothing of music and regard it merely as a way of passing time and necessarily treat it as an art of pleasure, as opposed to an art of beauty.[88] The distinction between the fine and pleasing arts, it would seem, is thus ultimately a matter of perception, not ontology. The true composer, in turn, "does not dole out mere tones to me, he gives me something more than mere aural sensations." Tones, he maintains, "are merely the means to set my imagination in motion, to give it wings, to enchant me."

> And as far as musical feeling is concerned, anyone who gets hung up on what is isolated or incidental and does not raise himself up to a summation of the great whole, of the full aesthetic effect, lags well behind and does not know musical pleasure. For indeed the pleasure of music depends greatly on the individual strength of the *capacity to apprehend and synthesize*. According to the various dispositions of the soul and the psyche, an intricate, substantial composition will please at times, while a simpler, more easily constructed one will please at others. At times it is a fugue, at times a naïve little song or a flowing rondo that pleases. A capacious mind and a cultivated taste are receptive to any and all of these.[89]

Michaelis never spells out exactly how the imagination functions in the act of listening, but he hints at it from time to time. Quite apart from its charms and emotional powers, the beauty in music that pleases us consists of "the succession, structure, contrast, harmony, elaboration, and resolution of tones. The pleasure of music resides here in the formal element, which by analogy has been called, justifiably, musical *ideas* and *figures*."[90] He observes at one point that the "artificialities" (*Kunstgriffe*) in Haydn's works make his music "piquant, and give it above all a humoristic spirit, which acts upon the power of imagination with extraordinary liveliness."[91] These *Kunstgriffe* would presumably have included violations of music's fourth wall, those unpredictable turns for which Haydn's works were so widely renowned, even during his lifetime. Music that calls attention to itself, in other words, is more likely to engage the listener's imagination.

Friedrich Schlegel recognized the philosophical implications of reflective listening when he declared that:

> Many people find it strange and laughable whenever musicians talk about the ideas in their compositions, and indeed there may well often be instances when one senses that they have more ideas in their music than they do about it. But whoever has a feeling for the wonderful affinity of all the arts

and sciences will at least not consider the matter from the flat perspective of so-called naturalness, according to which music is supposedly merely the language of the senses. That individual will not consider it impossible that all purely instrumental music has a certain tendency toward philosophy. Doesn't purely instrumental music have to create a text for itself? And is its theme not developed, confirmed, varied, and contrasted in the same way as the object of contemplation in a philosophical succession of ideas?[92]

Jean Paul, in turn, has one of the characters in his novel *Flegeljahre* (1804–05) pose this question: "But how did you listen? Forwards and backwards, or just as it went along past you? The public, like cattle, hears only the present, not the two polar opposites of time, only musical syllables, no syntax. A good auditor of the word commits to memory the antecedent portion of a musical phrase in order to grasp as beautiful the consequent."[93]

This kind of reflective listening, which Kant either could not or would not recognize, allowed later writers to apply virtually all his concepts about aesthetics in general to instrumental music in particular. It also fatally undermined the long-standing conception of music without a text as a form of wordless oratory. For it is one thing to construct a musical work or movement along the lines of an oration, but the expectation that lay listeners should actually perceive this structure marks a radical departure from earlier assumptions about listening in the concert hall.

This new attitude plays a prominent role in the critic Johann Karl Triest's extended survey of music in German-speaking lands in the eighteenth century, published serially in Rochlitz's *Allgemeine musikalische Zeitung* in 1801. Triest never actually cites Kant by name, but his account reflects a firm grasp of the philosopher's aesthetics. He places great emphasis on imagination, noting that the fine arts allow us to bring our "mental powers into harmony" through a synthesis of the senses and reason, the former of which gives "the imagination material for free play," the latter of which brings order to what we perceive."[94] Triest explicitly rejects Kant's division between instrumental and vocal music, for "every fine art (including music)" can bear a "dual definition . . . partly as *pure* art," in which its sensuous material stimulates "the free and beautiful play of the imagination" and "partly (in keeping with its *empirical* origins)" as an "aesthetic means to other ends, especially the beautified representation of one or more subjects (their feelings and actions)," in which case it would qualify as "*applied* art."[95]

Triest's categories of "pure" and "applied" art correspond not to the presence or absence of words in any given work of music but rather to whether or not listeners perceive that work as in some way representational. Thus a work of instrumental music might qualify as "applied" if its purpose is to evoke a particular object, and a work of vocal music could qualify as "pure" if its "text says nothing" and serves "merely . . . as a vehicle for the employment of the voice."[96] In this sense Triest's categories correspond to Kant's idea of "pure" and "adherent" beauty, with the important difference that Triest places greater weight on the perception of music than on its ontology. Listeners, in other words, have the option to attend to the relationship of the music to a text, a program, or an evocative title, or to ignore these altogether.

Not surprisingly, then, Triest argues that because it is not bound to any verbal text, instrumental music engages the listener's imagination more freely than vocal music. But sensuousness remains subordinate to understanding. "The *least* effect" of instrumental music's "play of tones," he says, is "a mere *tickling of the senses* . . . A greater effect is created when the understanding is stimulated to examine the correctness, beauty, or artistic skill of the series of tones (for example in the case of works or passages in strict counterpoint)."[97] Once again, the implied mode of perception is synoptic, or more broadly speaking, reflective. Only in recent decades, Triest maintains, has music "assumed a fuller, more voluptuous form" by synthesizing the contrapuntal complexity and artistry of the early years of the century with the melodic simplicity and naturalness of mid-century.[98] Through its artful integration of variety and unity, the new style is complex enough to provide material for the imagination yet not so complex as to overwhelm the understanding.

When Triest goes on to apply Kant's notion of the aesthetic idea explicitly to instrumental music, he points to Carl Philipp Emanuel Bach as the first composer to have incorporated such ideas into his works:

THE PLEASURE OF REFLECTION

No, Bach did not make an effort to compose in a dark and difficult manner; instead these characteristics flowed naturally from his ideas, in which the mechanical (merely reckoning) musician was as incapable of following him as was the musician who sought only sensuous delight. What was stirring in him was a kind of *aesthetic* idea, i.e., one that combines concepts and emotion, and that does not allow itself to be expressed in words, although it comes very *close* to the *specific* emotion that song can depict for us, and of which it is, as it were, the archetype. He translated this to his keyboard (or into notes), whereby his intimate familiarity with the tonal mechanism almost automatically furnished him with the necessary forms. Since his *poetic spirit* restrained him from using common ideas whenever he was permitted to compose freely, it was inevitable that those people who did not possess a kindred spirit would fail to understand it and even with repeated practice would barely recognize what a rich trove of ideas it contained. Bach was another Klopstock, who used tones *instead of* words ... This does not outweigh, but rather adds to his great achievement, namely his demonstration that pure music is no mere shell for applied music, or abstraction from it, but that it could achieve great aims by itself. He showed that it had no need to contort itself prosaically, or at best rhetorically, as a mere game for the senses or the intellect, but instead had the capacity to raise itself up to the level of poetry, which is the more pure, the less it is dragged down into the realm of common perception by words (which always contain second meanings).[99]

The reference to Friedrich Gottfired Klopstock is to a poet whose works were celebrated for their complexity and depth: this was not poetry to be grasped readily on first reading. Instead, it provided material for the understanding and imagination to work in harmony.

Triest's observations at the turn of the new century reflect a growing acceptance that borders on an imperative to listen to instrumental music as an object, as an artform whose value goes beyond its sensuous and emotional appeal. By ignoring Kant's fundamental distinction between vocal and instrumental music, and by applying the concept of aesthetic ideas to the latter, Triest effectively elevates music without words into the pantheon of the fine arts.

By the time Johann Nikolas Forkel got around to publishing the second volume of his *Allgemeine Geschichte der Musik* in 1801, Kantian principles of aesthetic judgment had been appropriated to instrumental music so widely that he seems not to have felt it necessary to go into much detail to justify his position. "The true business of music," he asserted, is to "transport us into beneficent states of mind."[100] And the nature of that pleasure is decidedly more than just sensory, for the "full pleasure" of the art is accessible only to those who make the effort to understand it.

> If we wish to have the full pleasure musical impressions can give us, we must, through attention and exercise, come to the aid of . . . our capacity, given to us by nature, to receive those impressions. Nature has only planted the seed for this in us; the cultivation of that seed is our own work, the work of our diligence and efforts.[101]
>
> In the end, a lack of appropriate practice and development of the organs of hearing is the most common cause of our lesser capacity to receive musical impressions. As far as music is concerned, one must say about a large portion of human beings that they have ears and hear not; not because they cannot hear but because they lack the necessary attention that is required for hearing as well as seeing, to determine if an object is to be distinguished in all its attributes from other objects of a similar kind.[102]

It is now the responsibility of listeners to make sense of what they are hearing. We are worlds removed from the standard formulations from only a few decades before of instrumental music as "the language of the heart."

In an unusually clear application of Kantian aesthetics to instrumental music, published in the *Allgemeine musikalische Zeitung* in 1811, the jurist Georg von Weiler flatly rejected the idea that symphonies, quartets, and the like exist in order to convey specific sentiments. Instead, the mind (*Geist*) perceives beauty in these genres:

> The free play of a melody through different keys and their juxtapositions, along with varied rhythms, surprising transitions and modulations, embellished figures, the relationship of the instruments toward each other, the sage distribution of effects, and so on—all these can understandably occupy the mind and keep it actively engaged without the necessity of it being presented with an emotion, a specific sentiment. But when it actually occurs to someone to set a verbal text to a quartet by Mozart, as a Frenchman has recently done (presumably to provide a certain justification for the composer) as a way of demonstrating that a work like this might permit one *to think something* as well: this betrays a complete misunderstanding about the aesthetic value of a work of music.[103]

THE PLEASURE OF REFLECTION 99

Commentaries like these from Reichardt, Michaelis, Triest, Forkel, and Weiler reinforce Karol Berger's thesis that it was in the second half of the eighteenth century that "European art music began to take seriously the flow of time from past to future" and that "musical form became primarily temporal." Berger sees this as part of a larger transformation in conceptions of time, one that moved from cyclical to linear, a conception reflected in contemporaneous compositional practices.[104] This new way of composing had major consequences for listening as well, for it demanded both memory and anticipation, along with the power of imagination to connect the two.

Post-Kantian music critics thus used Kantian categories and concepts to justify the art of instrumental music. But they largely rejected Kant's insistence, noted earlier, that "taste is always still barbaric when it needs the addition of *charms* and *emotions* for satisfaction, let alone if it makes these into the standard for its approval."[105] The sensory pleasure of music remained an essential element of the aesthetic experience for most of these critics, and they recognized that music could satisfy on more than one level.

Georg August Griesinger's brief response to Kant in a note published in the *Allgemeine musikalische Zeitung* in 1800 exemplifies this more tolerant attitude toward sensory pleasure. Griesinger took umbrage at Kant's tendency to equate all instrumental music with *Tafelmusik*, literally "table music," that is, music for a banquet, or as we would call it today, background music. It was possible, Griesinger argued, to enjoy instrumental music either as an art of pleasure or as an art of beauty, depending on the circumstances. Rather than categorize works of music themselves, he preferred to categorize the ways in which they could be experienced.

> As a work of *beautiful* art, music wants to please only through its form, that is, through its structure and the purity of its tones. As a work of *pleasurable* art it wants to delight by arousing charms and emotions. In the former, it acts upon the taste of reflection; in the latter, it acts upon the taste of the senses . . . For this reason one becomes indignant when some Midas interrupts the solemn stillness of a concert or at the opera by

making noise and chatting in a venue where the music puts itself on display primarily as an art of beauty, where every ear should be listening carefully to comprehend the sequence, choice, and concatenation of the notes that the genius of the composer has conjured up as if by magic.

The demands music is entitled to make as a *pleasurable* art, by contrast, are far more modest. In this case, music is not a work of poetic power that exists for its own sake, but rather only as a means by which to achieve some sort of particular goal. It wants to elicit and nourish feelings and sentiments; it is not a free beauty but rather an adherent beauty, i.e., it establishes in advance a concept of what it should be and a perfection that corresponds to that concept . . . In this regard, *Tafelmusik* has unmistakable value . . . Or should music never be allowed under any circumstances to present itself as a *pleasurable* art? Neither sculpture nor painting nor even poetry subjects itself to such rigor.[106]

Here, Griesinger rejects the notion that reflective listening is inherently superior to resonant listening, for both are appropriate according to the prevailing circumstances. In making this distinction, Griesinger nevertheless implicitly endorses the ideal of reflective listening in the concert hall, and growing numbers of the music-loving public would come to accept this ideal as well, even going so far as to learn how to listen in what (for them) was a new way, one that involved the mind as well as the heart.

These long-term changes in the musical world did not take place in isolation. A similar phenomenon was already well underway in the late eighteenth century in literature, where critics were making an increasingly overt distinction between "light" and "refined" modes of reading, a distinction Martha Woodmansee has since called "the policing of reading," an inculcation of moral value into not only what readers should read but also how they should read.[107] In the visual arts, connoisseurship was also gaining a broader footing around this time. This was, after all, the Age of Winckelmann, who taught his contemporaries new ways of seeing.[108] By the early nineteenth century, critical journals aimed at lay audiences were proliferating in all the arts, a reflection of the rapid expansion of public culture.[109] "Informed" consumption would soon become the accepted standard, and music, as we shall see in the next chapter, was no exception.

4

The Prestige of Reflection

Everybody passes judgment upon music, some through blind instinct
and very hastily, others by means of a cultivated taste and with reflection.
Who would dare to say that the first sort of judgment is better than the
second?"

—François-Joseph Fétis (1830)[1]

Listeners' assumptions about their responsibilities in the concert hall
changed only gradually over the course of the nineteenth century,
but it is fair to say that by 1850 concert audiences routinely accepted
reflective listening as the preferred mode of perception. Whether or not
they actually listened in this way necessarily varied from individual to
individual. This was, nevertheless, the standard to which any serious
music-lover aspired. Composers no longer bore the sole burden of in-
telligibility. Many, in fact, encouraged the belief that their works were
meant to be interpreted, not only by performers (as had always been the
case) but now by listeners as well.

From Oratory to Poetry

In the years around 1800, an ever-growing number of critics began to
treat musical works as objects to be contemplated as well as experienced.
The long-standing parallels between listening to an oration and listening
to a work of instrumental music became increasingly tenuous around

Music's Fourth Wall and the Rise of Reflective Listening. Mark Evan Bonds, Oxford University Press.
© Oxford University Press 2025. DOI: 10.1093/9780197806401.003.0005

this time: whereas orators had to convince an audience on the spot, composers were starting to exercise varying degrees of license to confront listeners with works that demanded reflection. The idea of having to listen to an oration twice or read a written version of it afterward in order to grasp its import was nothing short of nonsensical ("I liked Marc Antony's speech but would need to hear it again in order to be certain I really understood what he was saying about Caesar"). But this was precisely the new standard critics began to apply to certain challenging works of music in the early nineteenth century. Calls for repeated hearings are the surest sign that oratory could no longer function as an adequate analogue of musical performance. This becomes particularly evident in the contemporaneous reception of Beethoven's early- and middle-period works. After a performance of the composer's Second Symphony in Leipzig in 1804, for example, Johann Friedrich Rochlitz hailed it as

> a remarkable, colossal work, of a depth, strength, and artful learnedness like few others—of a difficulty in intent and execution for the composer as well for a large orchestra . . . most surely unlike any other known symphony. It wants to be played again and again, even by the most skilled orchestra, until the marvelous sum of original and at times strangely grouped ideas conjoin sufficiently, round themselves out, and now emerge as a great unity in the way they had appeared in the composer's mind. But it also wants to be heard again and again until even the educated listener will be able to follow the detail in the whole and the whole in the detail and enjoy it with the requisite leisure of enthusiasm.[2]

Another critic, writing from Vienna in 1807, declined to pass judgment on "an entirely new symphony by Beethoven"—the Fourth—after only a single hearing.[3] A different critic noted in 1824 that a "new quartet" by Schubert (likely the String Quartet in A minor, D. 804) would have to be heard "many times in order to be soundly judged."[4] The conceptual model of instrumental music as a wordless oration is clearly no longer in play here, for a speech or musical performance either "works" on first hearing or it does not.

THE PRESTIGE OF REFLECTION 103

Reactions like these would remain the exception rather than the rule for some time yet, but the fact that critics were making them at all points to the early stages of a sea-change in the protocols of listening. One particularly striking instance of this new attitude appears in an early review of Beethoven's String Quartet in B♭ Major, op. 130. The anonymous Viennese critic declared the work's finale (later published separately as the *Grosse Fuge*, op. 133) to be "incomprehensible, like Chinese."

> When the instruments have to struggle with enormous difficulties in the regions of the North and South Poles, when each of them presents a different figuration and crosses the others *per transitum* irregularly amidst countless dissonances, when the players, suspicious of themselves, do not attack entirely cleanly: then truly the Babylonian confusion has been consummated.[5]

Yet this same critic, having accused Beethoven of writing in what amounts to a foreign language, goes on to concede that "we do not want to dismiss things too hastily. Perhaps the time will come when that which on first sight seemed to us opaque and muddled will be recognized as clear and pleasing forms."[6] The last comment reads like a paraphrase of 1 Corinthians 13:12: For now we hear through a glass, darkly.

The idea of suspending judgment until a subsequent hearing implies a depth to be fathomed, and while an oration might well possess depth—the best ones in fact do—that quality was not meant to inhibit listeners from passing immediate judgment on what they had just heard. In the realm of oratory, depth was a means toward an end and not an end in its own right.

Critics of the time recognized this move away from the conceptual model of oratory. Triest, in his 1801 survey of music in German-speaking lands in the eighteenth century, explicitly noted that the music of recent times had shifted from the principles of rhetoric to the principles of poetry, a genre that demanded imagination of its listeners. It fell to C. P. E. Bach, according to Triest, to bring a new "poetic spirit" to music, even though many in the public rejected it. A portion of Triest's commentary, cited earlier, is worth revisiting in this context:

> Because his *poetic spirit* restrained him from using common ideas when-
> ever he was permitted to compose freely, it was inevitable that those people
> who were not of a kindred spirit would fail to understand it, and even after
> repeated practice, they could barely recognize what a rich trove of ideas
> were concealed in it. Bach was another Klopstock, who used tones *instead
> of* words. Is it the fault of the singer of odes if his lyrical leaps seem like
> nonsense to the rough multitude?[7]

This is an extraordinary indictment for its time: if listeners cannot comprehend what Bach has written, it is *they* who are to blame, not the
composer. The "lyrical leaps" (*Schwunge*) Triest finds in Bach's music
are closely associated with the genre of the ode. These are moments of
surprise and excess, moments that shock.[8] Triest's language, moreover,
is bitingly dismissive: "der rohe Haufen" translates literally as "the raw
heap," with *Haufen* the equivalent of a crowd or mob and *roh* suggesting
elements of crudeness and coarseness. Proper listening is a sign of a cultivated mind.

Poems in general and odes in particular demand reflection: they
are to be lingered over, interpreted, committed to memory, repeated.
Poetry calls attention to itself as language because it uses language in
ways that stand outside ordinary speech. Poems compel us to reflect
on the vehicle of language itself. What really counts, in other words,
is not so much *what* is expressed but *how* it is expressed. There is,
after all, no rhetoric of poetry, for as Walter J. Ong reminds us, a
poem is "a thing for contemplation," whereas an oration, through its
application of rhetoric, aims at the "production of action in another
individual," and specifically an action that is "something other than
contemplation."[9] Contemplation implies depth, and the growing
perception of depth in instrumental music around 1800—the perception of instrumental music as an object worthy of reflection—
manifests the broader move away from the conceptual framework of
oratory.

This is not to say that poetry is incapable of giving unmediated
pleasure. William Wordsworth famously argued on many occasions for
the directness and immediacy of the art's emotional power:

THE PRESTIGE OF REFLECTION   105

> The Poet writes under one restriction only, namely, the necessity of giving immediate pleasure to a human . . . Nor let this necessity of producing immediate pleasure be considered as a degradation of the Poet's art. It is far otherwise. . . . We have no sympathy but what is propagated by pleasure . . . We have no knowledge, that is, no general principles drawn from the contemplation of particular facts, but what has been built up by pleasure, and exists in us by pleasure alone.[10]

The insistence of Wordsworth's tone speaks to the strength of the position he was attacking. He wanted to restore to poetry a fourth wall that had long since crumbled—to the extent that it had ever existed at all. For while poetry can (and does) make use of rhetorical strategies and devices, it operates under a fundamentally different set of assumptions than oratory. Poetry encourages freedom from convention and embraces degrees of ambiguity and even obscurity in ways that oratory simply does not, or in the case of music prior to 1800, largely had not. Poetry makes no attempt to masquerade as "natural": it is inherently self-conscious and meant to be perceived as such.

In this sense, the image of music as poetry and the composer as a "tone-poet" or *Tondichter* (as Beethoven liked to think of himself) further hastened the dismantling of music's fourth wall. Critics helped propagate this neologism, not because instrumental compositions translated semantic meaning into sound—some did, most did not—but rather because the works composers were producing were now meant to be heard as objects to be contemplated. By these lights, composers were no longer orators but oracles, revealing higher truths in a veiled manner. Oracles demand interpretation: their pronouncements are crafted not within the framework of rhetoric but within the framework of riddles. Listeners must necessarily make an effort to grasp their import.

Learning to Listen

The growing presumption of depth in instrumental music cast ever-growing doubt on the hedonistic surface of sensory pleasure. Intellectual pleasure—based on reflection, taste, and judgment—presumes a contrast with any pleasure that might emanate directly from the material itself. Simply "by calling the surface a surface," as the musicologist Robert Fink points out, "we have already crystallized an anxiety."[11]

How, then, could listeners overcome that anxiety and plumb those depths? The expectation that the music-loving public should make at least some effort to acquire listening skills was slow to develop. Johann Nikolaus Forkel's lectures in Göttingen in the 1770s and 1780s found no immediate successors. Forkel was very much an outlier, and even his modest efforts met with resistance from none other than Johann Friedrich Reichardt, who took him to task for outlining a series of topics too limited for those with knowledge of the art and too advanced for those who knew nothing of it. Reichardt questioned both the utility and feasibility of the enterprise: he valued the dilettante's naïve and natural response to music precisely because it was naïve and natural. The kind of learning outlined in *Ueber die Theorie der Musik*, Reichardt argued, was worse than no learning at all, for it would rob dilettantes of their spontaneity without providing them the rigorous technical grounding that would foster true understanding. To his way of thinking, such listeners would be better served by reading about the history and aesthetics of music.[12] Johann Friedrich Rochlitz, too, harbored reservations about just how much technical knowledge amateurs could usefully absorb without a thorough study of harmony, counterpoint, and the like.[13]

In the meantime, journals helped musical amateurs develop their listening skills, albeit in an indirect and unsystematic manner. There is a strong undercurrent of self-improvement in this literature. Heinrich Christoph Koch, in his *Journal der Tonkunst* (1795), noted that "healthy eyesight" does not ensure "true pleasure" in taking in works of visual art and that, by the same token, a healthy sense of hearing is not sufficient to ensure pleasure in listening to music. Amateurs must cultivate for themselves "a certain degree of artistic feeling" in order to "deem works of art beautiful and enjoy the pleasure they provide."[14] Koch, like other journal editors of his time, was no disinterested third party: in

THE PRESTIGE OF REFLECTION 107

encouraging the public to learn more about music, he was at the same time promoting his own journal. Like Forkel and Reichardt, he identified an emerging market for journals aimed at the music-loving public, even if their various enterprises were ultimately short-lived. Rochlitz recognized the opportunities as well and in 1798 launched what turned out to be the first long-running journal of its kind, the *Allgemeine musikalische Zeitung*. Its success was due not only to the quality of its content but also to the ever-growing public demand for knowledge about music.

In the inaugural volume of his journal, Rochlitz created a taxonomy of listeners to explain just how and why opinions about any given work of music could vary so widely. The lowest category, he maintained, consists of those who attend concerts solely out of vanity or fashion and would rather chat than actually attend to the music. The next level comprises those connoisseurs who are traditionalists, fixated on rules, conventions, and the repertory of their youth. This group consists of men (and no women) who are mostly advanced in age and who find the music of the present to be "without charms." It also includes "virtuosos who are nothing more than virtuosos." The next higher group consists of those "who listen only with their ears, good, harmless little people" who enjoy dancing. And then finally come those who listen "with their entire soul," who know and understand their position between the poles of the intellectual and the sensuous.[15]

The prestige of reflective listening is evident throughout the journals of the time, even in such unexpected venues as an 1806 notice of a treatise on thoroughbass, in which the unnamed reviewer endorses the book's recommendation that even "mediocre keyboard players, including those of the fair sex, no less," should possess a knowledge of harmony on the grounds that it "provides much delight," and

> only in this way can one learn to recognize the whole of the composition. Indeed, one could add to this that without this body of knowledge, no true insight into music is possible at all. It follows that the pleasure in products of this art would have to remain only a sensory and purely agreeable charm, a mere play of the so-called lower senses, never able to become the play actually intended by the art.

The reviewer goes on to note that it is a lack of musical knowledge that has compelled so many "philosophers, critics, and their imitators," to follow the lead of Kant and relegate instrumental music to the category of the merely pleasurable arts.[16]

Critical notices of newly published music gradually began to take on a new tone, becoming longer, more detailed, and often more technical. A lengthy review of Beethoven's Third Piano Concerto, op. 37, published in the *Allgemeine musikalische Zeitung* in 1805, is full of notated examples, as is a review of the *Eroica* Symphony from 1807 in the same journal.[17] E. T. A. Hoffmann's 1810 review of the Fifth Symphony falls within this broader trend of greater technical detail. His account includes no fewer than twenty-two musical examples, one of them in full score. While rightly hailed as a landmark of analysis, it also sent its initial readers a more subtle message about the art of listening. The opening portion of the review treats the work from the perspective of its effect, which includes the oft-quoted assertion that "Beethoven's music sets in motion the lever of horror, fear, revulsion, and pain" and "awakens that infinite longing that is the essence of romanticism."[18] The bulk of the review, however, seeks to explain just *how* the music creates that effect and goes into considerable technical detail in pursuit of this goal. Hoffmann makes a special effort to demonstrate the overarching coherence of the symphony as a whole, manifested most obviously by the repeated and varied manipulations of the short-short-short-LONG rhythm that underlies the opening theme of the first movement and many subsequent ideas as well, including ones in the later movements. This is precisely the kind of synoptic listening earlier writers had been encouraging, a kind of listening that synthesizes memory, anticipation, and imagination.

A wave of other new journals followed the lead of the *Allgemeine musikalische Zeitung* in helping their readers become better listeners. These included the *Allgemeine musikalische Zeitung, mit besonderer Rücksicht auf den österreichischen Kaiserstaat* (Vienna, 1817–24), *The Harmonicon* (London, 1823–33), *Cäcilia* (Mainz, 1824–48), the *Berliner Allgemeine musikalische Zeitung* (Berlin, 1824–30), and the *Revue musicale* (Paris,

1827–35). The goal of music criticism, as articulated in 1824 by Adolph Bernhard Marx in the inaugural issue of his *Berliner Allgemeine musikalische Zeitung*, was "the understanding of the nature of every artistic means, of every artwork, of every artist, and finally of all art." Taste, he conceded, can change from generation to generation, but music lovers have an obligation to understand the aesthetics of any given period.[19] Listening entails responsibility.

Marx's new journal and many others like it reflect an exponential growth in public music culture in the early decades of the nineteenth century, itself the product of many social and technological changes: a steep decline of aristocratic patronage, increasing access to mass-produced pianos for the home, more cost-effective printing technologies that allowed for relatively inexpensive published music, expanding networks of public transportation, and growing populations in general.[20] An increasing number of general-interest journals of the time also included music in their coverage.[21]

There is even evidence that at least some listeners were beginning to follow the course of what they were hearing with the aid of the recently developed medium of the miniature ("pocket") score. Griesinger reported from Vienna to the Leipzig publisher Breitkopf & Härtel in 1802 that Pleyel's "very elegant pocket edition in octavo" of Haydn's string quartets was being used in concert halls by "amateurs and connoisseurs" alike.[22]

By 1830, these developments had at last created a viable European market for an extended "how-to-listen" guide, and the Belgian music historian and critic François-Joseph Fétis met that demand in spectacularly successful fashion with his *La musique mise à la portée de tout le monde: Exposé succinct de tout ce qui est nécessaire pour juger de cet art, et pour en parler sans l'avoir étudié*. His book went through two subsequent authorial editions (1834, 1847) and was translated into German (1830), Russian (1833), Spanish (1840), English (1842), and Italian (1858).[23] Fétis's book, the first extended account of its kind, bears all the elements that would come to characterize music appreciation texts down to the present day. While their organization and points of emphasis might vary, their principles have remained unchanged. They justify themselves on the grounds that an enhanced knowledge of music will enhance the pleasure of listening. They imply and occasionally state outright that sensory pleasure by itself is insufficient. They present in layperson's terms the basic elements of music and point to selected works as paradigmatic examples of the art. Finally, they encourage listeners to approach music as an object to be understood. For Fétis's text and its many successors, there is no fourth wall in music.

Fétis defines music as "the art of *moving the emotions by combinations of sounds*."[24] He prefers to think of music not in terms of what it expresses—what is "in" the music itself—but rather in terms of its effect on listeners, one that ideally transcends an exclusively sensory pleasure. "If there were nothing more in music than a principle of vague sensation," and if the art existed "merely to gratify the sense of hearing," he points out, "it would not deserve any more consideration than the culinary art. There would, in fact, be but little difference between the merit of a musician and that of a cook. But it is not so. It is not the ear alone which is affected by music. If music unites certain qualities, it produces emotion, in an indeterminate manner indeed, but more powerfully than painting, sculpture, or any other art."[25]

Judgment, however, is central. "To feel," Fétis points out, "is the vocation of all humanity; to judge is the province of the skillful." The effects of instrumental music "are in truth felt only by those who have been educated in it."[26] Fétis assures readers early on that there is a great difference between "vague feeling, which has no other origin than unreflected sensations, and that certainty of judgment which results from positive knowledge." Only by studying music's principles can we "increase our enjoyment" in the process of "forming our taste."[27] The purpose of his book, Fétis declares, is "to point out the means of increasing enjoyment, and of directing the judgment without the necessity of a long novitiate, which one rarely has the time and the inclination to go through."[28] The implication behind all of this is that one's social standing will improve, for "to speak of what one is ignorant of is a mania which affects the whole world, because no one is willing to appear ignorant of any thing.

THE PRESTIGE OF REFLECTION 111

This is seen in politics, in literature, in the sciences, and especially in the fine arts."[29] Everybody passes judgment upon music, some through blind instinct and very hastily, others by means of a cultivated taste and with reflection. Who would dare to say that the first sort of judgment is better than the second?"[30]

Judgment, moreover, is inseparable from perception itself, at least in the case of those who have made the effort to familiarize themselves with the elements of music. The analysis of one's response to the music is "made with the rapidity of lightning once we have acquired the habit of it; it becomes an element in our mode of feeling to such a degree that it is itself transformed into a sensation."[31] The skilled listener

> does not limit himself to apprehending some of the details of forms, to distinguishing the rhythm of the melodies, the more or less dramatic expression, etc. The musician comprehends all the details of harmony, takes notice of a sound in a chord which is not properly resolved, or of a happy employment of an unexpected dissonance, of an uncommon modulation, and of all the niceties of the simultaneity or succession of sounds; he distinguishes the different qualities of sound of the instruments, applauds or censures innovations upon rules, or the abuse of resources; in short, the immense details of all that constitutes the grand musical masses are present to his mind as if he were carefully examining them upon paper. Is it supposed that he makes these remarks with difficulty, that this prevents him from relishing the general effect of the composition, and that he derives less pleasure from it, than one who blindly gives himself up to his sensations? Not at all. He never even thinks of all these things; they are present to his thoughts, as if by enchantment, without his knowing it, and even without any attention on his part. What a wonderful effect of an organization improved by study and observation! All that would seem likely to weaken the sensation and to increase the share of the understanding turns to the advantage of this very sensation.[32]

This is all very Kantian: perception and judgment are essentially simultaneous. Fétis in fact at several points encourages listeners to set aside their emotional responses altogether when judging what they hear. "If we manage to defend ourselves from all the weaknesses which mislead our judgment and injure our sensations, we will then truly commence the act of intelligence by analyzing our sensations and judging their nature."[33] As listeners, "we ought always to abstain from forming an opinion until we have examined our consciences and separated from our heart and mind everything that might paralyze the action of the understanding."[34]

> Let a man of the world, instead of giving himself up, without reserve, to the vague pleasure which he receives from an air or a duet, set himself to examine its construction, to consider the arrangement and the repetition of its phrases, the principal rhythms, the cadences, etc. At first this labor will be painful and will break in upon his enjoyment; but by degrees a habit of attention will be formed which will soon become spontaneous. Then that which at first seemed to be merely a matter of dry calculation will become the foundation of a ready judgment, and the source of the liveliest gratification.[35]

Listening has become a form of labor. But we must persevere: "To learn to analyze the principle of musical sensations is doubtless a study which diverts attention from what may please the senses; this study disturbs the pleasure which one would experience in the hearing of music; but of what consequence is it if it suspends this pleasure only to render it more vivid? The study will every day become less painful when we shall have formed the habit of it, and the time will come when the analysis will be made unconsciously, and without disturbing our sensations."[36]

> I would say of instrumental music what I have had occasion to repeat several times: we must have patience to hear it without prepossessions, even though it should not please. With perseverance, we shall at length enjoy it, and then we may begin to analyse it; for this kind of music also has its melodies, its rhythm, its symmetrical quantities, its varieties of form, its effects of harmony, and its modes of instrumentation.[37]

At the beginning of his book's final chapter, Fétis acknowledges that the kind of listening he endorses requires conscious effort, but he insists that this will ultimately lead to a higher form of pleasure:

> I am sure that many readers, in running over the preceding chapter, will have said—"What does this man mean with his analyses? Does he wish to spoil our pleasure by a continual toil, incompatible with the enjoyment of the arts? These must be felt, not analyzed. Away with these observations, and these comparisons, which are at best adapted only to those dry

THE PRESTIGE OF REFLECTION   113

souls who can find nothing else in music, or to the professors of counter-point. We wish to enjoy, and not to judge, and therefore we have no need of reasonings." This is all very well. Heaven knows that I have no wish to disturb your pleasures . . .

Does any one persuade himself that I am so destitute of sense as to desire to substitute an analysis of the products of the arts for the pleasures which they give? No, no; such has not been my intention; but, being certain that we see only that which we have learned to look at, that we hear only that to which we know how to listen—that our senses, in short, and consequently our sensations, are developed only by exercise—I have sought to show how that of hearing should be directed, to render it more capable of compre-hending the impressions of music . . . .[38]

Fétis's preferred mode of listening is worlds removed from the oratorical framework of a previous generation. We must attend to the mechanism of the art we are hearing, to the elements behind the effect. Music's fourth wall has vanished.

Considering the immense commercial success of *La musique mise à la portée de tout le monde*, imitations were remarkably slow to ap-pear, at least in the form of monographs. The mission of educating the concert-going public nevertheless flourished in the realm of journalistic criticism, a genre Fétis himself would continue to cultivate with extraor-dinary energy. The 1830s witnessed the founding of yet another wave of new music journals that would go on to enjoy long runs, most notably the *Neue Zeitschrift für Musik (Leipzig, 1834–)*, the *Revue et Gazette musicale de Paris* (Paris, 1835–80), *Le ménestrel* (Paris, 1833/4–1940), *La France musicale* (Paris, 1837–70), and *The Musical World* (London, 1836–91). The feuilletons of general-interest newspapers routinely cov-ered new works of music, and the phenomenon of the composer-critic became increasingly common: Hector Berlioz, Robert Schumann, Franz Liszt, and Richard Wagner all took to prose to promulgate their opinions on the art of music, and not merely their own. By exposing general audi-ences to the composer's workshop, showing the ways in which creators of music thought about their art, these composer-critics helped under-mine the premise of music's fourth wall in subtle but effective ways. Schumann's lengthy review of Berlioz's *Symphonie fantastique* (1835) builds on Hoffmann's earlier review of Beethoven's Fifth Symphony and similarly constitutes, among other things, a roadmap for listeners, a way for them to make sense of a new and highly unconventional work. The same may be said of Liszt's later (1855) and equally lengthy essay—it would be misleading to call it a review—that takes Berlioz's *Harold en Italie* as its point of departure. As Alexandra Hui has recently observed, "much nineteenth-century music criticism was a reexamination of the proper form of listening."[39]

Not everyone embraced this new approach. Johann Christian Lobe, the author of a widely respected treatise on composition, could note in 1852 that "one should not *think* while listening to music but instead feel, *enjoy*." Intellectual satisfaction from music's form and the manipulation of thematic ideas, he acknowledged, could indeed heighten one's pleasure, but he took to task those composers who wrote only for connoisseurs.[40] Lobe's position reflects the prevailing attitude throughout most of the nineteenth century and helps explain the relative neglect or puzzlement over many of Beethoven's later works, particularly the string quartets.

By the closing decades of the century, however, public concert life had grown sufficiently to create a robust market for how-to-listen books. The increasing complexity of music's formal and harmonic language and the proliferation of heterogeneous idioms made the demand all the greater.[41] The principal self-justification for such guides has remained consistent down to the present: heightened understanding leads to heightened pleasure. Only the phrasing differs. A few representative examples:

> W. S. B. Mathews, *How to Understand Music: A Concise Course in Musical Intelligence and Taste* (Chicago: Author, 1880), 5.
>> The object of all this study is two-fold; first, to develop in the public a consciousness of the inherent relation between music and feeling; and second, to do this by means of master-works, which, of course, form the only complete and authoritative illustrations of this relation. In this way musical perceptions are sharpened, the student is introduced to the best parts of musical literature, and thereby his taste and musical feeling are cultivated.

THE PRESTIGE OF REFLECTION

Henry Edward Krehbiel, *How to Listen to Music: Hints and Suggestions to Untaught Lovers of the Art* (New York: C. Scribner's Sons, 1896), 15–16.

> There is something so potent and elemental in the appeal which music makes that it is possible to derive pleasure from even an unwilling hearing or a hearing unaccompanied by effort at analysis; but real appreciation of its beauty, which means recognition of the qualities which put it in the realm of art, is conditioned upon intelligent hearing. The higher the intelligence, the keener will be the enjoyment, if the former be directed to the spiritual side as well as the material.

Gustav Kobbé, *How to Appreciate Music* (New York: Moffat, Yard, 1906), 23.

> Among these [music-lovers] is an ever-growing number that "wants to know," that no longer is satisfied simply with allowing music to play upon the senses and the emotions, but wants to understand why it does so. To satisfy this natural desire which, with many, amounts to a craving or even a passion, and to do so in wholly untechnical language to the average reader, is the purpose of this book.

Edward Dickinson, *The Education of a Music Lover: A Book for Those Who Study or Teach the Art of Listening* (New York, C. Scribner's Sons, 1911), vii–viii.

> It goes without saying that so extensive a survey of musical art as I propose is not intended for those who hear music only for transient, superficial pleasure. Not that I would condemn such pleasure;—the instant joy, the sudden elevation of mood which fine music brings, even to those who know nothing about its principles, is not to be despised; the effect is not altogether evanescent, since every impression upon the senses alters the mental constitution, and even a slight visitation of truth or beauty leaves us a little higher in reason's scale than we were before. But still, this fugitive experience does not quite satisfy a person who is constantly bent on self-improvement, and he will be inclined to ask how he can add something more tangible to his momentary satisfactions, and draw from music that which will call into play his active powers of observation and reflection and give his understanding something solid to feed upon.

William Henry Hadow, "Introduction" to Percy Scholes, *The Listener's Guide to Music* (London: Oxford University Press, 1919), vii.

> Berlioz divided bad critics into "ceux qui ne sentent pas" and "ceux qui ne savent pas," and any one who will take the trouble may at least keep out of the latter class. If he does he will find to his reward that admiration grows as knowledge grows, and that the keener his perception

and the more sympathetic his judgement, the fuller and more enduring will his pleasure become.

Ethel Peyser, *How to Enjoy Music: A First-Aid to Music Listeners* (New
York: G. P. Putnam's Sons, 1933), vii.
This little book is designed for the listener who knows absolutely
nothing about music, save that he knows it is beautiful and that he is
exposed to something from which he receives less than is his due. I aim
merely to give him a way to get an earhold so that he may listen with a
little more intelligence and less strain and thus may enjoy more deeply.

Hugh M. Miller, *Introduction to Music: A Guide to Good Listening* (New
York: Barnes and Noble, 1958), 1:
. . . [T]o obtain the greatest enjoyment from music you must have some
understanding of it . . . No matter how sublime an experience a musical performance proves to be for you, any additional understanding
which you can bring to the music will enhance your ultimate pleasure.

Joseph Machlis, *Music: Adventures in Listening* (New York: W. W. Norton,
1966), 4–5:
[T]he great composers did not write their music to serve as a background for other activities . . . [S]ounds are forming patterns, and you
cannot understand them unless you hear how the patterns are related.

Mark Evan Bonds, *Listen to This* (Upper Saddle River, NJ: Prentice-Hall,
2009), ix:
Smart listening can help us enjoy whatever music we like even more.
The better we know how a piece works, the more deeply it will move us.

Roger Kamien, *Music: An Appreciation*, 12th ed. (New York: McGraw-
Hill, 2018), 2:
Perceptive, aware listening makes any musical experience more intense
and satisfying.

Comparable books with comparable statements scarcely exist for lovers of the theater or cinema, where the fourth wall has remained largely
intact. Those audiences can, of course, read up on the ins-and-outs of
acting, scriptwriting, stage design, film editing, and the like, but knowledge of these techniques is not considered essential for the enjoyment
of these arts. The presumption of technical knowledge as a prerequisite
of pleasure is unique to music and, more specifically, to one particular
repertory, that of so-called classical music.

THE PRESTIGE OF REFLECTION 117

Guides to the standard repertory also helped reinforce the similarities of the concert hall and the museum, that ultimate collection of objects to be taken in, studied, and understood. Prominent among these guides are George P. Upton's genre surveys, which include *The Standard Operas* (1886), *The Standard Oratorios* (1886), *The Standard Cantatas* (1887), and *The Standard Symphonies* (1888), and Hermann Kretzschmar's enormously successful multi-volume *Führer durch den Konzertsaal*, begun in 1887 and with regularly updated editions still in print today. Kretzschmar declared at one point that he felt confident in assuming that his readers possessed at least some degree of familiarity with the basics of musical form, "or at least the ability to tell the difference between doors and windows."[42]

The music historian Christian Thorau has aptly likened such guides to those published for vacationing tourists. In both cases, readers want to know the salient features of the objects they behold.[43] Henry Edward Krehbiel, author of one such guidebook, drew an explicit parallel between "travelers who do not see and listeners who do not hear."[44] Composer biographies served a similar didactic function.[45]

Program notes, which made their first appearance in the 1840s, also helped objectify the works audiences heard. The publisher, critic, and composer Charles Henry Purday had already made a strong case for them in a letter to the editors of *The Musical World* as early as 1836.

> It has often occurred to me that an important advantage would accrue to art, and society in general, if some means were adopted, to render musical performances as intellectual as they are sensual. Surely the most delightful art in the world was never intended merely to please the senses and gratify the ear. But such seems to be the principal object which the majority who frequent our concerts and music meetings have in view, if we may judge from the inattention observable in their conduct. This remark applies more particularly to instrumental than to vocal compositions; as in the latter case a direct appeal is made to the reasoning faculties. The public are not to be blamed for taking little interest in that which they do not understand. Although they know that the composition which has just been performed, is the effusion of some such extraordinary mind as that of a Mozart, a Haydn, or a Beethoven, with whose names they are familiar, from the circumstance of having their works so frequently brought before their notice—but are as ignorant (generally speaking) of the true

character, design, and end of those stupendous efforts of genius, as are the Hottentots of their existence: consequently, the performance of them, if listened to at all, is heard with indifference. . . . I would propose that a prologue, if I may use the term, should preface every performance of the works of the great masters, giving a brief and pithy analysis of the composition to be performed, showing its relative character to the mind of the musician, the feelings by which he was actuated in the production of his work, and the circumstances (where known) under which it was brought out: this would, by the novelty, in the first place, attract attention, and by frequent repetition, keep that attention alive and lead us in tracing the mind of the author through the productions of his pen; and the design of his work would thus be made clear to the understanding of the amateur, and infuse in him the desire to become more intimately acquainted with the classical compositions of the great masters.[46]

Purday's hope was fulfilled, if only gradually. Between 1845 and 1881, John Ella, who organized chamber music concerts at London's Musical Union, had printed in every concert program this passage from Pierre Baillot's *L'art du violon* of 1834: "It is not enough for the artist to be well prepared for the public; the public must also be well prepared for what it is going to hear."[47] Program notes with at least rudimentary analytical features would eventually become a standard feature in British, European, and North American concert halls by the turn of the twentieth century.[48] Even if left unread, they had an impact, for they are tokens of the ideal that knowledge is necessary—or at the very least useful—to the full experience of what is about to transpire, a reminder that listeners have an obligation to meet the music on *its* terms.

Social Prestige

The social motivations behind the prestige of reflective listening can scarcely be overestimated. With the precipitous decline of aristocratic patronage in the post-Napoleonic era, concerts open to a ticket-buying public allowed members of the bourgeoisie the opportunity to participate in a culture that had long been the province of the elite. Taste became a defining feature of social distinction, and taste could be acquired.[49]

THE PRESTIGE OF REFLECTION 119

Music lovers who sought to set themselves apart from the majority of listeners embraced the idea of listening as a skill, for it gave them a basis on which to pass a judgment that rested on something beyond pleasure. "Kant's principle of pure taste," as Pierre Bourdieu observed, "is nothing other than a refusal, a disgust—a disgust for objects which impose enjoyment and a disgust for the crude, vulgar taste which revels in this imposed enjoyment."

> Pure pleasure—ascetic, empty pleasure which implies the renunciation of pleasure, pleasure purified of pleasure—is predisposed to become a symbol of moral excellence, and the work of art a test of ethical superiority, an indisputable measure of the capacity for sublimation which defines the truly human man . . . Art is called upon to mark the difference between humans and non-humans . . .[50]

In the wake of Kant, resonant listening became increasingly suspect. The jurist Georg von Weiler, writing in 1811, looked down on such "pathological" listening as merely sensuous, unconnected except coincidentally to beauty, whereas "aesthetic" listening allowed an "open field" for the imagination of the listener.[51] E. T. A. Hoffmann was similarly dismissive of the typical amateur's approach to listening. In reworking his 1810 review of Beethoven's Fifth Symphony into his quasi-fictional *Kreisleriana* of 1813, he scorned "the musical rabble intimidated by Beethoven's powerful genius," a genius it "rebels against to no avail."

> But what if it is only *your* feeble regard which fails to grasp the deep inner coherence of every Beethoven composition? What if it is entirely *your* fault that you do not understand the master's language, which is intelligible to the initiated but not to you, and if the portal to the innermost sanctum remains closed to you?[52]

Elsewhere in his *Kreisleriana*, Hoffmann puts these words into the sardonic mouth of his fictional music director and quasi-alter-ego, Johannes Kreisler:

> The goal of art is of course above all nothing other than to provide human beings with pleasurable entertainment and thus distract them in a pleasant manner from their more serious dealings, or more specifically their only respectable dealings, namely those that secure them bread and

social respectability in such a way that they might afterwards return with doubled attention and effort to the true goals of their being, i.e., to be a diligent cogwheel in the windmill of the state and (I continue this metaphor) to twirl around and be twirled around. Now, no art is more adept at achieving this goal than music. To read a novel or a poem—assuming one's choice is fortunate enough not to include those that contain the fantastically tasteless, like so many of the most recent exemplars, and thus do not arouse in the slightest our imagination, which is truly the worst component of our original sin and to be exterminated with every effort—this reading, I maintain, has the unpleasant aspect that one is in a sense obliged to think about something while one reads: but this is clearly contrary to the goal of distraction.[53]

Hoffmann could scarcely have insulted the musical public in this way in his own journalistic criticism, but he clearly felt at liberty to do so through the persona of his fictional Kreisler.

Along similar lines, but in a more measured vein, the Swiss composer and pedagogue Hans Georg Nägeli urged listeners to resist "sinking" into a "deeper sphere of sensuousness." Proper listening, he maintained, involves "intellectual efforts," and the "highest feeling for art" exists only in connection with a "longing for ideals." This desire, however, "is satisfied only through the ability to perceive tones in the totality of their connections to the artwork as a whole."[54] The listener's "intellectual striving therefore aims to grasp in each artwork every single particular in relationship to the whole. His efforts are directed only toward coherence, order, variety in unity, a richness of ideas. His intellectual activity consists of a steady comparison, differentiation, correlation, association, subordination, and superordination."[55] Synoptic listening is now the ideal mode of perception.

In a dialogue published a year later under the title "Should One Think about Something while Listening to Instrumental Music?" Friedrich Louis Bührlen, a frequent contributor to the *Allgemeine musikalische Zeitung*, has the brighter of the two interlocutors urge his companion to listen from the composer's perspective, to become "a spiritual-intellectual relative of the artist if you wish to grasp the riches of art." His companion promises to listen this way the next time he hears a symphony by Beethoven.[56]

The divide between "higher" and "lower" approaches to listening grew stronger with each passing decade. With typical thoroughness, Johann Friedrich Rochlitz laid out the difference between the two in a lengthy essay of 1831. "High" taste entails judgments of reason, while "common" taste relies solely on the external senses.[57] The growing prestige of reflective, intellectual listening would eventually lead to an increasingly open rejection of resonant, sensory listening. "The vital question for our art," the composer and critic A. B. Marx declared in 1841, "is simply this: *if its spiritual-intellectual or sensuous side will predominate.*"[58]

This discourse often took place on the terrain of repertory, most openly in the repeated critical contrasts between Beethoven and Rossini from the 1820s onward. These two composers stood as figureheads of two different approaches, not only to composing but to listening as well. German writers were inclined to regard the sensuous appeal of Rossini's music as a fundamental defect. August Wilhelm Ambros, a leading critic of the mid-century, was typical in viewing the two composers as complete opposites, for while Beethoven had expressed himself "in music and through music" according to the "laws of proportion and beauty," Rossini had "raised the principle of purely sensory pleasure in music to categorical legitimacy." For Ambros, Rossini's output marked the beginning of the end of music. "When dessert is served, the meal is over."[59] The critic Franz Brendel agreed: music in Italy had recently "sunk into sensuousness," whereas Germany had experienced a new uplift through the works of Beethoven.[60]

Not everyone felt a need to apologize for sensory pleasure. Stendhal, a great advocate of Rossini's music, bemoaned the seriousness of his time and poked fun at the beautiful and the sublime as grandiloquent concepts. "The quality in music that makes it the most enthralling pleasure the soul can know, and that gives it so marked an advantage over even the finest poetry . . . lies in the powerful element of physical intoxication which it contains . . . The joy which music affords is violent and intense, but curiously unstable and quickly evanescent."[61] The hugely popular French composer Adolphe Adam expressed a similar belief that "the unique goal of music is to charm the ear and move the heart."[62]

122 MUSIC'S FOURTH WALL

The attack on sensory pleasure reached its most virulent—and influential—form in Eduard Hanslick's *Vom Musikalisch-Schönen*, first published in 1854 and revised across no fewer than ten subsequent authorial editions, the last appearing in 1902. Though ultimately an ontology of music, the treatise addresses the question of listening at many points, particularly in chapter five, which contrasts "aesthetic" and "pathological" modes of perception. Many of Hanslick's concepts can be traced back to the generation of thinkers who had applied Kantian principles to music in the late eighteenth and early nineteenth centuries.[63] Like Kant, Hanslick identified imagination as the true faculty for the perception of beauty, preferring the more current term *Phantasie* in place of *Einbildungskraft*.[64] "Without intellectual activity, there is no aesthetic enjoyment at all," he declared. For Hanslick, listening was an art in its own right. To be "intoxicated" by music "requires only weakness."[65]

More than any other single publication, *Vom Musikalisch-Schönen* helped establish reflective listening as the preferred—and indeed, the only acceptable—mode of perception in the concert hall. Though Hanslick mentions Kant only once, and in passing at that, his treatise stands out as the most influential application of Kantian thought to the question of musical listening. "Aesthetic contemplation," he declared, "should never conceive of music as a cause but rather always as effect, not as something that produces, but rather as a product."[66] He painted a withering picture of listeners who succumb to the easy charms of the senses:

> Half awake, nestled into their armchairs, those enthusiasts let themselves be carried away and rocked by the vibrations of the tones, instead of contemplating them keenly. The way it swells ever more loudly, attenuates, jubilates, or quivers away, it transports them into an indefinite state of feeling, which they are naïve enough to consider purely intellectual. They constitute the most "appreciative" audience and the one likely to most assuredly discredit the dignity of music. The aesthetic characteristic of *intellectual* enjoyment is lacking in their hearing. A fine cigar, a spicy delicacy, a warm bath achieves for them, unconsciously, the same thing as a symphony. From those who sit there mindlessly at leisure to others who are

THE PRESTIGE OF REFLECTION   123

deeply enraptured, the principle is the same: pleasure in the *elemental* in music.[67]

In the end, Hanslick conceded that it is possible to listen to the same work in different ways. Johann Strauss, Jr., he observed, had written "charming, indeed intellectually stimulating music in his better waltzes, but it ceases to be so as soon as we only want to dance in time to it."[68] Resonant listening, in other words, can accommodate physical movement, but reflective listening cannot.

This distinction manifested itself in the changing behavior of nineteenth-century audiences, who in different locales and at different rates became increasingly still and silent. Clapping in rhythm with the music remained (and remains) perfectly acceptable in certain venues and repertories but utterly scorned in others. In this respect, the nineteenth-century concert hall was something of a battleground, for restless and talkative audiences remained a feature of concert life for some considerable time. Even toward the end of the nineteenth century, as Katharine Ellis has pointed out, silence was still unusual enough to be considered worthy of comment; the "gold standard" of concert etiquette, as she puts it, remained "valued" but in practice "elusive."[69] Reflective listening provided the ideal vehicle by which to emphasize the social distinction between listeners able to judge works on the basis of something more than their own personal responses and the shackles of emotion. Had A. B. Marx lived long enough, he would have been pleased to see that the spiritual-intellectual side of music had won out over the sensuous, at least in the concert hall and at least in theory, even if not always in practice.

Epilogue

The Resilience of Resonance

> Art has gone to the devil ever since connoisseurs first appeared. By drilling artistic intelligence into the public we can succeed only in making it completely stupid. I would say instead that I ask nothing more of the public than *healthy senses and a human heart*.
>
> —Richard Wagner (1850)[1]

The rise of reflective listening came at a certain cost. At least some commentators of the eighteenth and nineteenth centuries recognized that a technical knowledge of music—or, more precisely, an awareness of music's technical elements while listening—could act as an impediment to feelings of transcendence. It is too often forgotten that Joseph Berglinger, Wackenroder's fictional composer, became disillusioned with his art precisely because of his professional expertise. As a young man, he had listened innocently, which is to say resonantly: "His soul, constantly in motion, became altogether a play of tones, as if freed from his body . . . or as if his body had become one with his soul." It was this feeling of transport that had inspired Berglinger to undertake intense training to learn the craft of the art, eventually rising to the position of music director (*Kapellmeister*) at a prominent German court. But he came to regard his success as merely outward, for he grew increasingly disenchanted with the mechanics of it all and longed for the days when he could listen naïvely again, his soul "altogether a play of tones."

Music's Fourth Wall and the Rise of Reflective Listening. Mark Evan Bonds, Oxford University Press.
© Oxford University Press 2025. DOI: 10.1093/9780197806401.003.0006

EPILOGUE · 125

In a letter to his confidant, the novella's narrator, Berglinger, expresses regret at his decision to "go behind the curtain" of the art. Instead of "flying freely," he must now "scramble about" the "unhelpful scaffold and cage" of music's "grammar." What he had imagined as a "glorious future" had become "a miserable present."[2] He promises that if anyone should happen to pose critical questions to him about his art, he would ask that person "not to make such an effort to learn feeling from books."[3]

Berglinger's is a cautionary tale of the wages of reflective listening. The story's narrator concludes by asking:

> Alas! Did it have to be precisely his *rich fantasy* that wore him down? Should I say that he was perhaps made more to *take pleasure* in art than to *practice* it? Are those in whom art operates like a veiled spirit of genius— quietly and secretively, without disturbing their earthly activities— perhaps more happily constituted?[4]

The realization that reflective perception had its drawbacks was not new, nor was it unique to music. In his *Paradoxe sur le comédien*, written in the 1770s, Denis Diderot had argued that a beholder's awareness of an actor's technical prowess compromised the vividness of the drama.[5] And early on in his *Essays on the Nature and Principles of Taste* (1790), Archibald Alison lamented that "the labour of criticism destroys" the "flow of imagination, in which youth, and men of sensibility, are so apt to indulge, and which so often brings them pleasure at the expense of their taste."

> The mind, in such an employment, instead of being at liberty to follow whatever trains of imagery the composition before it can excite, is either fettered to the consideration of some of its minute and solitary parts; or pauses amid the rapidity of its conceptions, to make them the objects of its attention and review. In these operations, accordingly, the emotion, whether of beauty, or sublimity, is lost, and if it is wished to be recalled, it can only be done by relaxing this vigour of attention, and resigning ourselves again, to the natural stream of our thoughts. The mathematician who investigates the demonstrations of the Newtonian philosophy, the painter who studies the design of Raphael, the poet who reasons upon the measure of Milton, all, in such occupations, lose the delight which these several productions can give; and when they are willing to recover their emotion, must withdraw their attention from those minute considerations, and leave their fancy to expatiate at will, amid all the great or pleasing conceptions, which such productions of genius can raise.[6]

126 EPILOGUE

Critics struggled to reconcile these two perspectives on works of art, the one based on immediacy, the other on distance. E. T. A. Hoffmann, as noted earlier, tried to do this in his 1810 review of Beethoven's Fifth Symphony, but the sharply contrasting language he used for each betrays the intractability of the problem. The first part of his review describes what amounts to a resonant response to the work: this symphony, Hoffmann tells us, opens up "the realm of the monstrous and immeasurable," and we "become aware of giant shadows that surge back and forth." We have been transported to a different world, listening to Beethoven's symphony as it plays out on the walls of Plato's cave, with the music projecting intimations of higher truths otherwise inaccessible to us.[7] But the second part of the review assumes a very different tone: it takes a step back from describing the experience of hearing the music and goes into considerable technical detail about harmonic progressions and thematic manipulations, with multiple notated excerpts. Hoffmann's use of technical (reflective) vocabulary to rationalize his emotional (resonant) response to the music would become a model for many subsequent critics, but in the end, it is not a conscious awareness of technical elements that reveals the shadows on the walls of Plato's cave; at the very least, we cannot keep both in our minds at the same time. The best we can do is vacillate between them. Attending to music as an object prevents us from becoming one with that object. Transcendent experiences are the byproducts of technical devices, but our awareness of those devices as devices—be they thematic, harmonic, timbral, formal, and so on—precludes our experience of them as transcendent.

It was for this reason that three of the major thinkers of the nineteenth century—Arthur Schopenhauer, Richard Wagner, and Friedrich Nietzsche—embraced the idea of resonant listening, each in his own way.

Schopenhauer, in the first volume of his *Die Welt als Wille und Vorstellung* (1818), posited that music was the only art that conveyed the essence of what he called the Will and not mere representations ("ideas") of it. True aesthetic contemplation, for him, eradicated the difference between subject and object. "We *lose* ourselves in this object completely, i.e. we forget our individuality, our will, and continue to exist only as pure

EPILOGUE   127

subject, the clear mirror of the object."[8] Music "passes before us like a paradise that is so utterly familiar and yet eternally foreign." It is "entirely comprehensible and yet so inexplicable."[9] Aesthetic experience is at its most intense in the act of listening to music, which carries the promise of forgetting the pain of earthly existence. Words set to music can only get in the way of such an experience, Schopenhauer maintained, for they compromise the art's ability to operate at its fullest. He pointed specifically to Rossini as the one composer whose music "speaks its *own* language so clearly and purely that it has no need of words at all and retains its full effect when performed on instruments alone."[10] As a species, "the composer reveals the innermost essence of the world and expresses the deepest wisdom in a language that his reason does not understand, just as a magnetic somnambulist explains things that he has no idea about when awake."[11]

Given music's importance within his worldview, Schopenhauer wrote surprisingly little about the art. But this, as Lydia Goehr points out, reflects his conviction that there is little that can be said about it, save perhaps indirectly, by analogy. "His mode of description," Goehr observes, "fundamentally protects music from being reduced to or translated into, and thus perhaps forever corrupted by, mundane and empirical description. As the language of the universal Will, music is the pure language of free subjectivity, feeling, spontaneity, and gesture; it is conceptless, non-intentional, and of preterlinguistic significance."[12] This is not, in the end, a mode of listening that attends to false endings, invertible counterpoint, unexpected thematic returns, or the like.

Wagner, a self-proclaimed disciple of Schopenhauer, also embraced the ideal of listeners losing themselves in the aesthetic experience. "Sympathetic listening," he observed, transports us into "that dreamlike state" in which we lose conscious control of our thoughts and actions.[13] He differentiated listeners not on the basis of their musical knowledge but on their commitment to sustained attention. In a remarkable letter of 1850 to Franz Liszt, he excoriated the "philistinism" of the public and the "asinine nature" of critics but in the next breath reversed course to declare that he would not accept any "perverse demands" that might entail "reproaching the public for its lack of artistic understanding." Nor would he accept a "salvation of art" through the "grafting of *artistic intelligence* onto the public from on high." He was opposed, in short, to the enterprise of music appreciation. "Art has gone to the devil ever since connoisseurs first appeared. By drilling artistic intelligence into the public we can succeed only in making it completely stupid. I would say instead that I ask nothing more of the public than *healthy senses and a human heart.*"[14]

Wagner was nevertheless caught between ideals and reality, and he effectively reversed himself in the very same letter yet again when he asked Liszt about the possibility of arranging for a "suitable review" of *Lohengrin* that would counter earlier unfavorable notices. Liszt responded with a pamphlet that one early critic hailed as "a *vade mecum* with which all can find their way through the labyrinth of Wagner's double-poetry," that is, both its text and its music.[15]

Wagner would later coin the term *Gefühlverständnis*—literally "feeling-understanding"—and plead for the no less paradoxical "emotionalization of understanding" (*Gefühlswerdung des Verstandes*).[16] "In drama," he declared, "we must become knowers through feeling. The mind tells us: *so it is* only when feeling has told us: *so it must be.*"[17] For "the artist appeals to feeling, not to understanding. If he is answered in terms of understanding, then that amounts to saying that he has not been *understood*, and our criticism is truly nothing other than the admission of the lack of understanding of the artwork, which can be understood only through feeling—albeit refined and not deformed feeling."[18]

To Wagner's mind, "educated feeling" is clearly superior to uneducated feeling, but his ambivalence about educating the public, given the friction between feeling and knowing, is on full display here. He was of two minds about the listeners' guides prepared by others to acquaint audiences with the significance of the various *Leitmotifs* of his later stage works, for he recognized the potential of such guides to facilitate an understanding of his creations even as he loathed the reductionistic nature of the enterprise.[19]

In the end, Wagner's theory of listening culminates in the aesthetics of the sublime, which is to say, an aesthetic experience that overpowers

EPILOGUE 129

the mind and thus aligns with resonant listening. In his 1870 essay on Beethoven, he maintained that music can be judged "solely by the category of the sublime, given that in the moment it suffuses us it arouses the highest ecstasy of a consciousness of boundlessness." By invoking the sublime, Wagner in effect advocated an approach by which listeners enter into the experience of listening with a willingness to be overwhelmed and transported. Music, as soon as it is perceived, "*immediately* detaches the intellect from all cognition of the relationships among everything outside us." Channeling Schopenhauer, Wagner declared that music, "as pure form liberated from all objectivity, cuts us off, as it were, from the external world and instead allows us now to look exclusively into our innermost selves and into the innermost essence of all things."[20] The sublime, by its very nature, stuns the mind and thus necessarily transcends understanding. As that which we cannot grasp, the sublime compels us to listen resonantly.

Nietzsche embraced resonant listening as well, particularly after his break with Wagner. "Our ears," he declared, "have become ever more intellectual, thanks to the extraordinary exercise of the intellect occasioned through the artistic developments of new music."

> Hence we now tolerate much greater loudness, much more "noise," because we are much better drilled to listen for the *reason in it* than our ancestors were. All of our senses have in fact now become somewhat dulled because they at once inquire after the reason for things, that is, for "what it means" and no longer "what it is." . . . What is the consequence of all this? The more capable of thought our eyes and ears become, the more they approach the boundary at which they become non-sensuous: joy has been transferred to the brain, the sensory organs themselves have become dull and weak, the symbolic increasingly takes the place of that which is—and by this path as certainly as any other we arrive at barbarism.[21]

Nietzsche had, by this point, come to loathe the image Wagner had created of himself as a vehicle of higher truths:

> With this extraordinary rise in the value of music that appeared to follow from Schopenhauerian philosophy, the value of *the musician* himself all at once went up in an unheard-of manner, too: from now on he became an oracle, a priest, indeed more than a priest, a kind of mouthpiece of the "in

itself" of things, a telephone from the beyond—henceforth he uttered not only music, this ventriloquist of God—he uttered metaphysics. Is it any wonder that he should one day finally utter *ascetic ideals*?[22]

To Nietzsche's mind, the belief that music could provide access to a higher realm of existence devalued the immediate, material experience of sound. When he discovered Georges Bizet's *Carmen* in 1881, he held it up as an antidote to Wagner's music dramas. *Carmen*, he observed, "builds, organizes, finishes: thus it constitutes the opposite of the polyp in music, the 'infinite melody'" promoted by Wagner.[23] "Il faut méditerraniser la musique," Nietzsche declared. "The return to nature, health, cheerfulness, youth, *virtue*!"[24] This is listening swept up in the immediacy of sound, without the burden of metaphysics. At this point in his life, Nietzsche was approaching music as a phenomenon to be experienced, not as an object to be contemplated.

* * *

While musical styles have changed radically since the time of Wagner and Nietzsche, music's fourth wall has not. It remains a touchstone of listening: are we conscious of it or not? The answer to that question fundamentally shapes the experience of what we hear.

Works that call attention to its composer's agency, as we have seen in Chapter 2, remind us of music's fourth wall and compel us to listen reflectively. And for a variety of reasons, composers from the late nineteenth century onward have become increasingly willing, even eager, to draw attention to their agency, at least in the concert hall: the contrast with popular music is striking. The classical music-appreciation industry—with its pre-concert lectures, program notes, repertory guides, classroom courses, textbooks, websites, podcasts, apps, and the like—is a multimillion-dollar annual enterprise that meets a need. But a pre-concert lecture or program notes for a rock concert? No. The typical audience member there approaches music as an event to be enjoyed at its fullest through experience, not through understanding.

To be sure, there are guidebooks, classroom courses, and textbooks on many varieties of popular music, including rock, country, bluegrass, and

EPILOGUE   131

particularly jazz, a genre that has become more and more classicized over time.[25] But even in the case of jazz, admirers rarely feel the need to apologize for their lack of knowledge: understanding is a welcome extra but an extra nevertheless. This attitude stands in stark contrast to that oft-heard declaration of "I don't know anything about classical music, but I enjoy it." The "but" is telling. Even those who, by their own admission, know little or nothing about the classical repertory (however they construe it) have come to believe that understanding is the key to a true aesthetic experience. Kant would be pleased.

Yet even in the realm of classical music, we can see in recent decades the beginnings of a resistance to the presumed superiority of reflective listening. Rose Rosengard Subotnik, in her influential *Deconstructive Variations* (1996), was among the first to point out the deeply problematic nature of what she called "structural listening," which subordinates sound to structure. Granted, this is an extreme manifestation of reflective listening, but it foregrounds all the more clearly the distance between auditor and object.[26] Subotnik's work resonated (if that term may be permitted) with younger scholars who similarly chafed at the abstraction and narrowness of this mode of perception.[27] More pointedly still, Carolyn Abbate has argued for the value of "drastic" (resonant) as opposed to "gnostic" (reflective) listening in an essay that has elicited widely divergent responses.[28] And Andreas Dorschel has advocated an acceptance of musical escapism as an act of renewal rather than denial.[29] In the meantime, advances in the cognitive neurosciences promise to help place personal responses to music on a more equal footing with objective evidence and universal principles.[30]

Resonant and reflective listening will continue to manifest themselves in a variety of ways for, in the end, there are no right or wrong ways of listening to music. Still, by understanding the rise of reflective listening in the minds of the musical public around the turn of the nineteenth century, we can better understand its manifold consequences for us today.

Notes

INTRODUCTION

1. Aaron Copland, *Music and Imagination* (Cambridge, MA: Harvard University Press, 1952), 9–10.

2. T. S. Eliot, "The Dry Salvages" (1941), from *Four Quartets*, in his *The Complete Poems and Plays, 1909–1950* (New York: Harcourt, Brace & World, 1962), 136.

3. My use of the term, as will become clear, differs considerably from that put forward by Anthony Gritten in his "Resonant Listening," *Performance Research* 15, no. 3 (2010), 115–22, which in turn employs the concept of resonance that figures so prominently in Jean-Luc Nancy 's *Listening*, trans. Charlotte Mandel (New York: Fordham University Press, 2007).

4. The attribution to Valéry, often asserted, has never been documented.

5. Jaak Panksepp, "The Emotional Sources of 'Chills' Induced by Music," *Music Perception* 13, no. 2 (1995), 171–207; Jerrold Levinson, "Musical Chills," in his *Contemplating Art: Essays in Aesthetics* (Oxford: Clarendon Press, 2006), 220–36; Jerrold Levinson, "Musical Frissons," *Revue française d'études américaines* 86 (2000), 64–76; Mihaly Csikszentmihalyi, *Flow: The Psychology of Optimal Experience* (New York: Harper & Row, 1990). For a review of more recent literature, see Leonard Tan and Hui Xing Sin, "Flow Research in Music Contexts: A Systematic Literature Review," *Musicae Scientiae* 25, no. 4 (2021), 399–428.

6. Alf Gabrielsson, *Strong Experiences with Music: Music is Much More than Just Music*, trans. Rod Bradbury (Oxford: Oxford University Press, 2011), 7.

7. On these and many other pitfalls that can color journalistic criticism, including commercial motivations, personal conflicts of interest, and nationalistic prejudices, see Katharine Ellis, "Music Criticism, Speech Acts and Generic Contracts," in *Nineteenth-Century Music Criticism*, ed. Teresa Cascudo García-Villaraco (Turnhout: Brepols, 2017), 3–21. On

the broader obstacles to writing a history of listening, see Leon Botstein, "Toward a History of Listening," *Musical Quarterly* 82 (1998), 427–31.

8. On Fontenelle's question and its afterlife, see Mark Evan Bonds, *Absolute Music: The History of an Idea* (New York: Oxford University Press, 2014), 74–78.

9. Noël-Antoine Pluche, *Le spectacle de la nature . . . tome septième, contenant ce qui regarde l'homme en société, nouvelle édition* (Paris: Veuve Estienne et fils, 1751), 115: "Le plus beau chant, quand il n'est qu'instrumental, devient presque nécessairement froid, puis ennuyeux, parce qu'il n'exprime rien. C'est un bel habit séparé du corps . . ."

10. Johann Georg Sulzer, "Instrumentalmusik," *Allgemeine Theorie der schönen Künste*, 2 vols. (Leipzig: M. G. Weidemanns Erben und Reich, 1771–74), 1:559. Sulzer acknowledged his collaboration with J. A. P. Schulz and Johann Philipp Kirnberger on entries regarding music, but the more general aesthetic observations on the art were ultimately Sulzer's responsibility.

11. Johann Nikolaus Forkel, "Genauere Bestimmung einiger musikalischer Begriffe. Zur Ankündigung des academischen Winterconcerts von Michaelis 1780 bis Ostern 1781," *Magazin der Musik* 1 (1783), 1069: "Der Liebhaber muß einen Dolmetscher haben, der ihm den Ausdruck der Kunst begreiflich macht; dazu dient ihm die Poesie. Folglich bleibt es unstreitig wahr, daß Instrumentalmusik in Absicht auf Eindruck, Wirkung und Nutzen, auf alle Weise der Vokalmusik weit nachstehe. Hier sind alle Kräfte der Kunst vereinigt; dort nur einige, und nur die schwächsten."

12. *KdU*, 5:329. More on this in Chapter 3.

13. Roger Mathew Grant, *Peculiar Attunements: How Affect Theory Turned Musical* (New York: Fordham University Press, 2020). On theories of attunement, see also Erik Wallrup, *Being Musically Attuned: The Act of Listening to Music* (Farnham, Surrey: Ashgate, 2015). On the broader forces that elevated the status of instrumental music, see Bellamy Hosler, *Changing Aesthetic Views of Instrumental Music in 18th-century Germany* (Ann Arbor, MI: UMI Research Press, 1981); John Neubauer, *The Emancipation of Music from Language: Departure from Mimesis in Eighteenth-century Aesthetics* (New Haven: Yale University Press, 1986); Mary Sue Morrow, *German Music Criticism in the Late Eighteenth Century: Aesthetic Issues in Instrumental Music* (Cambridge: Cambridge University Press, 1997); Mark Evan Bonds, *Music as Thought: Listening to the Symphony in the Age of Beethoven* (Princeton, NJ: Princeton University Press, 2006); Mark Evan Bonds, *Absolute Music*; Tomás McAuley, *The*

NOTES TO PAGES 7–12   135

Music of Philosophy: German Idealism and Musical Thought (New York: Oxford University Press, forthcoming).

14. Samuel Pepys, *The Diary of Samuel Pepys*, ed. Robert Latham and William Matthews, 11 vols. (Berkeley: University of California Press, 1973–2000), 9:94 (entry for February 27, 1668). For many similar examples, including ones well beyond the chronological and geographic limits implied by its title, see Gretchen L. Finney, "Ecstasy and Music in Seventeenth-Century England," *Journal of the History of Ideas* 8 (1947), 153–86. See also Bruce R. Smith, "Early Modern Period," *OHWMP*, 157–79. For examples of spiritual transcendence promoted through music, see Andrew Dell'Antonio, *Listening as Spiritual Practice in Early Modern Italy* (Berkeley: University of California Press, 2011).

15. Hector Berlioz, *À travers chants* (Paris: Michel Lévy frères, 1862), 92: "Or, *il faut vibrer* soi-même avec les instruments et les voix, et par eux, pour percevoir de véritables sensations musicales."

16. Hector Berlioz, *À travers chants*, 6: "À l'audition de certains morceaux de musique, mes forces vitales semblent d'abord doublées; je sens un plaisir délicieux, où le raisonnement n'entre pour rien; l'habitude de l'analyse vient ensuite d'elle-même faire naître l'admiration; l'émotion croissant en raison directe de l'énergie ou de la grandeur des idées de l'auteur, produit bientôt une agitation étrange dans la circulation du sang; mes artères battent avec violence; les larmes qui, d'ordinaire, annoncent la fin du paroxysme, n'en indiquent souvent qu'un état progressif, qui doit être de beaucoup dépassé. En ce cas, ce sont des contractions spasmodiques des muscles, un tremblement de tous les membres, un *engourdissement total des pieds et des mains*, une paralysie partielle des nerfs de la vision et de l'audition, je n'y vois plus, j'entends à peine; vertige . . . demi-évanouissement . . . On pense bien que des sensations portées à ce degré de violence sont assez rares." Translated by Piero Weiss in Piero Weiss and Richard Taruskin, eds., *Music in the Western World: A History in Documents*, 2nd ed. (Belmont, CA: Schirmer, 2008), 297–98. Ellipses in the original.

17. See Mark Evan Bonds, *The Beethoven Syndrome: Hearing Music as Autobiography* (New York: Oxford University Press, 2020). On Schumann specifically, see Benedict Taylor, *Music, Subjectivity, and Schumann* (Cambridge: Cambridge University Press, 2022).

18. Paris: Alexandre Mesnier, 1830.

19. Richard Taruskin, *The Oxford History of Western Music*, 5 vols. (Oxford: Oxford University Press, 2010), volume 4, chapter 9 ("Lost—or Rejected—Illusions"); Nancy November, *Cultivating String Quartets in Beethoven's Vienna* (Woodbridge, Suffolk: Boydell, 2017), 27, 214.

20. W. Dean Sutcliffe, *Instrumental Music in an Age of Sociability: Haydn, Mozart and Friends* (Cambridge: Cambridge University Press, 2020), 31, 397–407.

21. Most notably in James H. Johnson, *Listening in Paris* (Berkeley: University of California Press, 1995); Peter Szendy, *Écoute: Une histoire de nos oreilles* (Paris: Editions L'Harmattan, 2000), transl. Charlotte Mandell as *Listen: A History of Our Ears* (New York: Fordham University Press, 2008); Matthew Riley, *Musical Listening in the German Enlightenment: Attention, Wonder and Astonishment* (Aldershot: Ashgate, 2004); Martin Kaltenecker, *L'oreille divisée: Les discours sur l'écoute musicale aux XVIIIe et XIXe siècles* (Paris: Musica falsa, 2010); Matthew Pritchard, "Music in Balance: The Aesthetics of Music after Kant, 1790–1810," *JM* 36 (2019), 39–67; and the essays in *OHML*.

22. Lydia Goehr, *The Imaginary Museum of Musical Works: An Essay in the Philosophy of Music* (Oxford: Clarendon Press, 1992), 206.

23. Judith Becker, *Deep Listeners: Music, Emotion, and Trancing* (Bloomington: Indiana University Press, 2004), 2, 11, 89, 43. See also Gilbert Rouget, *Music and Trance: A Theory of the Relations Between Music and Possession*, trans. Derek Coltman, Gilbert Rouget, and Brunhilde Biebuyck (Chicago: University of Chicago Press, 1985).

24. Carolyn Abbate, "Music—Drastic or Gnostic?" *Critical Inquiry* 30 (2004), 508.

25. Carolyn Abbate, *In Search of Opera* (Princeton, NJ: Princeton University Press, 2001), 52.

26. Veit Erlmann, *Reason and Resonance: A History of Modern Aurality* (New York: Zone Books, 2010), 9–10. On the broader social implications of resonance in general, see Hartmut Rosa, *Resonance: A Sociology of Our Relationship to the World*, transl. James C. Wagner (Cambridge, Polity Press, 2019).

27. Nicholas Cook, *Music, Imagination, and Culture* (Oxford: Clarendon, 1990), 152.

28. Jerrold Levinson, *Music in the Moment* (Ithaca, NY: Cornell University Press, 1997).

29. This distinction is central to Heinrich Besseler's "Grundfragen des musikalischen Hörens," *Jahrbuch der Musikbibliothek Peters* 32 (1925–26), 35–52, trans. Matthew Pritchard with Irene Auerbach as "Fundamental Issues of Musical Listening (1925)," *Twentieth-Century Music* 8, no. 1 (2011), 49–70. See also Thomas Turino, *Music as Social Life: The Politics of Participation* (Chicago: University of Chicago Press, 2008).

NOTES TO PAGES 15–18

30. See, for example, Rebecca Cypess and Nancy Sinkoff, eds., *Sara's World: Gender, Judaism, and the Bach tradition in Enlightenment Berlin* (Rochester, NY: University of Rochester Press, 2018); Anja Bunzel and Natasha Loges, eds., *Musical Salon Culture in the Long Nineteenth Century* (Woodbridge, Suffolk, and Rochester, NY: Boydell Press, 2019); and Rebecca Cypess, *Women and Musical Salons in the Enlightenment* (Chicago: University of Chicago Press, 2022), especially chapter 2, "Sensuality, Sociability, and Sympathy: Musical Salon Practices as Enactments of Enlightenment."

31. On this point, see Simon Høffding, "Performative Passivity: Lessons on Phenomenology and the Extended Musical Mind with the Danish String Quartet," in *Music and Consciousness 2: Worlds, Practices, Modalities*, ed. Ruth Herbert, David Clarke, and Eric Clarke (New York: Oxford University Press, 2019), 127–42; and Anthony Gritten, "Does the Performer Have to Listen?" *Music & Practice* 6 (2022), 1–20.

32. For examples, see Frieder von Ammon, "Opera on Opera (on Opera): Self-Referential Negotiations of a Difficult Genre," in *Self-Reference in Literature and Music*, ed. Walter Bernhart and Werner Wolf (Amsterdam and New York: Rodopi, 2010), 65–85.

33. Stendhal [Henri Beyle], *Vie de Rossini*, 2 vols. (Paris: Auguste Boulland, 1824), 1:6: " . . . mais de nos jours, le talent de la musique instrumentale s'est tout-à-fait réfugié dans la tranquille et patiente Allemagne. Au milieu des forêts de la Germanie, il suffit à ces âmes rêveuses, de la beauté des sons, *même sans mélodie*, pour redoubler l'activité et les plaisirs de leur imagination vagabonde."

CHAPTER I

1. Anonymous, "Wien in Junius 1783," *Magazin der Musik*, 1, no. 2 (1783), 843: "Das starke Händeklatschen nach einem Concert ist der sicherste Beweis, daß nur das Gehör beschäftigt war. Musik, die ins Herz dringt, muß uns vergessen machen, daß wir Hände haben."

2. Wilhelm Heinrich Wackenroder, "Das merkwürdige musikalische Leben des Tonkünstlers Joseph Berglinger," in his *Herzensergiessungen eines eines kunstliebenden Klosterbruders*, in Wackenroder, *Sämtliche Werke und Briefe: Historisch-kritische Ausgabe*, 2 vols., ed. Silvio Vietta and Richard Littlejohns (Heidelberg: Winter, 1991), 1:133: "Der geringste Ton entschlüpfte ihm nicht, und er war von der angespannten Aufmerksamkeit am Ende ganz schlaff und ermüdet. Seine ewig bewegliche Seele war ganz

NOTES TO PAGES 18–21

ein Spiel der Töne;—es war, als wenn sie losgebunden vom Körper wäre und freyer umherzitterte, oder auch, als wäre sein Körper mit zur Seele geworden,—so frei und leicht ward sein ganzes Wesen von den schönen Harmonieen umschlungen, und die feinsten Falten und Biegungen der Töne drückten sich in seiner weichen Seele ab."

3. Hans Ulrich Gumbrecht, *Production of Presence: What Meaning Cannot Convey* (Stanford, CA: Stanford University Press, 2004). On the broader phenomenon of resonance from a sociological perspective, see Rosa, *Resonance*.

4. On the concept of transendence throughout the history of music, see the essays in Férdia J. Stone-Davis, ed., *Music and Transcendence* (Farnham, Surrey: Ashgate, 2015).

5. Sulzer, "Sinnlich," *Allgemeine Theorie der schönen Künste*, 2:1084: "Das Empfinden geht unmittelbar unsern innern Zustand an; denn bey jeder neuen Empfindung sind wir uns einer Veränderung in uns selbst bewußt; das Erkennen geht auf etwas, das wir als von uns getrennt, ansehen. Beym Erkennen sind wir Zuschauer dessen, was vorgeht; beim Empfinden sind wir selbst das Ding, mit dem etwas veränderliches vorgehet, und dieses Veränderliche beobachten wir nicht, als etwas, das von uns verschieden ist, sondern als etwas, das in unserer Würksamkeit liegt." Listeners of the time could and did associate purely musical sounds with visual images, as documented by Deirdre Loughridge in her *Haydn's Sunrise, Beethoven's Shadow: Audiovisual Culture and the Emergence of Musical Romanticism* (Chicago: University of Chicago Press, 2016), a tendency that marks one further step toward the eventual priority of reflective listening.

6. Sulzer, "Musik," *Allgemeine Theorie der schönen Künste*, 2:785, 780: "Es ist nicht möglich sie [Tanzmelodien] anzuhören, ohne ganz von dem Geiste der darin liegt, beherrscht zu werden: man wird wieder Willen gezwungen, das, was man dabey fühlt, durch Gebehrden und Bewegung des Körpers auszudrücken . . . Die Natur hat eine ganz unmittelbare Verbindung zwischen dem Gehör und dem Herzen gestiftet . . . . Das Gehör ist also weit der tauglichste Sinn, Leidenschaft zu erwecken." Johann Nicolaus Forkel, in his *Allgemeine Geschichte der Musik*, 2 vols. (Leipzig: Schwickert, 1788–1801), 1:3, paraphrases the second sentence quoted above.

7. See Erlmann, *Reason and Resonance*; Bonds, *Absolute Music*, 30–38; and the essays in "L'ouïe dans la pensée européene au XVIIIe siècle," special issue of the *Revue germanique internationale* 27 (2018).

8. Herder, *Kalligone* (1800), in his *Werke in zehn Bänden*, ed. Martin Bollacher et al. (Frankfurt am Main: Deutscher Klassiker Verlag,

NOTES TO PAGES 21–22 139

1985–2000), 8:703: "Die Musik spielt in uns ein Clavichord, das unsere eigene innigste Natur ist." Idem, 8:813: "Nicht 'von aussen werden die Empfindungen der Musik erzeugt,' sondern in uns, in uns."

9. Herder, *4. Kritisches Wäldchen* (1769), in his *Werke in zehn Bänden*, 8:355: "Das Ohr ist der Seele am nächsten—eben weil es ein *inneres* Gefühl ist." Ibid., 8:336: "Die Wollust der Tonkunst liegt tief in uns verborgen: sie wirkt in der Berauschung."

10. Herder, "Liebe und Selbstheit" (1781), in his *Werke in zehn Bänden*, 4:409: "So ists mit dem Genuß der Düfte, ja selbst der Töne. Wir ziehen sie in uns, wir trinken den Strom ihrer Wollust mit langen Zügen: und nur dann sagen wir, daß wir Musik *genießen*, wenn sie unser Herz zerschmelzt, wenn sie mit dem innern Saitenspiel unsrer Empfindungen Eins wird. Der Strom des Wohllauts, so fein er sey, wird indes auch *verschlungen*; er dauert etwa nur in den harmonischen Wirkungen, in den angenehmen Vibrationen fort, die er auf uns machte."

11. F[riedrich] L[ouis] B[ührlen], "Reflexionen über das Wesen der Musik," *AmZ* 17 (1815), 779–80: "Was sie [die Musik] ausspricht, das kann nie fern, verjüngt, kalt vor uns stehen; es tritt nahe, es zwingt unser Gemüth, sich ihm harmonisch auszudehnen; es erregt . . . unsere Gefühle, und bewirkt so, dass wir uns gewissermassen mit dem Gegenstand verschmelzen müssen . . . Ihrer [der Musik] Natur nach dringt sie . . . unmittelbar in die Seele."

12. Henry Home, Lord Kames, *Elements of Criticism*, 4th ed., 2 vols. (Edinburgh: A. Kincaid & J. Bell, 1769), 1:90, 93, 94, 97. On the widespread acceptance of the principle of ideal presence, not only in Great Britain but also on the continent, see Eric Rothstein, "'Ideal Presence' and the 'Non Finito' in Eighteenth-Century Aesthetics," *Eighteenth-Century Studies* 9 (1976), 307–32.

13. Sulzer, "Comödie," *Allgemeine Theorie der schönen Künste*, 1:216–17: "Der Zuschauer muß bey jeder dramatischen Vorstellung vergessen, daß er etwas durch Kunst veranstaltetes sehe; nur denn, wenn er gar keinen Begriff, weder von dem Dichter, noch von dem Schauspieler, als Schauspieler hat, genießt er die Lust der Vorstellung ganz. So bald ihm das geringste vorkommt, wobey er ansteht, ob der Dichter oder der Schauspieler völlig in der Natur geblieben sey, so wird er von dem Schauplatz der Natur auf eine durch Kunst gemachte Bühne versetzt, wo er aus einem Zuschauer ein Kunstrichter wird. Dadurch wird jeder Eindruck, den das Schauspiel auf ihn macht, plötzlich geschwächt, weil er aus einer würklichen Welt in eine eingebildete herüber gebracht wird."

14. Sulzer, "Natürlich (Schöne Künste)," *Allgemeine Theorie der schönen Künste*, 2:813: "Sie müssen uns täuschen, daß wir ihre Würklichkeit zu empfinden vermeinen."

15. Friedrich Just Riedel, *Theorie der schönen Künste*, 2nd ed. (Vienna and Jena: Cuno, 1774), 151: "Eine *Phantasie* ist eine lebhafte und anschau-ende Vorstellung, in welcher wir das Objekt selbst sehen und ihm auf eine idealische Art gegenwärtig sind und diese Phantasie, diese mentale Gegenwart, als Effekt auf Seiten unserer betrachtet, heißt *Täuschung*; oder *Illusion*. Wir vergessen, wenn wir getäuschet werden, daß wir nur eine Nachahmung, oder willkührliche Erdichtung uns vorstellen; unsere Phantasie versetzet uns in Scene selbst, die der Künstler uns abgebildet hat." For more on this point, see Jochen Schulte-Sasse, "Aesthetic Illusion in the Eighteenth Century," in *Aesthetic Illusion: Theoretical and Historical Approaches*, ed. Frederick Burwick and Walter Pape (Berlin and New York: Walter de Gruyter, 1990), 105–21.

16. Karl Philipp Moritz, "Versuch einer Vereinigung aller schönen Künste und Wissenschaften unter dem Begriff des in sich selbst Vollendeten" (1785), in his *Schriften zur Ästhetik und Poetik*, ed. Hans Joachim Schrimpf (Tübingen: Max Neimeyer, 1962), 5: "... das *angenehme Vergessen unsrer selbst* bei Betrachtung eines schönen Kunstwerks...." Ibid., "... und eben dies Verlieren, dies Vergessen unsrer selbst, ist der höchste Grad des reinen und uneigennützigen Vergnügens, welches uns das Schöne gewährt." For commentary on these and other similar passages, see Harri Mäcklin, "Aesthetic Self-Forgetfulness," *BJA* 61 (2021), 527–41.

17. Georg Joseph Vogler, "Thätige Geschmaks-Bildung für die Beurtheiler der Tonstücken," *Betrachtungen der Mannheimer Tonschule* 1 (1778), 293–94: "Die Gewalt der Harmonie erhebt uns in die Sphäre, wir hören die Engel singen—wir singen mit—dort schimmert der Glanz des Allerhöchsten, wir sind ganz verblendet, vom Glanze verblendet—nach Willkühr des mächti-gen Harmoniker verblendet—will er es der allmögende Tonschöpfer: so fallen, rollen, rumpeln wir in den Abgrund, in die Tiefe der Tiefe—wir hören die Teufel heulen, mit Verzweiflung heulen,—das Abentheuerliche—sind wir nicht vielleicht selbsten—es war nur eine Täuschung, eine hinreissende Täuschung, die uns die Kräften des Verstandes benahm, blos um mit dem fühlbaren Herzen, fühlbar zu denken, statt denken, zu fühlen ... "

18. Christopher Small, *Musicking: The Meanings of Performing and Listening* (Middletown, CT: Wesleyan University Press, 1998), 4.

19. Nicholas Cook, *Beyond the Score: Music as Performance* (New York: Oxford University Press, 2013), chapters 1 ("Plato's Curse") and 2 ("Page and Stage").

NOTES TO PAGES 24–25

20. John Dewey, *Art as Experience* (New York: Minton, Balch, 1934), 249.

21. Montesquieu, *Essai sur le goût* (published 1758), ed. Charles-Jacques Beyer (Geneva: Librairie Droz, 1967), 65: "La perfection des arts est de nous présenter les choses qu'elles nous fassent le plus de plaisir qu'il est possible."

22. Sulzer, "Künste; Schöne Künste," *Allgemeine Theorie der schönen Künste*, 2:613: "die vornehmsten Werkzeuge zur Glückseligkeit der Menschen."

23. John Locke, *An Essay Concerning Human Understanding* (1689), ed. Peter H. Nidditch (Oxford: Clarendon Press, 1975), 274–75.

24. Ritchie Robertson, *The Enlightenment: The Pursuit of Happiness, 1680–1790* (New York: Harper, 2021), xvii.

25. Thomas M. Kavanagh, *Enlightened Pleasures: Eighteenth-century France and the New Epicureanism* (New Haven, CT: Yale University Press, 2010), 1.

26. Gabrielle Emilie le Tonnelier de Breteuil, Marquise Du Châtelet, *Discours sur le bonheur* (1744–46). In *Huitième Recueil philosophique et littéraire de la Société Typographique de Bouillon* (Bouillon: Société Typographique de Bouillon, 1779), 8:2: "Il faut commencer par se bien dire à soi-même et par se bien convaincre que nous n'avons rien à faire en ce monde qu'à nous y procurer des sensations et des sentiments agréables. Les moralistes qui disent aux hommes: réprimez vos passions, et maîtrisez vos désirs, si vous voulez être heureux, ne connoissent pas le chemin du bonheur." See also Robert Mauzi, *L'idée du bonheur dans la littérature et la pensée françaises au XVIIIe siècle* (Paris: Armand Colin, 1960).

27. Johann Mattheson, *Der vollkommene Capellmeister* (Hamburg: Herold, 1739), 129, 133, 207.

28. David Hume, *A Treatise of Human Nature* (1739–40), ed. Lewis Amherst Selby-Bigge and P. H. Niddich, 2nd ed. (Oxford: Oxford University Press, 2014), 472.

29. Charles Burney, *A General History of Music*, 4 vols. (London: Author, 1776–89), 3:v.

30. Letter of 26 September 1781 to Leopold Mozart, in *Briefe und Aufzeichnungen: Gesamtausgabe*, 2nd ed., 8 vols., ed. Wilhelm A. Bauer, Otto Erich Deutsch, and Ulrich Konrad (Bärenreiter: Deutscher Taschenbuch Verlag, 2005), 3:162: "[W]eil aber die Leidenschaften, heftig oder nicht, niemal bis zum Eckel ausgedrückt seyn müssen und die Musick, auch in der schaudervollsten lage, das Ohr niemalen beleidigen, sondern doch dabey vergnügen Muß, folglich allzeit Musick bleiben Muß . . ."

31. Kames, *Elements of Criticism*, 1:137.

32. Sulzer, "Musik," 2:782–83: "Ueberhaupt also würket die Musik auf den Menschen nicht in so fern er denkt, oder Vorstellungskräfte hat, sondern in so fern er empfindet. Also ist jedes Tonstück, das nicht Empfindung erwecket, kein Werk der ächten Musik . . . Der Zuhörer, für den ein Tonstück gemacht ist, wenn er auch nichts von der Kunst versteht, nur muß er ein empfindsames Herz haben, kann allemal entscheiden, ob ein Stück gut oder schlecht ist: ist es seinem Herzen nicht verständlich, so sag er dreiste, es sey dem Zweck nicht gemäß, und tauge nichts; fühlet er aber sein Herz dadurch angegriffen, so kann er ohne Bedenken es für gut erklären; der Zweck ist dadurch erreicht worden."

33. Charles Batteux, *Les beaux-arts réduits à un même principe*, 2nd ed. (Paris: Durand, 1747), 277: "Toute Musique et toute Danse doit avoir une signification, un sens." Jean Leronde d'Alembert, "De la liberté de la musique" (1758), in his *Oeuvres*, 5 vols. (Paris: Belin, 1821–22), 1:544: "Les auteurs qui composent de la musique instrumentale ne feront qu'un vain bruit, tant qu'ils n'auront pas dans la tête . . . une action ou une expression à peindre."

34. Christian Gottfried Krause, *Von der musikalischen Poesie* (Berlin: Johann Friedrich Voss, 1752), 54: "Die Musik hingegen rühret unmittelbar, und übertrifft darinn die Mahlerey unendlich . . . Bey Anhörung eines musikalischen Stückes bekümmert man sich nicht, ob es eine Bewegung in der Körperwelt nachahme, sondern nur, ob es schön sey, gefalle und rühre? Unser Inneres, unsere ganze Seele will daran Theil haben."

35. Johann Adam Hiller, "Abhandlung von der Nachahmung der Natur in der Musik," *Historisch-kritische Beyträge zur Aufnahme der Musik* 1 (1754–55), 523: "Die Musik hat geheime Zugänge zu dem Herzen, die wir noch nicht entdecket haben, und die wir vor ihr zu beschützen nicht im Stande sind. Es giebt Empfindungen, die sich besser fühlen als ausdrücken lassen . . . Man gebe Achtung, auf das, was in dem Herzen bey Anhörung mancher Musiken vorgehet. Man ist aufmerksam, sie gefällt. Sie suchet weder Traurigkeit noch Freude, weder Mitleiden noch Wuth zu erregen, und doch werden wir von ihr gerührt. Wir werden so unvermerkt, so sanft von ihr gerührt, daß wir nicht wissen, was wir empfinden; oder besser, daß wir unsrer Empfindung keinen Namen geben können. Dieses Gefühl der Töne ist uns unbekannt, aber es erwecket uns Vergnügen, und das ist uns genug. Es läßt sich, in der That, das Einnehmende in der Musik nicht alles benennen, noch unter gewisse Titel bringen. Die Musik hat dahero ihr Amt allemal gethan, wenn sie nur unser Herz befriediget hat."

36. Ibid.: "Das Herz, spricht Herr Batteux, hat seine eigene Weise, etwas zu verstehen, die von den Worten nicht abhängt; und wenn es gerührt ist, so

hat es alles begriffen." The passage in the original French is from Batteux, *Les beaux-arts*, 285–86: "Le coeur a son intelligence indépendante des mots; & quand il est touché, il a tout compris."

37. Caspar Ruetz, "Sendschreiben eines Freundes an den andern über einige Ausdrücke des Herrn Batteux von der Musik," *Historisch-kritische Beyträge zur Aufnahme der Musik* 1 (1754), 296: "Diß ist die schlechteste Art der Zuhörer, die man nur immer haben kann, welche an statt sich den Empfindungen zu überlassen, alles erkläret haben wollen. Was soll denn dieser Satz bedeuten? . . . Was für eine Leidenschaft enthält diese Figur? Was bedeutet dieser Gang? Wer eine gute Musik nicht fühlen kann, noch will, dem kann es gleich viel seyn, was dieser oder jener Satz bedeute. Man erfinde zuvor eine Sprache, dadurch man eine jedwede Empfindung benennen, und von andern unterscheiden kann."

38. Boyé, *L'expression musicale, mise au rang des chimères* (Amsterdam: s.n., 1779), 23: "L'objet principal de la Musique est de nous plaire physiquement, sans que l'esprit se mette en peine de lui chercher d'inutiles comparaisons. On doit la regarder absolument comme un plaisir des sens & non de l'intelligence."

39. Carl Ludwig Junker, *Über den Werth der Tonkunst* (Bayreuth and Leipzig: Johann Andreas Lübecks sel. Erben, 1786), 53: "Ueberlasse dich also blos dem Genuß! empfinde blos. Zergliedre nie in den Augenblicken des Genusses die einzelnen Begriffe; nie den Antheil, den die Denkkräfte deiner Seele, am Vergnügen haben. Suche nie deine Empfindungen zu reinen deutlichen Vorstellungen aufzuheitern. Du mußt dich in dem Zustand einer gewissen Verwirrung befinden; diese muss dir die Lust des Auszirkelns benehmen! Ueberlasse das Geschäft der Zergliedrung, dem Philosophen, dem Aesthetiker, auf seiner Studierstube. Denn—ewig wahr bleibts: eine Empfindung in einzelne zerlegt, aus denen sie zusammengesetzt ist, hört auf dieselbe zu seyn; und das Vergnügen des Genußes, beruhet auf dunklen Gefühlen."

40. Jean-François Marmontel, *Élémens de littérature* (1787), ed. Sophie Le Ménahèze (Paris: Desjonquères, 2005), 266 ("Chant"): "Que la musique instrumentale flatte l'oreille sans présenter à l'âme aucune image distincte, aucun sentiment décidé . . . c'en est assez."

41. Plato, *Republic*, trans. G. M. A. Grube and C. D. C. Reeve, in his *Complete Works*, ed. John M. Cooper (Indianapolis and Cambridge: Hackett, 1997), 1047 (II: 411a–b). The reference to the "feeble warrior" is to the *Iliad*, xvii.588.

42. Wilhelm Heinrich Wackenroder, "Ein Brief Joseph Berglingers," in Wackenroder and Tieck, *Phantasien über die Kunst, für Freunde der*

NOTES TO PAGES 29–31

Kunst (1799), in Wackenroder, *Sämtliche Werke und Briefe*, 1:225: "Die Kunst ist eine verführerische, verbotene Frucht; wer einmal ihren innersten, süßesten Saft geschmeckt hat, der ist unwiederbringlich verloren für die thätige, lebendige Welt. Immer enger kriecht er in seinen selbsteignen Genuß hinein, und seine Hand verliert ganz die Kraft, sich einem Nebenmenschen wirkend entgegenzustrecken.—Die Kunst ist ein täuschender, trüglicher Aberglaube; wir meinen in ihr die letzte, innerste Menschheit selbst vor uns zu haben, und doch schiebt sie uns immer nur ein schönes *Werk* des Menschen unter, worin alle die eigensüchtigen, sich selber genügenden Gedanken und Empfindungen abgesetzt sind, die in der thätigen Welt unfruchtbar und unwirksam bleiben. Und ich Blöder achte dies Werk höher, als den Menschen selber, den Gott gemacht hat."

43. E. T. A. Hoffmann, "*Recension: Sinfonie . . . par Louis van Beethoven . . . Oeuvre 67 . . . ,*" *AmZ* 12 (4 July 1810), 633: "das wundervolle Reich des Unendlichen." On the antecedents of Hoffmann's review, see Bonds, *Music as Thought*, 44–62.

44. Wilhelm Heinrich Wackenroder, "Die Wunder der Tonkunst," in Wackenroder and Tieck, *Phantasien über die Kunst*, in Wackenroder, *Sämtliche Werke und Briefe*, 1:205–6: "O, so schließ' ich mein Auge zu vor all' dem Kriege der Welt,—und ziehe mich still in das Land der Musik, als in das *Land des Glaubens*, zurück, wo alle unsre Zweifel und unsre Leiden sich in ein tönendes Meer verlieren,—wo wir alles Gekrächze der Menschen vergessen, wo kein Wort- und Sprachengeschnatter, kein Gewirr von Buchstaben und monströser Hieroglyphenschrift uns schwindlig macht, sondern alle Angst unsers Herzens durch leise Berührung auf einmal geheilt wird.—Und wie? Werden hier Fragen uns beantwortet? Werden Geheimnisse uns offenbart?—Ach nein! Aber statt aller Antwort und Offenbarung werden uns luftige, schöne Wolkengestalten gezeigt, deren Anblick uns beruhigt, wir wissen nicht wie;—mit kühner Sicherheit wandeln wir durch das unbekannte Land hindurch,—wir begrüßen und umarmen fremde Geisterwesen, die wir nicht kennen, als Freunde, und alle die Unbegreiflichkeiten, die unser Gemüth bestürmen, und die die Krankheit des Menschengeschlechtes sind, verschwinden vor unsern Sinnen, und unser Geist wird gesund durch das Anschaun von Wundern, die noch weit *unbegreiflicher* und erhabener sind."

CHAPTER 2

1. Jean Paul Richter, *Vorschule der Ästhetik*, ed. Norbert Miller (Hamburg: Felix Meiner, 1990), 131–32: "So spricht z.B. *Sterne* mehrmals lang und

erwägend über gewisse Begebenheiten, bis er endlich entscheidet: es sei ohnehin kein Wort davon wahr. Etwas der Keckheit des vernichtenden Humors Ähnliches, gleichsam einen Ausdruck der Welt-Verachtung kann man bei mancher Musik, z.B. der Haydnschen, vernehmen, welche ganze Tonreihen durch eine fremde vernichtet und zwischen Pianissimo und Fortissimo, Presto und Andante wechselnd stürmt." The comments on Haydn appeared in the first edition of the *Vorschule* (1804); those on Sterne were added for the second edition (1813).

2. Oliver Taplin, "Fifth-Century Tragedy and Comedy: A Synkrisis," *Journal of Hellenic Studies* 106 (1986): 164. My thanks to Barbara Kowalski (New York University) for this reference.

3. Mark Ringer, *Electra and the Empty Urn: Metatheater and Role-Playing in Sophocles* (Chapel Hill: University of North Carolina Press, 1998).

4. See Helmut G. Asper, *Hanswurst: Studien zum Lustigmacher auf der Berufsschauspielerbühne in Deutschland im 17. und 18. Jahrhundert* (Emsdetten: Lechte, 1980).

5. Victor I. Stoichita, *The Self-Aware Image: An Insight into Early Modern Metapainting*, trans. Anne-Marie Glasheen (London: Harvey Miller, 2015).

6. "Reverse Side of a Framed Painting," ca. 1670–75, now in the National Museum, Copenhagen. A color image is available in Stoichita, *The Self-Aware Image*, 299.

7. Lorenzo Pericolo, "What is Metapainting? *The Self-Aware Image* Twenty Years Later," in Stoichita, *The Self-Aware Image*, 12. See also Götz Pochat, "Aesthetic Illusion and the Breaking of Illusion in Painting (Fourteenth to Twentieth Centuries)," in *Immersion and Distance: Aesthetic Illusion in Literature and Other Media*, ed. Werner Wolf, Walter Bernhart, and Andreas Mahler (Amsterdam and New York: Radopi, 2013), 237–61.

8. Wayne C. Booth, "The Self-conscious Narrator in Comic Fiction before *Tristram Shandy*." *Publications of the Modern Language Association* 67 (1952): 163–85.

9. Jan Plamper, *The History of Emotions: An Introduction*, trans. Keith Tribe (New York: Oxford University Press, 2015), 24. See also John Mullan, *Sentiment and Sociability: The Language of Feeling in the Eighteenth Century* (Oxford: Clarendon Press, 1988); William M. Reddy, *The Navigation of Feeling: A Framework for the History of Emotions* (Cambridge: Cambridge University Press, 2001), 141–72.

10. Robert Darnton, *The Great Cat Massacre and other Episodes in French Cultural History* (New York: Basic Books, 1984), 243, 242.

11. See also John Preston, *The Created Self: The Reader's Role in Eighteenth-Century Fiction* (New York: Barnes & Noble, 1970); Richard A.

NOTES TO PAGES 33–35

Lanham, *Tristram Shandy: The Games of Pleasure* (Berkeley: University of California Press, 1973); Wolfgang Iser, *Laurence Sterne: Tristram Shandy*, trans. David Henry Wilson (Cambridge: Cambridge University Press, 1988); Thomas Keymer, ed., *Laurence Sterne's Tristram Shandy: A Casebook* (Oxford and New York: Oxford University Press, 2006).

12. See Janet Todd, *Sensibility: An Introduction* (London: Methuen, 1986), especially chapter 8, "The Attack on Sensibility," 129–46.

13. George A. Kennedy, *Classical Rhetoric and Its Christian and Secular Tradition from Ancient to Modern Times* (Chapel Hill: University of North Carolina Press, 1980), 4–5.

14. Marin Mersenne, *Harmonie universelle, contenant la théorie et la pratique de la musique* (1636), 3 vols. (Paris: Centre national de la recherche scientifique, 1963), 365 (*recte 361*): "Il faut considerer *la lettre* toute entiere, & le dessein ou l'intention de c qu'elle contient, & où elle porte l'esprit, afin de luy accommoder une modulation, & des mouvemens si propres, qu'estant chantée elle ait du moins autant de force sur les auditeurs, comme si elle estoit recitée par un excellent Orateur." Translation from D. A. Duncan, "Persuading the Affections: Mersenne's Advice to the Harmonic Orator," in *French Musical Thought, 1600–1800*, ed. Georgia Cowart (Ann Arbor: University of Michigan Research Press, 1989), 154. See also Patricia M. Ranum, *The Harmonic Orator: The Phrasing and Rhetoric of the Melody in French Baroque Airs* (Hillsdale, NY: Pendragon, 2001).

15. On the perceived parallels of music and oratory in the eighteenth century, see Mark Evan Bonds, *Wordless Rhetoric: Musical Form and the Metaphor of the Oration* (Cambridge, MA: Harvard University Press, 1991); Dietrich Bartel, *Musica Poetica: Musical-rhetorical Figures in German Baroque Music* (Lincoln: University of Nebraska Press, 1997); *Haydn and the Performance of Rhetoric*, ed. Tom Beghin and Sander M. Goldberg (Chicago: University of Chicago Press, 2007).

16. Jean-Baptiste Du Bos, *Réflexions critiques sur la poësie et sur la peinture*, 2 vols. (Paris: Jean Mariette, 1719), 2:320: "Que penseroit-on du *Musicien qui soûtiendroit* que ceux qui ne sçavent pas la musique sont incapables de décider si le menuet qu'il a composé plaist où s'il ne plaist pas? Quand un Orateur fait bailler & dormir son auditoire, ne passe-t il pas pour constant qu'il a mal harangué, sans qu'on songe à s'informer si les personnes que son discours a jettées sur le costé sçavoient la rhétorique[?]"

17. Marcus Fabius Quintilian, *The Institutio oratoria of Quintilian*, 3 vols., trans. H. E. Butler (London: William Heinemann; Cambridge, MA: Harvard University Press, 1953), 3:209 (VIII.ii.22).

NOTES TO PAGES 36–37

18. Johann Joseph Fux, *Gradus ad Parnassum* (Vienna: Joannis Petri van Gehlen, 1725), 240; Marcus Tullius Cicero, *Rhetorica ad Herennium*, trans. Harry Caplan (Cambridge, MA: Harvard University Press, 2014), 233.

19. Fux, *Gradus ad Parnassum*, 241: "Dico itaque Compositionem illam boni Gustûs praerogativam jure sibi vendicare, quae Praeceptis nixa, trivialium, atque extravagantis insolentiae abstinens, ad sublimiora tendens, naturali tamen ratione incedens, artis etiam peritis oblectamenti praestandi potestatem habet."

20. Johann Joachim Quantz, *Versuch einer Anweisung die Flöte traversiere zu spielen* (Berlin: J. F. Voss, 1752), 102: "Die Vernunft lehret, daß wenn man durch die bloße Rede von jemanden etwas verlanget, man sich solcher Ausdrücke bedienen müsse, die der andere versteht. Nun ist die Musik nichts anders als eine künstliche Sprache, wodurch man seine musikalischen Gedanken dem Zuhörer bekannt machen soll. Wollte man also dieses auf eine dunkele oder bizarre Art, die dem Zuhörer unbegreiflich wäre, und keine Empfindung machte, ausrichten: was hülfe alsdenn die Bemühung, die man sich seit langer Zeit gemachet hätte, um für gelehrt angesehen zu werden? Wollte man verlangen, daß die Zuhörer lauter Kenner und Musikgelehrte seyn sollten, so würde die Anzahl der Zuhörer nicht sehr groß seyn: man müßte sie denn unter den Tonkünstlern von Profession, wiewohl nur einzeln aufsuchen."

21. Johann Adam Hiller, "Abhandlung von der Nachahmung der Natur in der Musik," 542–43: "Es sey allemal ein Gesang, der die Empfindungen des Herzens künstlich auszudrücken bemüht ist . . . [S]o wird der ohnfehlbare Beyfall aller Zuhörer, so wohl der Kunstverständigen, als derer die sie nicht verstehen, der Musik und dem Künstler zugleich Ehre machen."

22. Anonymous, "Arts. Musique," *L'Avantcoureur*, 16 January 1764, 39: "Cette musique a le double mérite de plaire aux vrais connoisseurs & à ceux qui ne jugent que par sentiment."

23. Leopold Mozart to Wolfgang Amadeus Mozart, letter of 11 December 1780, in *Briefe und Aufzeichnungen*, 3:53: "Ich empfehle dir Bey deiner Arbeit nicht einzig und allein für das musikalische, sondern auch für das *ohnmusikalische Publikum* zu denken, – du weist es sind *100 ohnwissende* gegen *10 wahre Kenner*, – vergiß also das so genannte *populare* nicht, das auch die *langen Ohren* Kitzelt."

24. Wolfgang Amadeus Mozart to Leopold Mozart, letter of 28 December 1782, in *Briefe und Aufzeichnungen*, 3:245–46: "die Concerten sind eben das Mittelding zwischen zu schwer, und zu leicht – sind sehr Brillant – angenehm in die ohren – Natürlich, ohne in das leere zu fallen – hie und

148 NOTES TO PAGES 37–39

da – können auch *kenner allein* satisfaction erhalten – doch so – daß die nichtkenner damit zufrieden seyn müssen, ohne zu wissen warum."

25. On the divided nature of audience attention in the eighteenth century, see William Weber, "Did People Listen in the 18th Century?" *Early Music* 25 (1997): 678–91; Peter Schleuning, *Der Bürger erhebt sich: Geschichte der deutschen Musik im 18. Jahrhundert*, 2nd ed. (Stuttgart: Metzler, 2000); Matthew Riley, *Musical Listening in the German Enlightenment*; James O. Young, "The 'Great Divide' in Music," *BJA* 45, no. 2 (2005): 175–84; Sutcliffe, *Instrumental Music in an Age of Sociability*, especially 346–70.

26. Bernard Lamy, *La rhétorique ou l'art de parler*, 4th ed. (Paris: Florentin & Pierre Delaulne, 1701), 354: "Le plus grand secret de l'éloquence est de tenir les esprits attentifs, & d'empêcher qu'ils ne perdent de vûë le but où ils faut les conduire."

27. Aristotle, *Rhetoric*, trans. W. Rhys Roberts (London: Oxford University Press, 1924), 121 (1404b).

28. Quintilian, *Institutio oratoria*, 3:203–15 (VIII.ii.12–iii.6). See also Katelijne Schiltz, *Music and Riddle Culture in the Renaissance* (Cambridge: Cambridge University Press, 2015), 43.

29. Georg Friedrich Meier, *Anfangsgründe aller schönen Wissenschaften*, 3 vols. (Magdeburg: Carl Hermann Hemmerde, 1748–50), 1:331: "Ein jeder, der schön denken will, muss dafür sorgen, daß ein jeder seiner Leser oder Zuhörer etwas neues, in seinen schönen Gedanken, antreffe. Wenn wir ein Gedicht lesen sollen, und wir vermuthen in demselben nichts neues, so werden wir gewiss das Lesen unterlassen."

30. Mattheson, *Der vollkommene Capellmeister*, 132, 214, 237; Heinrich Christoph Koch, *Versuch einer Anleitung zur Composition*, 3 vols. (Rudolstadt: Löwische Erben und Schirach; Leipzig: A.F. Böhme, 1782–93), 2:23–26.

31. Mattheson, *Der vollkommene Capellmeister*, 36: "Kann wohl ein aufmerksamer Zuhörer zum Vergnügen bewegt werden, wenn man ihm beständig einen Lärm mit dem Taktschlagen, es sey der Füsse oder der Arme erreget? Wenn er ein dutzend Geiger vor sich siehet, die keine andere Verdrehungen des Leibes machen, als ob sie böse Krankheiten hätten? Wenn der Clavierspieler das Maul krümmet, die Stirne auf und nieder ziehet, und sein Antlitz dermassen verstellet, dass man die Kinder damit erschrecken mögte?"

32. Charles Burney, *The Present State of Music in Germany, the Netherlands, and United Provinces*, 2nd ed., 2 vols. (London: T. Becket, J. Robson, and G. Robinson, 1775), 2:270–71.

NOTES TO PAGES 39–41

33. Mattheson, *Der vollkommene Capellmeister*, 233: "Doch ist die Verwunderung über eine ungewöhnliche Fertigkeit auch eine Art der Gemüths-Bewegung . . ."

34. James Beattie, *Essays: On Poetry and Music as they Affect the Mind*, 3rd ed. (London: E. and C. Dilly, 1779), 153.

35. Annette Richards, *The Free Fantasia and the Musical Picturesque* (Cambridge: Cambridge University Press, 2001), 140.

36. Quintilian, *Institutio oratoria*, 2:119 (IV.ii.126).

37. Meier, *Anfangsgründe aller schönen Wissenschaften*, 1:429: "Man muss alles dasjenige vermeiden, wodurch die Aufmerksamkeit von der Betrachtung der Sache selbst abgelenkt, und vornehmlich auf die Betrachtung der Zeichen und Bilder, in welche der Gegenstand eingehüllt ist, gelenkt werden könnte." For further discussion of this passage, see Riley, *Musical Listening in the German Enlightenment*, 23.

38. Sulzer, "Kraft," *Allgemeine Theorie der schönen Künste*, 2:602: ". . . daß der Gegenstand eine ästhetische Kraft hat, wenn er vermögend ist unsere Aufmerksamkeit von der Betrachtung seiner Beschaffenheit abzulenken und sie auf die Würkung zu richten, die der Gegenstand auf uns, vornehmlich auf unseren inneren Zustand macht."

39. For a survey of this trope across many centuries, see Paolo D'Angelo, *Sprezzatura: Concealing the Effort of Art from Aristotle to Duchamp*, trans. Sarin Marchetti (New York: Columbia University Press, 2018).

40. Quintilian, *Institutio oratoria*, 2:37 (IV.i.57).

41. Joseph Riepel, *Gründliche Erklärung der Tonordnung insbesondere, zugleich aber für die mehresten Organisten insgemein* (Frankfurt: s. n., 1757), 42: "Denn das Sprichwort heißt: *Die Kunst soll verdeckt seyn.* Damit nämlich die Natur allzeit die Vorhand behalte."

42. Quantz, *Versuch einer Anweisung die Flöte traversiere zu spielen*, 16: ". . . daß der Zuhörer keinen ängstlichen Fleiß dabey bemerke: sondern daß überall die Natur hervorleuchte."

43. Sulzer, "Trio," *Allgemeine Theorie der schönen Künste*, 2:1180–81: "Die strenge Fuge . . . hat in einem Kammertrio . . . außer auf den Kenner, dem die Kunst allenthalben willkommen ist, keine Kraft auf den Liebhaber von Gefühl; weil er durch keine Veranstaltung zu großen Empfindungen vorbereitet ist . . . Daher erfodert das Kammertrio eine Geschicklichkeit des Tonsetzers, die Kunst hinter dem Ausdruck zu verbergen."

44. *Mercure de France*, 15 June 1779: "A l'égard du troisième, où brille toute la science du contrepoint, l'Auteur a obtenu les suffrages des Amateurs d'un genre de musique qui peut intéresser l'esprit, sans jamais aller au coeur."

Cited in Otto Erich Deutsch, ed. *Mozart: Die Dokumente seines Lebens* (Kassel: Bärenreiter, 1961), 165.

45. Kames, *Elements of Criticism*, 2:418.

46. Archibald Alison, *Essays on the Nature and Principles of Taste* (Edinburgh: Bell and Bradfute, 1790), 86.

47. Gotthold Ephraim Lessing, *Hamburgische Dramaturgie*, 36. Stück (1 September 1767), in his *Werke*, 5 vols., ed. Franz Bornmüller (Leipzig and Vienna: Bibliographisches Institut, 1884), 4:161, 162: "Und wie schwach muss der Eindruck sein, den das Werk gemacht hat, wenn man in eben dem Augenblicke auf nichts begieriger ist, als die Figur des Meisters dagegen zu halten? Das wahre Meisterstück, dünkt mich, erfüllet uns so ganz mit sich selbst, dass wir des Urhebers darüber vergessen; dass wir es nicht als das Produkt eines einzeln Wesens, sondern der allgemeinen Natur betrachten . . . Die Täuschung muss sehr schwach sein, man muss wenig Natur, aber desto mehr Künstelei empfinden, wenn man so neugierig nach dem Künstler ist."

48. Daniel K. L. Chua, "Haydn as Romantic: A Chemical Experiment with Instrumental Music," in *Haydn Studies*, ed. W. Dean Sutcliffe (Cambridge: Cambridge University Press, 1998), 146. For a concise overview of ways in Haydn called attention to his art, see Mary Hunter, "Self-Reflexivity," in *The Cambridge Haydn Encyclopedia*, ed. Caryl Clark and Sarah Day-O'Connell (Cambridge: Cambridge University Press, 2019), 348–49.

49. Steven Everett Paul, "Wit, Comedy, and Humour in the Instrumental Music of Franz Joseph Haydn" (PhD diss., University of Cambridge, 1980); Gretchen A. Wheelock, *Haydn's Ingenious Jesting with Art: Contexts of Musical Wit and Humor* (New York: Schirmer Books, 1992); Richards, *The Free Fantasia and the Musical Picturesque*, 101–44; Scott Burnham, "Haydn and Humor," in *The Cambridge Companion to Haydn*, ed. Caryl Clark (Cambridge: Cambridge University Press, 2005), 61–76; Wolfram Steinbeck, "Witz und Werk: Zur Konstitution musikalischer Form in Haydns Symphonik," in *Joseph Haydn im 21. Jahrhundert: Bericht über das Symposium der Österreichischen Akademie der Wissenschaften, der Internationalen Joseph Haydn-Privatstiftung Eisenstadt und der Esterhazy-Privatstiftung vom 14. bis 17. Oktober 2009 in Wien und Eisenstadt*, ed. Christine Siegert, Gernot Gruber, and Walter Reicher (Tutzing: Hans Schneider, 2013), 231–63; Raymond Knapp, *Making Light: Haydn, Musical Camp, and the Long Shadow of German Idealism* (Durham, NC: Duke University Press, 2018). For an insightful survey of rhythmic wit in the string chamber music of Haydn and Mozart, see Danuta Mirka, *Metric Manipulations in Haydn and Mozart: Chamber Music for Strings,*

NOTES TO PAGES 43–47

1787–1791 (New York: Oxford University Press, 2009), chapter 8 ("Wit, Comedy, and Metric Manipulations in Haydn's and Mozart's Personal Styles").

50. Notable accounts include Wheelock, *Haydn's Ingenious Jesting with Art*, 10–13 *et passim*; Gerhard J. Winkler, "Op. 33/2: Zur Anatomie eines Schlußeffekts," *Haydn-Studien* 6, no. 4 (1994): 288–97; Férdia Stone-Davis, "Music and World-Making: Haydn's String Quartet in E-flat Major (op. 33 no. 2), in Stone-Davis, ed. *Music and Transcendence*, 125–45; Naomi Waltham-Smith, *Music and Belonging: Between Revolution and Restoration* (New York: Oxford University Press, 2017), 61–64.

51. Joseph Haydn, *Symphonies 88–92*, Berliner Philharmoniker, Simon Rattle, conductor (Warner/EMI Classics 094639423729), 2007; https://www.youtube.com/watch?v=brBjPeV3K18,https://www.prestomusic.com/classical/products/7957221--haydn-symphonies-nos-88-92

52. On silence in music in general, see Fabian Oliver Kurze, "In die Stille geleiten: Darstellungsprinzipien und Erfahrungsweisen eines musikalischen Grundphänomens" (PhD diss., Tübingen, 2018).

53. On the sources and possible implications of the melody, see Geoffrey Chew, "The Night-Watchman's Song Quoted by Haydn and its Implications," *Haydn-Studien* 3 (1973–74): 106–24. On the Symphony no. 60 in general, see Elaine Sisman, "Haydn's Theater Symphonies," *JAMS* 43 (1990): 311–21; Wheelock, *Haydn's Ingenious Jesting with Art*, 154–73; and Knapp, *Making Light*, 91–93.

54. Koch, *Versuch einer Anleitung zur Composition*, 2:40–41, 39: ". . . nur durch schöne Empfindungen eure Zuhörer zu vergnügen, sey euer einziger Zweck." On Koch's critique, see Felix Diergarten, "'At Times Even Homer Nods Off': Heinrich Christoph Koch's Polemic against Joseph Haydn," *Music Theory Online* 14, no. 1 (2008), https://www.mtosmt.org/issues/mto.08.14.1/mto.08.14.1.diergarten.html.

55. Koch, *Versuch einer Anleitung zur Composition*, 2:41: "Anstatt also mit der Kunst auf das Herz zu würken, sucht man den Verstand der Zuhörer mit Witz zu beschäftigen."

56. See James Webster, *Haydn's "Farewell" Symphony and the Idea of Classical Style: Through-Composition and Cyclic Integration in His Instrumental Music* (Cambridge: Cambridge University Press, 1991), 39–45. For an overview of hypotheses about the motivations behind the finale, see Mark Evan Bonds, "Life, Liberty, and the Pursuit of Happiness: Revolutionary Ideals in Narratives of the 'Farewell' Symphony," in *Joseph Haydn & die "Neue Welt": Musik- und Kulturgeschichtliche Perspektiven*, ed. Walter Reicher and Wolfgang Fuhrmann (Vienna: Hollitzer, 2019), 283–301.

NOTES TO PAGES 47–52

57. See Webster, *Haydn's "Farewell" Symphony*, 267–87.

58. For a hypothetical listener's changing expectations toward this movement as it unfolds, see Webster, *Haydn's "Farewell" Symphony*, 300–13.

59. Albert Christoph Dies, *Biographische Nachrichten von Joseph Haydn* (Vienna: Camesina, 1810), 92: "Der urplötzliche Donner des ganzen Orchesters schreckte die Schlafenden auf, alle wurden wach und sahen einander mit verstörten und verwunderten Mienen an. . . . [S]o benützten Einige diesen Vorfall als Stoff zum Tadel, und sagten: Haydn habe bisher immer, auf eine galante Art überrascht, doch dieses Mahl sey er sehr grob gewesen."

60. For further examples of such responses, see Andreas Ballstaedt, "'Humor' und 'Witz' in Joseph Haydns Musik," *Archiv für Musikwissenschaft* 55 (1998): 212–13.

61. On the slow movement of Symphony no. 93, see Melanie Lowe, *Pleasure and Meaning in the Classical Symphony* (Bloomington: Indiana University Press, 2007), 146–53.

62. On instrumental recitatives in Haydn's quartets, see Nancy November, "Instrumental Arias or Sonic Tableaux: 'Voice' in Haydn's String Quartets Opp. 9 and 17," *M&L* 89 (2008): 346–72.

63. H. C. Robbins Landon, *Haydn: Chronicle and Works*, 5 vols. (London: Thames and Hudson, 1976–80), 2:566; Webster, *Haydn's "Farewell" Symphony*, 167; Elaine Sisman, "Haydn, Shakespeare, and the Rules of Originality," in *Haydn and His World*, ed. Elaine Sisman (Princeton, NJ: Princeton University Press, 1997), 30.

64. James Webster, "Haydn and the Rhetoric of Improvisation," in *Haydn and the Performance of Rhetoric*, ed. Tom Beghin and Sander M. Goldberg (Chicago: University of Chicago Press, 2007), 208. See also Elaine Sisman's insightful observations on a number of other works by Haydn that create the same impression, in her "Haydn, Shakespeare, and the Rules of Originality."

65. For multiple further examples of this, see Wolfgang Fuhrmann, "Haydn und sein Publikum," Habilitationsschrift, Bern, 2010. I am grateful to Professor Fuhrmann for sharing with me a copy of this work in advance of its publication.

66. Burney, *A General History of Music*, 4:601–02.

67. Burney, *A General History of Music*, 4:602.

68. For a survey of contemporaneous critiques of mixtures of high and low, serious and comic, see Wheelock, *Haydn's Ingenious Jesting with Art*, 19–51.

69. Burney, *A General History of Music*, 4:266.

NOTES TO PAGES 52–54

70. Domenico Scarlatti, "Lettore," in his *Essercizi per gravicembalo* ([London: B. Fortier, 1738]), [v]: "Non aspettarti, o Dilettante o Professor che tu sia, in questi Componimenti il profondo Intendimento, ma bensì lo scherzo ingegnoso dell'Arte, per addestrarti alla Franchezza sul Gravicembalo." My thanks to Massimo Ossi (Indiana University) for helping me parse this sentence.

71. Johann Adam Hiller, "Zehnte Fortsetzung des Entwurfs einer musikalischen Bibliothek," *Wöchentliche Nachrichten und Anmerkungen die Musik betreffend* 3 (3 October 1768), 107: ". . . Comische und Tändelnde . . . Es ist wahr, man findet wohl gearbeitete, prächtige und affectvolle Sätze darunter . . . aber sollte nicht das seltsame Gemisch der Schreibart, des Ernsthaften und Comischen, des Erhabenen und Niedrigen, das sich so oft in einem und eben demselben Satze beysammen findet, bisweilen eine üble Wirkung thun?"

72. Johann Adam Hiller, "Verzeichnis der im Jahr 1766 in Italien aufgeführten Singspiele," *Wöchentliche Nachrichten und Anweisungen, die Musik betreffend* 2 (13 July 1767): 14: "[D]ennoch aber möchten wir wohl wünschen, dass er sich nicht so sehr an andern Orten, wo er nicht hingehört, eindringen möchte; oder dass die Componisten nicht alle Augenblicke Comisches und Ernsthaftes in einerley Stück unter einander würfen. Wie viel Concerte, Sinfonien u. d. g. bekommen wir heut zu Tage zu hören, die uns die Würde der Musik in gesetzten und prächtigen Tönen fühlen lassen; aber ehe man es vermuthet, springt Hans Wurst mitten darunter, und erregt durch seine pöbelhaften Possen um so vielmehr unser Mitleid, je ernsthafter die vorhergegangene Rührung war."

73. See Asper, *Hanswurst*, and Beatrice Müller-Kampel, *Hanswurst, Bernardon, Kasperl: Spasstheater im 18. Jahrhundert* (Paderborn: Ferdinand Schöningh, 2003).

74. Johann Christoph Stockhausen, *Critischer Entwurf einer auserlesenen Bibliothek für die Liebhaber der Philosophie und schönen Wissenschaften*, 4th ed. (Berlin: Haude und Spener, 1771), 464–65: "Jetzt nehmen die Sachen von Heiden, Toeschin, Cannabisch, Filz, Pugnani, Campioni sehr überhand. Man darf aber nur halber Kenner seyn, um das Leere, die seltsame Mischung vom comischen und ernsthaften, tändelnden und rührenden, zu merken, welche allenthalben herrscht."

75. Carl Spazier, "Über Menuetten in Sinfonien," *Musikalisches Wochenblatt* 2, no. 12 (1791): 91: "Ich soll also z.B. durch den Komponisten in eine bestimmte Gemüthsverfassung vermittelst eines Instrumentalstücks versetzt werden. . . . In sofern kann ich auch fordern, dass alle wesentlichen

154   NOTES TO PAGES 54–56

oder zufälligen Theile darin zu dem erforderlichen Zwecke übereinstimmen, und dass nichts darin vorkomme, was den Hauptzweck störe."

76. Carl Ludwig Junker, *Zwanzig Componisten: Eine Skizze* (Bern: Typographische Gesellschaft, 1776), 64–65, 66: "Das wird niemand in Abrede seyn, daß die einzig herrschende Gesinnung (oder weil von der Tonkunst die Rede ist) die einzig herrschende Empfindung Haydens abstechend, bizarr sey; —daß sie sich ohne Zurückhaltung äußre. . . . Laune muß die einzig herrschende Empfindung seyn. Wie wenn wir sie aber nicht durchgehends in allen Haydnschen Produkten, als das einzige, hervorstechende Gepräge fänden? So ist es ein Beweiß, nicht; —daß ich den Unterscheidungs-Charakter falsch bestimmt hätte; sondern, daß diese Empfindung nicht, zu allen Zeiten in gleichem Grad herrschend, —in gleichem Grad so deutlich kenntlich seyn müsse, und daß Humor seine Ebbe und Flut haben könne; —Ebbe und Flut, die durch Lage, physischen und moralischen Einfluß, und überhaupt durch Umstände des Lebens, bestimmt und abgeändert werden kann; — — nicht unterdrückt . . .

"Und keine Fähigkeit, keine Eigenschaft, keine Kraft, leidet mehr Abänderung, mehr zufällige Bestimmung, als Empfindung; — weil keine mehr von der Bestimmung der sinnlichen Rührung abhängt, als sie. Aber man nenne mir auch nur ein einziges Produkt von Hayden, wo Laune nicht immer merklicher Zug wäre? Man wird keines finden.

"Wenn nur eine einzig bestimmte Empfindung nie der Vorwurf einer Sinfonie seyn kann, so kann auch Laune überhaupt, nicht das wahre Gepräge derselben seyn, und Haydens Sinfonien werden, weil seine Empfindung zu einseitig ist, — weniger als Sinfonien seyn."

77. Georg August Griesinger, *Biographische Notizen über Joseph Haydn* (Leipzig: Breitkopf & Härtel, 1810), 107: "Eine *arglose Schalkheit*, oder was die Britten Humour nennen, war ein Hauptzug in Haydns Charakter. Er entdeckte leicht und vorzugsweise die komische Seite eines Gegenstandes, und wer auch nur Eine Stunde mit ihm zugebracht hatte, mußte es bemerken, daß der Geist der österreichischen National-Heiterkeit in ihm athme. In seinen Kompositionen zeigt sich diese Laune ganz auffallend, und besonders sind seine Allegro's und Rondeaux oft ganz darauf angelegt, den Zuhörer durch leichtfertige Wendungen des anscheinenden Ernstes in den höchsten Grad des Komischen zu necken, und fast bis zur ausgelassenen Fröhlichkeit zu stimmen. Ebenso ist die früher erwähnte Abschieds-Symphonie ein durchgeführter musikalischer Scherz."

78. Carl Ditters von Dittersdorf, *Lebensbeschreibung: Seinem Sohne in die Feder diktiert* (Leipzig: Breitkopf & Härtel, 1801), 238: "[Kaiser]: Tändelt

NOTES TO PAGES 56–57   155

er [Haydn] nicht manchesmal gar zu viel?" "[Ich]: Er hat die Gabe zu tän-
deln, ohne jedoch die erhabene Kunst herabzuwürdigen."

79. Anonymous, "Ankündigung," *Wiener Zeitung*, 23 February 1791,
463: "Haydn [hat] seinen Ruhm . . . dadurch vergrössert, daß er Kunst,
Tändeley und Geschmack mit der leichtesten Ausführung zu verbinden
gewußt hat, dergestalt, daß sowohl der Künstler, als der blosse Liebhaber
vollkommen befriediget seyn wird."

80. See Wolfgang Fuhrmann, "Originality as Market-Value: Remarks on the
Fantasia in C Hob. XVII:4 and Haydn as Musical Entrepreneur," *Studia
Musicologica* 51 (2010): 303–16.

81. Anonymous, "Hayden (in Salzburg)," in *Musikalischer Almanach auf
das Jahr 1782* ("Alethinopel," i.e., Leipzig: 1782), 19, 20: "Musikalischer
Spaßmacher, aber, so wie Yorik, nicht fürs Bathos, sondern fürs hohe
Komische; und dies ist in der Musik verzweifelt schwer. Deswegen fühlen
auch so wenig Leute—daß Haydn Spaß mache, und wenn er ihn mache . . .
Selbst seine Adagios, wo der Mensch eigentlich weinen sollte, haben oft
das Gepräge des hohen Komischen."

82. See the epigraph to the present chapter.

83. Anonymous, "Recensionen. *Variations tirés des derniers Quatuors de
Mr. Joseph Haydn, arrangés pour le Clavecin ou Pianof. par Mr. l'Abbé
Gelinek*. Vienna: Cappi etc.," *AmZ* 4 (15 June 1802): 618–19: "Es giebt
freylich wohl eine sehr angenehme Weise, an sich unbedeutende Ideen
kontrapunktisch und künstlich durchzuführen; es ist aber die humoris-
tische, in welcher J. Haydn so einzig ist, und wo Einem, selbst bey dem
seriösesten Schein, das Bewusstseyn bleibt, es sey doch nur Scherz damit.
Wer davon Beyspiele haben will, die man gleich bey der Hand haben kann,
der vergleiche mehrere Finale oder die meisten sogenannten Menuetten
in Haydns neueren Sinfonien, oder den, gerade in dieser Rücksicht, aller-
liebsten Klaviersatz, Haydns Werke, Ausg. Breitkopf-Härtel, Heft IV, S.
25 folgg. Dann gleicht diese Ernsthaftigkeit in der Absicht und Würkung
dem tragischen Schein mancher Partien in den Lustspielen der Spanier
oder in Gozzi's Mährchen. So etwas lässt sich aber, ohne von der Natur
mit der Gabe dieses Humors ausgerüstet zu seyn, durchaus nicht mit
Glück machen."

84. See Thomas Austin O'Connor, "Is the Spanish *Comedia* a Metatheater?"
Hispanic Review 43 (1975): 275–89. On the early modern *comedia* as
"parodic of itself as a process of representation," see Catherine Connor
(Swietlicki), "*Postmodernism avant la lettre*: The Case of Early Modern
Spanish Theater," *Gestos* 9 (1994): 43–59. On Gozzi's influence on
German letters, see Tiziana Corda, *E. T. A. Hoffmann und Carlo Gozzi:*

156 NOTES TO PAGES 57–60

Der Einfluss der Commedia dell'Arte und der Fiabe Teatrali in Hoffmanns Werk (Würzburg: Königshausen & Neumann, 2012).

85. Letter of 27 June 1790 to Marianne von Genzinger, in Joseph Haydn, *Gesammelte Briefe und Aufzeichnungen*, ed. Dénes Bartha (Kassel: Bärenreiter, 1965), 243: "Nun trifft es mich abermahl, daß ich zu Hauß bleiben muss. Was ich dabey verliehre, können sich Euer gnaden selbst einbilden. Es ist doch traurig, immer Sclav zu seyn: allein, die Vorsicht will es." On the double-edged nature of court appointments for composers, see Mark Evan Bonds, "The Court of Public Opinion: Haydn, Mozart, Beethoven," in *Beethoven und andere Hofmusiker seiner Generation*, ed. Birgit Lodes, Elisabeth Reisinger, and John D. Wilson (Bonn: Beethoven-Haus, 2018), 7–24.

86. Griesinger, *Biographische Notizen über Joseph Haydn*, 13: "Wer mich gründlich kennt, der muß finden, daß ich dem Emanuel Bach sehr vieles verdanke, dass ich ihn verstanden und fleisig studiert habe." On broader issues of Bach's influence, see A. Peter Brown, *Joseph Haydn's Keyboard Music: Sources and Style* (Bloomington: Indiana University Press, 1986), chapter 7 ("Joseph Haydn and C. P. E. Bach: The Question of Influence").

87. See Hans-Günter Ottenberg, *C.P.E. Bach*, trans. Philip J. Whitmore (Oxford: Oxford University Press, 1987), 108, 139–42, 166; Susan Wollenberg, "A New Look at C. P. E. Bach's *Musical Jokes*," in *C. P. E. Bach Studies*, ed. Stephen L. Clark (Oxford: Clarendon Press, 1988), 295–314.

88. Burney, *The Present State of Music in Germany, the Netherlands, and United Provinces*, 2:266.

89. Sutcliffe, *Instrumental Music in an Age of Sociability*, 398–99.

90. See Hermann Danuser, "Das imprévu in der Symphonik: Aspekte einer musikalischen Formkategorie in der Zeit von Carl Philipp Emanuel Bach bis Hector Berlioz," *Musiktheorie* 1 (1986): 64–67.

91. Sutcliffe, *Instrumental Music in an Age of Sociability*, 400–01.

92. Anonymous, "Nachrichten: Auszüge aus Briefen, Todesfälle: Wien, den 29. January 1787," *Magazin der Musik* 2 (1787): 1273–74: ". . . nur Schade, daß er sich in seinem künstlichen und wirklich schönen Satz, um ein neuer Schöpfer zu werden, zu hoch versteigt, wobey freilich Empfindung und Herz wenig gewinnen, seine neuen Quartette für 2 Violin, Viole und Baß, die er Haydn dedicirt hat, sind doch wohl zu stark gewürzt—und welcher Gaum kann das lange aushalten."

93. See Werner Wolf, "Metamusic? Potentials and Limits of 'Metareference' in Instrumental Music: Theoretical Reflections and a Case Study (Mozart's *Ein musikalischer Spaß*)," in *Self-reference in Literature and Music*, ed.

NOTES TO PAGES 60–62

Walter Bernhart and Werner Wolf (Amsterdam and New York: Rodopi, 2010), 1–32.

94. See Balázs Mikusi, "The G Minor Minuet of Mozart's 'Haffner' Serenade: Yet Another Musical Joke?" *The Musical Times* 147 (2006): 47–55.

95. Anonymous, "Wien. 17 April 1805. Fortsetzung," *Der Freimüthige* 3 (17 April 1805): 332: "Die Musik könne so bald dahin kommen, daß jeder, der nicht genau mit den Regeln und Schwierigkeiten der Kunst vertraut ist, schlechterdings gar keinen Genuß bei ihr finde, sondern durch eine Menge unzusammenhängender und überhäufter Ideen, und einen fortwährenden Tumult aller Instrumente zu Boden gedrückt, nur mit einem unangenehmen Gefühle der Ermattung den Konzertsaal verlasse." Translation from *The Critical Reception of Beethoven's Compositions by His German Contemporaries*, 2 vols., ed. Wayne M. Senner, Robin Wallace, William Meredith (Lincoln: University of Nebraska Press, 1999–2001), 2:16.

96. Anonymous, "Nachrichten. Wien, am 9. April," *AmZ* 7 (1 May 1805), 501–02.

97. Anonymous, "Tre Sonate per il Clav. o Foretpiano con un Violino . . . dal S. Luigi van Beethoven. Op. 12," *AmZ* 1 (5 June 1799), 571: " . . . ein bisarrer mühseliger Gang! . . . ein Suchen nach seltener Modulation, ein Ekelthun gegen gewöhnliche Verbindung, ein Anhäufen von Schwierigkeit auf Schwierigkeit, dass man alle Geduld und Freude dabey verliert."

98. Anonymous. "Philharmonic Concerts. Eighth Concert, Monday, June 6, 1825," *The Harmonicon*, no. 31 (July 1825): 118.

99. For further discussions of works by Beethoven that call attention to the hand behind them, see Karol Berger, "Beethoven and the Aesthetic State," *Beethoven Forum* 7 (1999): 17–44; and Tobias Janz, "'Music about Music': Metaization and Intertextuality in Beethoven's *Prometheus Variations* op. 35," in *Metareference across Media: Theory and Case Studies*, ed. Werner Wolf (Amsterdam and New York: Rodopi, 2009), 211–33.

100. See Mark Evan Bonds, "Irony and Incomprehensibility: Beethoven's 'Serioso' String Quartet in F minor, Op. 95, and the Path to the Late Style," *JAMS* 70 (2017): 285–356; on Marx's comments, see 287–89.

101. Carl Czerny, "Further Recollections of Beethoven," *Cock's Musical Miscellany* 1, no. 6 (2 August 1852): 65–66, quoted in *Beethoven aus der Sicht seiner Zeitgenossen in Tagebüchern, Briefen, Gedichten und Erinnerungen*, ed. Klaus Martin Kopitz and Rainer Cadenbach, 2 vols. (Munich: G. Henle, 2009), 1:215.

102. For numerous examples of this phenomenon, see Bonds, *The Beethoven Syndrome*.

NOTES TO PAGES 63–64

103. Ludwig Rellstab, "Ueber Beethovens neuestes Quartett," *BAmZ* 2 (25 May 1825): 165–66: "Die feierliche Empfindung durchdrang jeden Anwesenden. Nur die hatten sich versammelt, die mit wahrer Erhebung und Andacht unsterbliche Werke des großen Mannes aufzufassen vermochten … Was uns auch darin fremd, dunkel, verworren erscheinen mag, es hat seine Klarheit und Nothwendigkeit in der Seele des Schaffenden, und dort müssen wir Belehrung suchen."

104. Berthold Hoeckner, "Schumann and Romantic Distance," *JAMS* 50 (1997): 55–132; Julian Johnson, "Narrative Strategies in E. T. A. Hoffmann and Robert Schumann," in *Resounding Concerns*, ed. Rüdiger Görner (Munich: Iudicium, 2003), 55–70; Erika Reiman, *Schumann's Piano Cycles and the Novels of Jean Paul* (Rochester, NY: University of Rochester Press, 2004). On the demands Schumann's music placed on contemporary listeners, see Ulrike Kranefeld, *Der nachschaffende Hörer: Rezeptionsästhetische Studien zur Musik Robert Schumanns* (Stuttgart: J. B. Metzler, 2000); Hermann Danuser, "Robert Schumann und die romantische Idee einer selbstreflexiven Kunst," in *Übergänge zwischen Künsten und Kulturen: Internationaler Kongress zum 150. Todesjahr von Heinrich Heine und Robert Schumann*, ed. Henriette Herwig et al. (Stuttgart: Metzler, 2007), 471–91.

105. See Johann Czerny, *Sterne, Hippel und Jean Paul: Ein Beitrag zur Geschichte des humoristischen Romans in Deutschland* (Berlin: Alexander Duncker, 1904); Hamilton H. H. Beck, *The Elusive "I" in the Novel: Hippel, Sterne, Diderot, Kant* (New York: Peter Lang, 1987). On Beethoven and Jean Paul, see Elisabeth Eleonore Bauer, "Beethoven—unser musikalischer Jean Paul: Anmerkungen zu einer Analogie," in *Beethoven: Analecta varia*, ed. Heinz-Klaus Metzger and Reiner Riehn (Munich: edition text + kritik, 1987), 83–105.

106. Ludwig Tieck, *Der gestiefelte Kater*, in his *Sämmtliche Werke*, 2 vols. (Paris: Baudry, 1841), 1:472:

> KÖNIG: Aber noch eins, sagen Sie mir nur, da Sie so weit weg wohnen, wie Sie unsre Sprache so geläufig sprechen können?
> NATHANAEL. Still!
> KÖNIG. Wie?
> NATHANAEL. Still! Still!
> KÖNIG. Ich versteh' nicht.
> NATHANAEL *leise zu ihm*. Seien Sie doch ja damit ruhig, denn sonst merkt es ja am Ende das Publikum da unten, daß das eben sehr unnatürlich ist …

LEUTNER. Am meisten erbosen mich immer Widersprüche und Unnatürlichkeiten. Warum kann denn nur der Prinz nicht ein bißchen eine fremde Sprache reden, die sein Dolmetscher verdeutschte?

107. Tieck, *Die verkehrte Welt*, in his *Sämmtliche Werke*, 1:496: "Wo, Henker, kommt das Gewitter her, davon steht ja kein einziges Wort in meiner Rolle. Was sind das für Dummheiten! Und ich und mein Esel werden darüber pudelnaß ... Maschinist! Maschinist! so halt er doch ins Teufels Namen inne!"

108. On violations of the fourth wall in the dramas of Tieck, see Frederick Burwick, *Illusion and the Drama: Critical Theory of the Enlightenment and Romantic Era* (University Park: Pennsylvania State University Press, 1991), 279–93; Roger Paulin, *Ludwig Tieck: A Literary Biography* (Oxford: Clarendon Press, 1985); and Sigmund Jakob-Michael Stephan, "The Early Romantic Comedy of Aesthetic Disobedience," *Oxford German Studies* 50, no. 3 (2021): 350–64. For a broader survey, see John L. Styan, *Drama, Stage and Audience* (Cambridge: Cambridge University Press, 1975), especially chapter 6 ("Non-illusory Theatre").

109. See Rudolf Lieske, *Tiecks Abwendung von der Romantik* (Berlin: E. Ebering, 1933).

110. Szendy, *Listen*, 27. See also Michael Talbot, "The Work-Concept and Composer-Centredness," in *The Musical Work: Reality or Invention?* ed. Michael Talbot (Liverpool: Liverpool University Press, 2000), 168–86.

111. See Julian Johnson, *Mahler's Voices: Expression and Irony in the Songs and Symphonies* (New York: Oxford University Press, 2009), especially chapters 4 ("Plural Voices") and 8 ("Performing Authenticity").

CHAPTER 3

1. Christian Friedrich Michaelis, "Vermischte Bemerkungen über Musik," *Berlinische Musikalische Zeitung* 2 (1806), 81: "Der Beurtheiler der Kunst muß, wenn er gerecht urtheilen will, mit dem Künstler über die von ihm ausgeführte Idee sympathesiren und gleich denken, muß den Künstler auch aus des Künstlers Standpunkte beurtheilen, muß weingstens ahnden, was dieser wollte, was diesen begeisterte."

2. The standard account of the early history of the concept remains Paul Oskar Kristeller, "The Modern System of the Arts: A Study in the History of Aesthetics," *Journal of the History of Ideas* 12 (1951), 496–527, and

NOTES TO PAGES 67–69

13 (1952), 17–46. See also Larry Shiner, *The Invention of Art: A Cultural History* (Chicago: University of Chicago Press, 2001).

3. *KdU*, 5:306 (§44): " . . . nicht eine Lust des Genusses, aus bloßer Empfindung, sondern der Reflexion . . . und so ist ästhetische Kunst, als schöne Kunst, eine solche, die die reflektierende Urteilskraft und nicht die Sinnenempfindung zum Richtmaße hat." Translation from *CPJ*, 185.

4. Jean-Baptiste Du Bos, *Réflexions critiques*, 2:306: "L'ouvrage plaist-il, ou ne plaist il pas? L'ouvrage est-il bon ou mauvais en general? C'est la même chose. Le raisonnement ne doit donc intervenir dans le jugement que nous portons sur un poëme ou sur un tableau que pour rendre raison de la decision du sentiment, & pour expliquer quelles fautes l'empêchent de plaire, & quels sont les agréments qui le rendent capables d'attacher." Translation altered slightly from Georgia Cowart, "Sense and Sensibility in Eighteenth-Century Musical Thought," *Acta musicologica* 56 (1984), 254. Krause quotes the opening of this passage (in German) with approval in his *Von der musikalischen Poesie*, 363.

5. Du Bos, *Réflexions critiques*, 2:308, 312–13: "Le coeur s'agite de lui même & par un mouvement qui precede toute deliberation, quand l'objet qu'on lui presente est réellement un objet touchant, soit que l'objet ait une existence réelle, soit qu'il soit un objet imité. Le coeur est fait, il est organisé pour cela. Son operation previent donc tous les raisonements, ainsi que l'operation de l'oeil & celle de l'oreille les devancent dans leurs sensations . . . Mais le merite le plus important des poëmes & des tableaux est de nous plaire . . . On connoît donc suffisament s'ils ont bien réüssi quand on connoît si l'ouvrage touche ou s'il ne touche pas." Translation slightly altered from Jean-Baptiste Du Bos, *Critical Reflections on Poetry and Painting*, trans. Thomas Nugent, 2 vols. (London: John Nourse, 1748), 2:239–40, 242.

6. Jean-Pierre Crousaz, *Traité du beau* (Paris: François L'Honoré, 1715), 8: "Les idées occupent l'Esprit, les sentimens interessent le Coeur, les idées nous amusent, elles exercent l'attention, & quelquefois la fatiguent, suivant qu'elles sont plus our moins composées, & plus ou moins combinées entre'elles; mais les sentimens nous dominent, ils s'emparent de nous, ils décident de notre sort & nous rendent heureux ou malheureux, selon qu'ils sont doux ou fâcheux, agréables ou desagréables. On exprime aisément ses idées, mais il est très-difficile de décrire ses sentimens, il est même impossible d'en donner par aucun discours une exacte connoissance à ceux qui n'en ont jamais éprouvé de semblables." Translation from Cowart, "Sense and Sensibility," 254. Johann Nikolaus Forkel published an extended

NOTES TO PAGES 69–71

excerpt of this treatise, in German translation, in his *Musikalisch-kritische Bibliothek* 1 (1778), 3–52, and 2 (1778), 3–125.

7. Johann Mattheson ("Aristoxenus der Jüngere"), *Die neueste Untersuchung der Singspiele nebst beygefügter musikalischer Geschmacksprobe* (Hamburg: Christian Herold, 1744), 123: "Der Geschmack . . . ist die innerliche Empfindung, Wahl und Beurtheilung, die unser Verstand, in sinnreichen Dingen, von sich spüren läßt. Wenn die Zunge ihren eigenen Verstand hat, wie Plinius will; so hat der Verstand gewissermaßen seine eigne Zunge, womit er seine Gegestände kostet und prüfet."

8. Johann Adolph Scheibe, *Critischer Musikus*, 2nd ed. (Leipzig: Bernhard Christoph Breitkopf, 1745), 767: "Der Geschmack ist die Fähigkeit des Verstandes, dasjenige zu beurtheilen, was die Sinne empfinden."

9. Johann Nikolaus Forkel, "Vorrede," *Musikalisch-Kritische Bibliothek* 1 (1778), xiv: ". . . außer *dem sinnlichen*, auch noch ein *intellektuelles Vergnügen* . . . "

10. Johann Nikolaus Forkel, *Ueber die Theorie der Musik, insofern sie Liebhabern und Kennern nothwendig und nützlich ist: Eine Einladungschrift zu musikalischen Vorlesungen* (Göttingen: Wittwe Vandenhoeck, 1777).

11. On Forkel's lectures, see Matthew Riley, "Johann Nikolaus Forkel on the Listening Practices of 'Kenner' and 'Liebhaber'," *Music & Letters* 84 (2003): 414–33; and Mark Evan Bonds, "Turning Liebhaber into Kenner: Johann Nikolaus Forkel's Lectures on the Art of Listening, ca. 1780–1785," in *OHML*, 145–62.

12. Johann Nikolaus Forkel, *Ankündigung seines akademischen Winter-Concerts von Michaelis 1779 bis Ostern 1780* (Göttingen: Dietrich, 1779), 4–5, 10: ". . . worinn die Vorzüge und Schönheiten dieser Stücke zu suchen sind"; "der wahre Gesichtspunkt"; "den Absichten und Zwecken gemäß."

13. Forkel, *Ankündigung seines akademischen Winter-Concerts*, 5: "Diese Verschiedenheit der Urtheile, des Geschmacks und der Empfindung äußert sich jedoch hauptsächlich *nur* bey bloßer *Instrumentalmusik*, wo die mannichfaltigen Combinationen der Töne einen Hörer fordern, der wenigstens schon so viel Kunstkenntniß und Uebung hat, daß er sie behalten, mit einander vergleichen, und dadurch ihre Bedeutung fühlen kann, welche sie nach der Absicht des Componisten haben sollen."

14. Forkel, *Allgemeine Geschichte der Musik*, 1:41: "Da jede musikalische Periode auch schon bey einer nur mäßigen Länge, die Aufmerksamkeit des Zuhörers anstrengt, wenn er ihr in allen ihren kleinsten Theilen gehörig folgen, und den ganzen Zusammenhang fassen und begreifen soll; so ist auch in dem Bau der Perioden die höchst mögliche Deutlichkeit und Klarheit nothwendig, weil ohne sie der Zuhörer entweder ermüdet

162 NOTES TO PAGES 71–72

oder zerstreut wird, folglich auf keine Weise im Stande ist, dem Gange des Ganzen zu folgen, und das vom Tonstücke erwartete Vergnügen zu erhalten. Diese allgemeine Uebersicht des Ganzen mit allen seinen einzelnen Theilen, muß soviel möglich erleichtert werden, um so mehr, da die Musik eine solche Sprache ist, zu welcher nur sehr wenige Zuhörer ein vollständiges Wörterbuch besitzen . . . " Translation altered slightly from Riley, *Musical Listening in the German Enlightenment*, 17.

15. Saint Augustine of Hippo, *Confessions*, Book 11, chapter 28. For commentary on this passage, see Karol Berger, "Toward a History of Hearing: The Classic Concerto, a Sample Case," in *Convention in Eighteenth- and Nineteenth-Century Music: Essays in Honor of Leonard G. Ratner*, ed. Wye J. Allanbrook, Janet M. Levy, William P. Mahrt (Stuyvesant, NY: Pendragon, 1992), 421–23.

16. René Descartes, *Compendium musicae* (Utrecht: à Zÿll und ab Ackers dÿck, 1650), 8–9.

17. Berger, "Toward a History of Hearing," 422.

18. Leon Botstein, "The Consequences of Presumed Innocence: The Nineteenth-century Reception of Joseph Haydn," in *Haydn Studies*, ed. W. Dean Sutcliffe (Cambridge: Cambridge University Press, 1998), 1–34.

19. Johann Friedrich Reichardt, "Neue merkwürdige musikalische Werke," *Musikalisches Kunstmagazin* 1 (1782), 84: "Die Musik ist an sich selbst schon als Musik eine Ergötzung, ohne daß sie Empfindungen und Leidenschaft nachahmt. Sie darf uns eben nicht traurig, lustig und Erstaunen machen, und kann doch durch ein blosses angenehmes Gemisch von Tönen unser Ohr auf eine liebliche Art so kützeln, dass wir ergötzt werden. Sie kann ferner durch ihre mannigfaltige und künstliche Verhältnisse der Töne untereinander, durch die Verwickelung und Auflösung derselben, auf eine angenehme Art unseren Verstand beschäftigen und uns dadurch auf eine edle Art ergötzen. Endlich kann sie beides verbinden. Dies ist die Ursache, warum wir an blosser Instrumentalmusik, die auch keine bestimmte Empfindung oder Leidenschaft ausdrückt, dennoch Vergnügen finden. Dies ist auch die Ursache, dass Mannheimer Instrumentalmusik, die das Ohr angenehm kützelt, dem blossen Liebhaber vorzüglich gefällt; daß sogenannte Berlinische Musik, die den Verstand beschäftigt, dem gelehrten Kenner vorzüglich gefällt; und daß vernünftige Verbindung von beiden, dem billigen und gefühlvollen Kenner die höchste Ergötzung bei der Instrumentalmusik gewährt." For a different translation and further commentary, see Matthew Pritchard, "Music in Balance: The Aesthetics of Music after Kant, 1790–1810," *JM* 36 (2019), 54. For additional criticisms similar to Reichardt's, see Klaus Winkler, "Alter und

NOTES TO PAGES 72–78 163

Neuer Musikstil im Streit zwischen den Berlinern und Wienern zur Zeit der Frühklassik," *Die Musikforschung* 33 (1980), 37–45.

20. Burney, *A General History of Music*, 3:v.

21. Burney, *A General History of Music*, 4:630.

22. Burney, *A General History of Music*, 3:vi–vii.

23. Burney, *A General History of Music*, 3:x–xi.

24. Burney, *A General History of Music*, 3:vi.

25. See the editors' Introduction to Adam Smith, "Of the Nature of that Imitation which Takes Place in What Are Called the Imitative Arts," in his *Essays on Philosophical Subjects*, ed. W. P. D. Wightman and J. C. Bryce (Oxford: Clarendon Press, 1980), 171–75.

26. Smith, "Of the Nature of that Imitation," 203, 198, 204–05.

27. Smith, "Of the Nature of that Imitation," 204. The closing reference to "an ancient philosopher and musician" is almost certainly to Saint Augustine.

28. See Bernd Sponheuer, *Musik als Kunst und Nicht-Kunst: Untersuchungen zur Dichotomie von "hoher" und "niederer" Musik im musikästhetischen Denken zwischen Kant und Hanslick* (Kassel: Bärenreiter, 1987), 97–100.

29. *KdU*, 5:223 (§13): "Der Geschmack ist jederzeit noch barbarisch, wo er die Beimischung der *Reize* und *Rührungen* zum Wohlgefallen bedarf, ja wohl gar diese zum Maßstabe seines Beifalls macht." Translation from *CPJ*, 108.

30. Kant, *Anthropologie in pragmatischer Hinsicht* (1798), in his *Gesammelte Schriften*, ed. Königlich Preußische Akademie der Wissenschaften (Berlin: Georg Reimer, 1900–), 7:251 (§73): "Affekten und Leidenschaften unterworfen zu sein, ist wohl immer Krankheit des Gemüts, weil beides die Herrschaft der Vernunft ausschließt." Translation from Kant, *Anthropology from a Pragmatic Point of View*, ed. and trans. Robert B. Louden and Manfred Kuehn (Cambridge: Cambridge University Press, 2006), 149.

31. Kant, *Metaphysik der Sitten* (1797), in his *Gesammelte Schriften*, 6:407: "Zur inneren Freiheit aber werden zwei Stücke erfordert: seine selbst in einem gegebenen Fall Meister (*animus sui compos*) und über sich selbst Herr zu sein (*imperium in semetipsum*), d. i. seine Affecten zu zähmen." Translation from Kant, *Metaphysics of Morals*, ed. and transl. Mary Gregor (Cambridge: Cambridge University Press, 1996), 166.

32. See Peter L. Oesterreich, "Das Verhältnis von ästhetischer Theorie und Rhetorik in Kants *Kritik der Urteilskraft*," *Kant-Studien* 83 (1992), 324–35.

164   NOTES TO PAGES 79–81

33. *KdU*, 5:328 (§53). On this point in relation to Kant's wider philosophical system, see Tomás McAuley, "Immanuel Kant and the Downfall of the *Affektenlehre*," in *Sound and Affect: Voice, Music, World*, ed. Judith Lochhead, Eduardo Mendieta, and Stephen Decatur Smith (Chicago: University of Chicago Press, 2021), 342–60.

34. *KdU*, 5:306 (§44).

35. *KdU*, 5:214 (§8). Ibid., 5:354 (§59): ". . . und sogar an Gegenständen der Sinne auch ohne Sinnenreiz ein freies Wohlgefallen finden lehrt." Translation from *CPJ*, 228.

36. *KdU*, 5:226 (§14): "Rührung . . . gehört gar nicht zur Schönheit." Translation from *CPJ*, 111. On the importance of imagination in Kant's aesthetics, see Jane Kneller, *Kant and the Power of Imagination* (Cambridge: Cambridge University Press, 2007).

37. *KdU*, §54.

38. Hannah Ginsborg, "Kant," in *The Routledge Companion to Philosophy and Music*, ed. Theodore Gracyk and Andrew Kania (London and New York: Routledge, 2011), 328–29.

39. Abigail Zitin, *Practical Form: Abstraction, Technique, and Beauty in Eighteenth-century Aesthetics* (New Haven, CT: Yale University Press, 2020), 159.

40. Alexander Gerard, *An Essay on Taste* (London: A. Millar; Edinburgh: A. Kincaid and J. Bell, 1759), 3–4. On imagination in general, see James Engell, *The Creative Imagination: Enlightenment to Romanticism* (Cambridge, MA: Harvard University Press, 1981).

41. Kant, *Anthropologie in pragmatischer Hinsicht*, 7:239: "1) Die sinnliche, 2) die intellectuelle Lust. Die erstere entweder (a) durch den Sinn (das Vergnügen), oder (b) durch die Einbildungskraft (der Geschmack); die zweite (nämlich intellectuelle) entweder (a) durch darstellbare *Begriffe* oder (b) durch *Ideen* . . ." Translation from Kant, *Anthropology from a Pragmatic Point of View*, 125.

42. *KdU*, 5:229–30 (§16).

43. *KdU*, 5:329 (§53): "die ganze Musik ohne Text."

44. *KdU*, 5:329 (§53). Translation altered slightly from *CJ*, 199.

45. *KdU*, 5:329–30 (§53).

46. *KdU*, 5:314 (§49): "[U]nter einer ästhetischen Idee aber verstehe ich diejenige Vorstellung der Einbildungskraft die viel zu denken veranlaßt, ohne daß ihr doch irgend ein bestimmter Gedanke, d.i. *Begriff* adäquat sein kann, die folglich keine Sprache völlig erreicht und verständlich machen kann.—Man sieht leicht, daß sie das Gegenstück (Pendant) von einer *Vernunftidee* sei, welche umgekehrt ein Begriff ist, dem keine *Anschauung*

NOTES TO PAGES 81–83

(Vorstellung der Einbildungskraft) adäquat sein kann." Translation from *CJ*, 182.

47. *KdU*, 5:314 (§49): "Die Einbildungskraft (als produktives Erkenntnisvermögen) ist nämlich sehr mächtig in Schaffung gleichsam einer anderen Natur, aus dem Stoffe, den ihr die wirkliche gibt." Translation from *CJ*, 182.

48. See in particular the comments in *KdU*, 5:331–32 (§54).

49. See Mojca Kuplen, "Reflective and Non-reflective Aesthetic Ideas in Kant's Theory of Art," *BJA* 61 (2021), 1–16.

50. *KdU*, 5:316 (§49): "Mit einem Worte, die ästhetische Idee ist eine, einem gegebenen Begriffe beigesellte Vorstellung der Einbildungskraft welche mit einer solchen Mannigfaltigkeit der Teilvorstellungen in dem freien Gebrauche derselben verbunden ist, daß für sie kein Ausdruck, der einen bestimmten Begriff bezeichnet, gefunden werden kann, der also zu einem Begriffe viel Unnennbares hinzu denken läßt, dessen Gefühl die Erkenntnisvermögen belebt und mit der Sprache, als bloßem Buchstaben, Geist verbindet." Translation from *CJ*, 185.

51. *KdU*, 5:314 (§49). See above, p. 81.

52. Kant, *KdU*, 5:326–27 (§53): "Unter allen behauptet die *Dichtkunst* . . . den obersten Rang. Sie erweitert das Gemüt dadurch, daß sie die Einbildungskraft in Freiheit setzt und innerhalb den Schranken eines gegebenen Begriffs unter der unbegrenzten Mannigfaltigkeit möglicher damit zusammenstimmender Formen diejenige darbietet, welche die Darstellung desselben mit einer Gedankenfülle verknüpft, der kein Sprachausdruck völlig adäquat ist, und sich also ästhetisch zu Ideen erhebt." Translation from *CJ*, 196.

53. Kant, *KdU*, 5:327 (§53): "Die Beredsamkeit, sofern darunter die Kunst zu überreden, d.i. durch den schönen Schein zu hintergehen (als *ars oratoria*), und nicht bloße Wohlredenheit (Eloquenz und Stil) verstanden wird, ist eine Dialektik, die von der Dichtkunst nur so viel entlehnt, als nötig ist, die Gemüter vor der Beurteilung für den Redner zu dessen Vorteil zu gewinnen, und dieser die Freiheit zu benehmen . . . [D]a sie [die Maschinen der Überredung] eben sowohl auch zur Beschönigung oder Verdeckung des Lasters und Irrtums gebraucht werden können, den geheimen Verdacht wegen einer künstlichen Überlistung nicht ganz vertilgen können. In der Dichtkunst geht alles ehrlich und aufrichtig zu. Sie erklärt sich: ein bloßes unterhaltendes Spiel mit der Einbildungskraft, und zwar der Form nach einstimmig mit Verstandesgesetzen treiben zu wollen, und verlangt nicht, den Verstand durch sinnliche Darstellung zu überschleichen und zu verstricken." Translation altered slightly from *CJ*, 197–98. The translation

166 NOTES TO PAGES 83–86

of "Beredsamkeit" as "rhetoric" rather than "oratory" or "oratorical eloquence" in *CPJ*, 204, obscures Kant's important distinction between primary and secondary rhetoric.

54. On the decline of the rhetorical model as a governing metaphor of musical
form, see Bonds, *Wordless Rhetoric*, 141–45.

55. See Frieder Zaminer, "Über die Herkunft des Ausdrucks 'Musik ver-
stehen'," in *Musik und Verstehen: Aufsätze zur semiotischen Theorie,
Ästhetik und Soziologie der musikalischen Rezeption*, ed. Peter Faltin and
Hans-Peter Reinecke (Cologne: Arno Volk, 1973), 314–19.

56. Peter Lichtenthal, *Der musikalische Arzt, oder: Abhandlung von dem
Einflusse der Musik auf den Körper, und von ihrer Anwendung in gewissen Krankheiten. Nebst einigen Winken, zur Anhörung einer guten Musik*
(Vienna: Christian Friedrich Wappler und Beck, 1807), 181: "Ein gutes
musikalisches Stück, ist mit einer Rede, die uns der Redner von der Kanzel
hält, eine und dieselbe Sache. Es besteht immer aus einem Thema, dieses
wird in einem gut gearbeiteten Satze immer mehr erweitert, verändert,
durchgeführt, wiederholt usw. Man findet in ihm . . . die nämlichen
Zwischensätze und Uibergänge, die nämlichen Figuren und Kadenzen wie
in einer Rede . . . "

57. Lichtenthal, *Der musikalische Arzt,* 196: "Bey Anhörung einer guten
Musik dürfen uns keine fremde Gegenstände zerstreuen, sondern wir
müssen genau mit einer allgemeinen Empfindung, mit deutlichen
Bewusstseyn, alles mögliche auffassen, was nur in unserer Macht steht.
Zum Beyspiel: wie ist das Thema? wie ist das Tempo? wie ist die Tonart,
wie sind die Harmonien, die Figuren, die Uibergänge, die Passagen?
welchen Plan hat der Kompositor, d. h. wie ist das Thema ausgeführt,
wie entspricht es dem Gegenstande, welcher hier gemalt werden soll? und
hauptsächlich, wie ist die Instrumentation? der Inbegriff von allen diesem
lehrt uns ob der Autor was gesagt habe oder nicht. Haben wir einmal
dieses Was und Wie eingesehen, so haben wir auch die Musik gehört."

58. Schiller, "Über das Pathetische" (1793), in his *Werke und Briefe in zwölf
Bänden*, ed. Otto Dann et al. (Frankfurt/Main: Deutscher Klassiker
Verlag, 1988–2004), 8:427: "Auch die Musik der Neuern scheint es vorzüglich nur auf die Sinnlichkeit anzulegen, und schmeichelt dadurch dem
herrschenden Geschmack, der nur angenehm gekitzelt nicht ergriffen,
nicht kräftig gerührt, nicht erhoben sein will. Alles *schmelzende* wird
daher vorgezogen, und wenn noch so großer Lärm in einem Konzertsaal
ist, so wird plötzlich alles Ohr, wenn eine schmelzende Passage vorgetragen
wird. Ein bis ins tierische gehender Ausdruck der Sinnlichkeit erscheint
dann gewöhnlich auf allen Gesichtern, die trunkenen Augen schwimmen,

der offene Mund ist ganz Begierde, ein wollüstiges Zittern ergreift den ganzen Körper, der Atem ist schnell und schwach, kurz alle Symptome der Berauschung stellen sich ein: zum deutlichen Beweise, daß die Sinne schwelgen, der Geist aber oder das Prinzip der Freiheit im Menschen der Gewalt des sinnlichen Eindrucks zum Raube wird. Alle diese Rührungen sage ich, sind durch einen edeln und männlichen Geschmack von der Kunst ausgeschlossen, weil sie bloß allein dem *Sinne* gefallen, mit dem die Kunst nichts zu verkehren hat."

59. Schiller, "Über Matthissons Gedichte" (1794), in his *Werke und Briefe in zwölf Bänden*, 8:1023: "Zwar sind Empfindungen, *ihrem Inhalte nach*, keiner Darstellung fähig; aber *ihrer Form nach* sind sie es allerdings, und es existiert wirklich eine allgemein beliebte und wirksame Kunst, die kein anderes Objekt hat, als eben diese Form der Empfindungen. Diese Kunst ist die *Musik*."

60. Christian Gottfried Körner, "Über Charakterdarstellung in der Musik" (1795), in his *Aesthetische Ansichten: Ausgewählte Aufsätze*, ed. Joseph P. Bauke (Marbach: Schiller-Nationalmuseum, 1964), 24–47. On Körner and his essay, see Jacob de Ruiter, *Der Charakterbegriff in der Musik: Studien zur deutschen Ästhetik der Instrumentalmusik 1740–1850* (Stuttgart: Franz Steiner, 1989); Robert Riggs, "'On the Representation of Character in Music': Christian Gottfried Körner's Aesthetics of Instrumental Music," *Musical Quarterly* 81, no. 4 (1997), 599–631. Riggs' essay includes a complete translation of Körner's text.

61. Schiller, "Zu Gottfried Körners Aufsatz 'Über Charakterdarstellung in der Musik'," in his *Werke und Briefe*, 8:1083: "Offenbar beruht die Macht der Musik auf ihrem körperlichen materiellen Teil.... [S]o wird die Musik nur aesthetisch durch Form . . . Ohne Form würde sie über uns blind gebieten; ihre Form rettet unsre Freiheit."

62. Schiller, "Zu Gottfried Körners Aufsatz," 1084: "Nimmst Du der Musik alle *Form*, so verliert sie zwar alle ihre *ästhetische* aber nicht alle ihre musikalische Macht.

"Nimmst Du ihr allen *Stoff*, und behältst bloß ihren reinen Teil, so verliert sie zugleich ihre ästhetische und ihre Musikalische Macht, und wird bloß ein Objekt des Verstandes. Dies beweist also, daß auf ihren körperlichen Teil mehr Rücksicht genommen werden muß, als Du genommen hast.

"Eben so urteilte auch Humboldt, und Göthe. Ich wünschte also, daß Du, wäre es auch nur im Vorbeigehen, die eigentümliche Macht der Musik, die bloß auf ihrer Materie beruht, noch berühren möchtest."

63. Schiller, *Über die ästhetische Erziehung des Menschen in einer Reihe von Briefen* (1795), in his *Werke und Briefe in zwölf Bänden*, 8:641 (22nd

168   NOTES TO PAGES 87–88

letter): "In einem wahrhaft schönen Kunstwerk soll der Inhalt nichts, die Form aber alles tun; denn durch die Form allein wird auf das Ganze des Menschen, durch den Inhalt hingegen nur auf einzelne Kräfte gewirkt. Der Inhalt, wie erhaben und weit umfassend er auch sei, wirkt also jederzeit einschränkend auf den Geist und nur von der Form ist wahre ästhetische Freiheit zu erwarten. Darin also besteht das eigentliche Kunstgeheimnis des Meisters, *dass er den Stoff durch die Form vertilgt*; und je imposanter, anmaßender, verführerischer der Stoff an sich selbst ist, je eigenmächtiger derselbe mit *seiner* Wirkung sich vordrängt, oder je mehr der Betrachter geneigt ist, sich unmittelbar mit dem Stoff einzulassen, desto triumphierender ist die Kunst, welche jenen zurückzwingt und über diesen die Herrschaft behauptet." In her *The Orchestral Revolution: Haydn and the Technologies of Timbre* (Cambridge: Cambridge University Press, 2013), Emily Dolan documents the power of timbre over listeners of the time (see in particular chapter 4, "The Republic of Sound"), though whether this would have encouraged resonant or reflective listening would necessarily have varied from individual to individual.

64. Schiller, *Über die ästhetische Erziehung des Menschen*, in his *Werke und Briefe*, 8:642 (22nd letter): "Eine schöne Kunst der Leidenschaft gibt es; aber eine schöne leidenschaftliche Kunst ist ein Widerspruch, denn der unausbleibliche Effekt des Schönen ist Freiheit von Leidenschaften."

65. Schiller, *Über die ästhetische Erziehung des Menschen*, in his *Werke und Briefe*, 8:642 (22nd letter): ". . . weil auch die geistreichste Musik *durch ihre Materie* noch immer in einer größern Affinität zu den Sinnen steht, als die wahre ästhetische Freiheit duldet . . . " The translation of *geistreich* as "ethereal" in Elizabeth M. Wilkinson and L. A. Willoughby's widely used edition (*On the Aesthetic Education of Man in a Series of Letters* [Oxford: Clarendon Press, 1967], 155) is misleading.

66. Schiller, "Über naive und sentimentalische Dichtung" (1795), in his *Werke und Briefe*, 8:745: "Ihr Ziel ist einerlei mit dem höchsten, wornach der Mensch zu ringen hat, frei von Leidenschaft zu sein, immer klar immer ruhig um sich und in sich zu schauen, überall mehr Zufall als Schicksal zu finden, und mehr über Ungereimtheit zu lachen als über Bosheit zu zürnen oder zu weinen."

67. Schiller, "Über den Gebrauch des Chors in der Tragödie," in his *Die Braut von Messina* (1803), in his *Werke und Briefe*, 5:283: "Die wahre Kunst aber hat es nicht bloß auf ein vorübergehendes Spiel abgesehen, es ist ihr ernst damit, den Menschen nicht bloß in einen augenblicklichen Traum von Freiheit zu versetzen, sondern ihn wirklich und in der Tat frei zu *machen*."

NOTES TO PAGES 89–90 169

68. Schiller, "Über den Gebrauch des Chors in der Tragödie," in his *Werke und Briefe*, 5:282: "Es soll ein Spiel bleiben, aber ein poetisches. Alle Kunst ist der Freude gewidmet, und es gibt keine höhere und keine ernsthaftere Aufgabe, als die Menschen zu beglücken. Die rechte Kunst ist nur diese, welche den höchsten Genuß verschafft. Der höchste Genuß aber ist die Freiheit des Gemüts in dem lebendigen Spiel aller seiner Kräfte."

69. August Wilhelm Schlegel, *Ueber dramatische Kunst und Litteratur: Vorlesungen*, 2 vols. (Heidelberg: Mohr und Zimmer, 1809–11), 1:115: "Der Chor ist mit einem Worte der idealisierte Zuschauer. Er lindert den Eindruck einer tief erschütternden oder tief rührenden Darstellung, indem er dem wirklichen Zuschauer seine eignen Regungen schon lyrisch, also musikalisch ausgedrückt entgegenbringt, und ihn in die Region der Betrachtung hinaufführt."

70. August Wilhelm Schlegel, *Ueber dramatische Kunst und Litteratur*, 2:71–72: "Die meisten Dichter . . . nehmen Partey, und verlangen von den Lesern blinden Glauben . . . . Je eifriger diese Rhetorik ist, desto leichter verfehlt sie ihren Zweck. Auf jeden Fall werden wir gewahr, daß wir die Sache nicht unmittelbar, sondern durch das Medium einer fremden Denkakt erblicken. Wenn hingegen der Dichter zuweilen durch eine geschickte Wendung die weniger glänzende Kehrseite der Münze nach vorne dreht, so setzt er sich mit dem auserlesenen Kreis der Einsichtsvollen unter seinen Lesern oder Zuschauern in ein verstohlnes Einverständniß; er zeigt ihnen, daß er ihre Einwendungen vorhergesehn und im voraus zugegeben habe; daß er nicht selbst in dem dargestellten Gegenstande befangen sey, sonder frey über ihm schwebe, und daß er den schönen, unwiderstehlich anziehenden Schein, den er selbst hervorgezaubert, wenn er anders wollte, unerbittlich vernichten könnte." On the growing importance of irony in early nineteenth-century aesthetics, see Bonds, "Irony and Incomprehensibility: Beethoven's 'Serioso' String Quartet in F minor, Op. 95."

71. Frederick Burwick, "Greek Drama: Coleridge, de Quincey, A. W. Schlegel," *Wordsworth Circle* 44 (2013), 3–12. Frederick Burwick, *Illusion and the Drama: Critical Theory of the Enlightenment and Romantic Era*, 303. Burwick's monograph surveys a long tradition of violations of the theater's fourth wall.

72. Friedrich Schlegel, "Athenäum Fragment 238," in *Kritische Friedrich-Schlegel-Ausgabe*, ed. Ernst Behler et al. (Munich: F. Schöningh, 1958–), 2:204: "So wie man aber wenig Wert auf eine Transzendentalphilosophie legen würde, die nicht kritisch wäre, nicht auch das Produzierende mit dem Produkt darstellte . . . so sollte wohl auch jene Poesie . . . mit der künstlerischen Reflexion und schönen Selbstbespiegelung, die sich im

170 NOTES TO PAGES 90–92

Pindar, den lyrischen Fragmenten der Griechen, und der alten Elegie, unter den Neuern aber in Goethe findet, vereinigen, und in jeder ihrer Darstellungen sich selbst mit darstellen, und überall zugleich Poesie und Poesie der Poesie sein."

73. For an insightful examination of what Matthew Pritchard has called this "dual conception of music" in the decades around 1800, see his "Music in Balance."

74. Johann Heinrich Gottlieb Heusinger, *Handbuch der Ästhetik*, 2 vols. (Gotha: Justus Perthes, 1797–1800), 1:135: "Musik ist die Kunst, durch Töne bestimmte Gefühle in den Zuhörern hervorzubringen . . . Als *schöner* Künstler begnügt sich der Tonkünstler nicht bloß mit Hervorbringung dieser Gefühle, sondern er bringt sie auf eine solche Art hervor, daß die Erregung derselben alle Gemüthskräfte des Menschen angemessen beschäftiget, d.h. seine Art Gefühle zu erwecken ist *schön.*" Ibid., 1:182: "Die größeste Kunst besteht darin, daß man den Zuhörer auf den Punct bringe, wo man ihn haben will."

75. Heusinger, *Handbuch der Ästhetik*, 1:182.

76. Johann Friedrich Reichardt, "Fingerzeige für den denkenden und for-schenden deutschen Tonkünstler," *Musikalisches Kunstmagazin* 2 (1791), 87–89. Johann Friedrich Reichardt, editorial note to Kant, "Von der Methodenlehre des Geschmacks," *Musikalisches Kunstmagazin* 2 (1791), 65: "Dieses vortreffliche, aufhellende Werk können forschende Künstler und Kunstkenner nicht eifrig genug studieren."

77. On Reichardt's relationship to Kant, see Walter Salmen, *Johann Friedrich Reichardt: Komponist, Schriftsteller, Kapellmeister und Verwaltungsbeamter der Goethezeit*, 2nd ed. (Hildesheim: Georg Olms, 2002), 190–91.

78. Anonymous, "Gedanken über die Oper," *AmZ* 1 (3 October 1798), 1; Immanuel Kant, "Fragmente über musikalische Gegenstände aus neuen, wichtigen, nichtmusikalischen Schriften: Aus Kants Anthropologie," *AmZ* 2 (9 December 1799), 23–25. See also Rochlitz's enthusiastic comments about Kant in his "Der Geschmack: Schreiben an einen Tonkünstler," *AmZ* 33 (3 August 1831), 502, albeit with certain reserva-tions about the philosopher's views on music.

79. Anonymous, "Aufschlüsse über Musik aus den Werken der Philosophen," *AmZ* 5 (17 November 1802), 130: "Was Kant über die Musik gelehrt hat, ist den Lesern der Musik[alischen] Zeitung schon bekannt worden."

80. On Michaelis' life and career, see Lothar Schmidt's commentary to his edition of Michaelis, *Ueber den Geist der Tonkunst und andere Schriften* (Chemnitz: Gudrun Schröder, 1997), 297–301.

NOTES TO PAGES 92–93

81. Christian Friedrich, Michaelis, *Ueber den Geist der Tonkunst, mit Rücksicht auf Kants Kritik der ästhetischen Urtheilskraft: Ein ästhetischer Versuch*, 2 vols. (Leipzig: Schäferische Buchhandlung, 1795–1800), 1:28–29.

82. Michaelis, *Ueber den Geist der Tonkunst*, 1:10: "Aesthetische Ideen machen den Geist der Musik aus."

83. *KdU*, 5:324 (§51): "... die Kunst des schönen Spiels der Empfindungen"; Michaelis, *Ueber den Geist der Tonkunst*, 1:16.

84. Michaelis, *Ueber den Geist der Tonkunst*, 1:54–55:"Die Erklärung der Musik als einer *hörbaren und verschönerten Darstellung menschlicher Gefühle und Leidenschaften*, scheint mir daher zu enge zu seyn ... Vielleicht könnte man die Tonkunst erklären, als die Kunst, *durch mannichfaltige Verbindung der Töne das Gefühl zu rühren, die Fantasie zu beleben und zu beschäftigen, und das Gemüt zu Ideen des Schönen und Erhabenen zu stimmen:* oder kürzer: *als die Kunst, durch verbundene Töne unmittelbar ästhetische Gefühle und mittelbar ästhetische Ideen zu eregen.*"

85. Michaelis, "Nachtrag zu den Ideen über die ästhetische Natur der Musik," *Eunomia: Eine Zeitschrift des 19. Jahrhunderts* 1 (1801), 346: "Diese *Unbestimmtheit* der musikalischen Darstellung ist der *Freiheit* unserer Phantasie sehr günstig; in sofern gleicht die musikalische Schilderung den *ästhetischen Ideen* des Dichters, welche uns in ein unendliches Feld der Gedanken blicken lassen; in sofern hat die Musik etwas *Idealisches*, etwas, was die Einbildungskraft befreit und beflügelt, über die beschränkte Wirklichkeit erhebt."

86. Michaelis, *Ueber den Geist der Tonkunst*, 2:63: "Die Musik kann nur in so fern *geistreich* und *schön* seyn, in wie fern sie ästhetische Ideen ausdrückt, also die Einbildungskraft in ein freies und harmonisches Spiel setzt, wodurch eine belebende Gedankenfülle dargestellt wird."

87. Michaelis, *Ueber den Geist der Tonkunst*, 2:7–8: "Der Standpunkt der *Freiheit* ist es, auf welchen uns der Künstler setzt; er bewegt unsere Gemüthskräfte zu lebendiger harmonischer Thätigkeit, und erregt unser Wohlgefallen an einer Darstellung, die wir uns auf seine Veranlassung selbst gebildet haben; er stellt uns in eine Welt, die sich uns nicht von außen aufdringt, sondern aus unserer Einbildungskraft in unserem Geist und Herzen aufgeht, ein Werk unserer Selbstthätigkeit ist; er erhebt uns in eine höhere Sphäre, in welcher wir uns als frei und selbsthandelnd erblicken, zur Selbständigkeit emporgerichtet finden ... Wir finden bei den Produkten der schönen Kunst uns selbst in dem freien Spiele unserer mit dem Verstande zusammenstimmenden Einbildungskraft, also entbunden der Fesseln, welche die gemeine Ansicht der Wirklichkeit uns anlegt, erhaben über den Zwang des sinnlichen Eindrucks ... "

172   NOTES TO PAGES 94–95

88. Michaelis, *Ueber den Geist der Tonkunst*, 2:16–17; see also 2:40.

89. Michaelis, "Vermischte Bemerkungen über Musik," *Berlinische Musikalische Zeitung* 1 (1805), 14: "Der wahre Tonkünstler zählt mir nicht bloß Töne zu, er gibt mir mehr als bloße Gehörempfindungen. Sie sind ihm bloß Mittel, meine Einbildungskraft in Bewegung zu setzen, sie zu beflügeln, mich zu begeistern . . . Und der ist im musikalischen Gefühl noch sehr zurück und kennt den musikalischen Genuß nicht, der bloß am Einzelnen oder am Zufälligen hängen bleibt, und sich nicht zur Zusammenfassung des großen Ganzen, des vollen ästhetischen Effekts erhebt. Denn freilich hängt das Wohlgefallen an einer Musik sehr ab von der individuellen Stärke des *Auffasungs-* und *Zusammenfassungs-Vermögens*. Daher nach Verschiedenheit der Seelendisposition und Gemüthsfähigkeit, bald eine verwickelte, reichhaltige, bald eine einfachere, leichter verbundene Composition, bald eine Fuge, bald ein naives Liedchen oder ein fließendes Rondo mehr gefallen kann. Das umfassende Gemüth und der gebildete Geschmack aber ist für beides und für alles empfänglich."

90. Michaelis, "Einige Gedanken über das Interessante und Rührende in der Musik," *Eunomia: Eine Zeitschrift des 19. Jahrhunderts* 4, no. 2 (August 1804), 151: "Das Schöne, welches uns, abgesehen von allem Reizenden und Rührenden, gefällt, besteht bloß in der glücklich angelegten Aufeinanderfolge, Zusammensetzung, Kontrastirung, Zusammenstimmung, Verwicklung und Auflösung der Töne. Hier haftet das Wohlgefallen an dem *Formellen* der Musik, welches man, der Analogie gemäß, mit Recht musikalische *Gedanken* und *Figuren* genannt hat."

91. Michaelis, "Vermischte Bemerkungen über Musik," *Berlinische Musikalische Zeitung* 1 (1805), 26: "Solche Kunstgriffe machen die Musik pikant, und geben ihr vorzüglich den humoristischen Geist, welcher außerordentlich belebend auf die Einbildungskraft wirkt."

92. Friedrich Schlegel, "Athenäum Fragment 444" (1798), in *Kritische Friedrich-Schlegel-Ausgabe*, 2:254: "Es pflegt manchem seltsam und lächerlich aufzufallen, wenn die Musiker von den Gedanken in ihren Kompositionen reden; und oft mag es auch so geschehen, daß man wahrnimmt, sie haben mehr Gedanken in ihrer Musik als über dieselbe. Wer aber Sinn für die wunderbaren Affinitäten aller Künste und Wissenschaften hat, wird die Sache wenigstens nicht aus dem platten Gesichtspunkt der sogenannten Natürlichkeit betrachten, nach welcher die Musik nur die Sprache der Empfindung sein soll, und eine gewisse Tendenz aller reinen Instrumentalmusik zur Philosophie an sich nicht unmöglich finden. Muß die reine Instrumentalmusik sich nicht selbst einen Text erschaffen? und

NOTES TO PAGES 95–96   173

wird das Thema in ihr nicht so entwickelt, bestätigt, variiert und kontrastiert, wie der Gegenstand der Meditation in einer philosophischen Ideenreihe?"

93. Jean Paul Richter, *Flegeljahre: Eine Biographie*, 4 vols. (Tübingen: Cotta, 1804–05), 2:133: "Aber wie hörtest du? Voraus und zurück, oder nur so vor dich hin? Das Volk hört wie das Vieh nur Gegenwart, nicht die beiden Polar-Zeiten, nur musikalische Sylben, keine Syntax. Ein guter Hörer des Worts prägt sich den Vordersatz eines musikalischen Perioden ein, um den Nachsatz schön zu fassen." See Nikolaus Bacht, "Jean Paul's Listeners," *Eighteenth-Century Music* 3 (2006), 201–12.

94. Johann Karl Friedrich Triest, "Bemerkungen über die Ausbildung der Tonkunst in Deutschland im achtzehnten Jahrhundert," *AmZ* 3 (1 January 1801), 227: "Die Sinnlichkeit lieferte der Einbildungskraft einen Stoff zum freyen Spiel und der Verstand suchte es mit seinen Regeln zu vereinigen." Translation altered slightly from Triest, "Remarks on the Development of the Art of Music in Germany in the Eighteenth Century," trans. Susan Gillespie, in *Haydn and His World*, ed. Elaine Sisman (Princeton, NJ: Princeton University Press, 1997), 323.

95. Triest, "Bemerkungen über die Ausbildung der Tonkunst," 227–28: "So erhielt also jede schöne Kunst, (mithin auch die Musik) eine doppelte Bestimmung. Sie war theils *reine* (für sich bestehende) Kunst, Bearbeitung eines sinnlichen Stoffs zum freyen und schönen Spiel der Einbildungskraft; theils diente sie (ihrem *empirischen* Ursprunge nach) nur als aesthetisches Mittel zu anderweitigen Zwecken, besonders zur verschönerten Darstellung eines oder mehrer Subjekte (ihrer Gefühle und Thaten) und war dann *angewandte* Kunst." Translation altered slightly from Triest, "Remarks on the Development of the Art of Music," 324.

96. Triest, "Bemerkungen über die Ausbildung der Tonkunst," 227: "Dies verstehe ich unter *reiner* Musik, wozu man sogar alle Gesangstücke rechnen kann, bey denen der Text nichts sagt, indem er nur als Vehikel zum Gebrauch der Singstimme dient." Translation from Triest, "Remarks on the Development of the Art of Music," 387.

97. Triest, "Bemerkungen über die Ausbildung der Tonkunst," *AmZ* 3 (4 March 1801), 397: "Die *niedrigste* Würkung desselben ist ein blosser *Sinnenkitzel* . . . Grösser ist die, wenn der *Verstand* dabey zur Untersuchung der Richtigkeit, Schönheit, Künstlichkeit der Tongänge gereizt wird (z. B. bey Stücken oder Passagen im gebundenen Styl)." Translation altered slightly from Triest, "Remarks on the Development of the Art of Music," 369.

174 NOTES TO PAGES 96–98

98. Triest, "Bemerkungen über die Ausbildung der Tonkunst," 399: "eine vollere üppigere Gestalt." Translation from Triest, "Remarks on the Development of the Art of Music," 370.

99. Triest, "Bemerkungen über die Ausbildung der Tonkunst," 300–01: "Nein, Bach sezte nicht mit Fleiss dunkel und schwer, sondern diese Eigenschaften waren eine natürliche Folge seines Ideenganges, worinn ihm der mechanische (blos rechnende) eben so wenig, als der nur sinnliche Ergötzung suchende Musiker folgen konnte. In ihm regte sich irgend eine *ästhetische* d. h. aus Begriff und Empfindung zusammengesezte, Idee, welche sich nicht in Worten ausdrücken lässt, ob sie gleich *nahe* an die *bestimmte* Empfindung streift, welche uns der Gesang darstellen kann, und wovon sie gleichsam das Urbild ist. Diese trug er auf sein Klavier (oder in Noten) über, indem ür seine innige Vertrautheit mit der Tonmechanik ihm die nöthigen Formen dazu fast von selbst zuführte. Da ihn nun sein *Dichtergeist* von gemeinen Ideen zurückhielt, wenn er frey komponiren durfte, so konnte es nicht fehlen, dass diejenigen, deren Geist dem seinigen nicht verwandt war, ihn nicht verstanden, und nur nach wiederholter Uebung kaum ahndeten, was für ein Gedankenreichthum darin verborgen wäre. Bach war ein andrer Kopstock, der Töne *statt* Worte gebrauchte . . . Doch dies wiegt sein hohes Verdienst nicht auf; es erhöht es vielmehr, nämlich, dass er zeigte: die reine Musik sey nicht blosse Hülle für die angewandte, oder von dieser abstrhirt, sondern könne für sich allein grosse Zwecke erreichen. Sie habe nicht nöthig, sich als blosses Sinnen- oder Verstandesspiel prosaisch oder höchstens rhetorisch herumzudrehen, sondern vermöchte sich zur *Poesie* zu erheben, die um desto reiner sey, je weniger sie durch Worte (die immer Nebenbegriffe enthalten) in die Region des gemeinen Sinnes hinabgezogen würde." Translation altered slightly from Triest, "Remarks on the Development of the Art of Music," 346.

100. Forkel, *Allgemeine Geschichte der Musik*, 2:9: "uns . . . in wohlthätige Gemüthszustände versetzen können . . . ist das eigentliche Geschäft der Musik."

101. Forkel, *Allgemeine Geschichte der Musik*, 2:9: "Wir müssen also . . . dem Vermögen, welches uns die Natur gegeben hat, musikalische Eindrücke zu empfangen, durch Aufmerksamkeit und Uebung zu Hülfe kommen, wenn wir den vollen Genuß wünschen, den sie uns verschaffen kann. Die Natur hat nur den Samen dazu in uns gelegt; die Entwickelung desselben ist unser eigen Werk, das Werk unseres Fleisses und unserer Uebungen."

102. Forkel, *Allgemeine Geschichte der Musik*, 2:8–9: "Endlich ist Mangel an gehöriger Uebung und Ausbildung der Gehörorgane am allerhäufigsten

die Ursache unserer geringeren Fähigkeit zu musikalischen Eindrücken. Von einem großen Theil der Menschen muß man in musikalischer Rücksicht sagen: Sie haben Ohren und hören nicht; nicht, weil sie nicht hören können, sondern weil es ihnen an der notwendigen Aufmerksamkeit mangelt, die beym Hören wie beym Sehen erforderlich ist, wenn ein Gegenstand nach allen seinen Merkmalen von anderen Gegenständen ähnlicher Art unterschieden werden soll."

103. Georg von Weiler, "Ueber den Begriff der Schönheit, als Grundlage einer Aesthetik der Tonkunst," *AmZ* 13 (13 February 1811), 121: "Es ist begreiflich, wie das freye Spiel mit einer Melodie in verschiedenen Tonarten und Zusammenstellungen, wie der mannigfaltige Rhythmus, überraschende Uebergänge der Modulation, passende Figuren, die Haltung der Instrumente gegen einander, die weise Vertheilung des Effectes u. dergl. den Geist beschäftigen und in Regsamkeit erhalten können, ohne dass es nöthig wäre, ihm eine Leidenschaft, eine bestimmte Empfindung, vorzuhalten. Wenn es aber sogar jemandem in den Sinn kömmt, einem Mozartschen Quatuor, wie unlängst ein Franzose es unternahm, einen Sprachtext unterzulegen, um (vermuthlich zu einiger Rechtfertigung des Tonsetzers) es anschaulich zu machen, dass sich bey einem solchen Tonstücke *auch etwas denken* lasse: so verräth es völligen Missverstand über den ästhetischen Werth eines Tonstücks." The reference to the text underlay of a Mozart string quartet is to Jérome-Joseph de Momigny's *Cours complet d'harmonie et de composition* (1805): see Edward Klorman, *Mozart's Music of Friends: Social Interplay in the Chamber Works* (Cambridge: Cambridge University Press, 2016), 52–70.

104. Karol Berger, *Bach's Cycle, Mozart's Arrow: An Essay on the Origins of Musical Modernity* (Berkeley: University of California Press, 2007), 9, 14.

105. *KdU*, 5:223 (§13). See above, p. 78.

106. [Georg August] Gr[iesinger], "Apologie der Tafelmusik," *AmZ* 2 (22 January 1800), 292, 293–94: "Als ein Werk der *schönen* Kunst will die Musik nur durch ihre Form, d. h. die Komposition und Reinheit der Töne gefallen. Als Werk der *angenehmen* Kunst will sie vergnügen, Reize und Rührungen erwecken. Dort wirkt sie auf den Reflexions-, hier auf den Sinnengeschmack . . . Man geräth deswegen auch in Unwillen, wenn in einem Konzert oder in der Oper, wo die Musik hauptsächlich als schöne Kunst prangen muss, und wo jedes Ohr lauschen sollte, um die Folge, Wahl und Zusammenstellung der Töne, welche der Genius des Kompositeurs hingezaubert hat, zu ergründen, irgend ein Midas durch Getös und Plaudern die feyerliche Stille unterbricht . . .

176　　　　　NOTES TO PAGES 100–101

"Weit geringer sind im Gegentheil die Ansprüche, welche die Musik als *angenehme* Kunst zu machen befugt ist. Als solche ist sie kein für sich selbst bestehendes Werk der dichtenden Kraft, sondern nur ein Mittel zu irgend einem beliebigen Zwecke. Sie will Gefühle und Empfindungen hervorbringen und nähren; sie ist auch keine freye, sondern eine anhängende Schönheit, d. h. sie setzt einen Begriff von dem, was sie seyn soll, und eine demselben gemässe Vollkommenheit voraus . . . . In dieser Rücksicht hat die Tafelmusik unverkennbaren Werth . . . Oder soll die Musik unter keiner Bedingung als blos *angenehme* Kunst auftreten dürfen? Einem solchen Rigorismus unterwirft sich weder die Plastik, noch die Mahlerey, noch selbst die Dichtkunst." The attribution to Griesinger is from the *Répertoire international de la presse musicale: Allgemeine musikalische Zeitung, 1798–1848*, 14 vols., ed. Ole Hass (Baltimore: RIPM, 2009), 1:45.

107. Martha Woodmansee, *The Author, Art, and the Market: Rereading the History of Aesthetics* (New York: Columbia University Press, 1993), chapter 4 ("Aesthetics and the Policing of Reading"). See also Jochen Schulte-Sasse, *Die Kritik an der Trivialliteratur seit der Aufklärung: Studien zur Geschichte des modernen Kitschbegriffs* (Munich: Wilhelm Fink, 1971); Christa Bürger et al., eds. *Zur Dichotomisierung von hoher und niederer Literatur* (Frankfurt am Main: Suhrkamp, 1982).

108. See Katherine Harloe, *Winckelmann and the Invention of Antiquity: History and Aesthetics in the Age of Altertumswissenschaft* (Oxford: Oxford University Press, 2013). See also Albert Dresdner, *Die Entstehung der Kunstkritik im Zusammenhang der Geschichte des europäischen Kunstlebens* (Munich: F. Bruckmann, 1915); Peter de Bolla, *The Education of the Eye: Painting, Landscape, and Architecture in Eighteenth-century Britain* (Stanford, CA: Stanford University Press, 2003).

109. Jürgen Habermas, *The Structural Transformation of the Public Sphere: An Inquiry into a Category of Bourgeois Society*, trans. Thomas Burger (Cambridge, MA: MIT Press, 1989).

CHAPTER 4

1. François-Joseph Fétis, *La musique mise à la portée de tout le monde: Exposé succinct de tout ce qui est nécessaire pour juger de cet art, et pour en parler sans l'avoir étudié* (Paris: Alexandre Mesnier, 1830), 75–76: "Tout le monde porte des jugemens sur la musique; les uns par un instinct aveugle et avec précipitation, les autres par un goût perfectionné et avec réflexion. Qui oserait dire que la première espèce de jugemens vaut mieux que l'autre?"

NOTES TO PAGES 101–103

Translation altered from the anonymous translation published as *Music Explained to the World, or: How to Understand Music and Enjoy its Performance* (Boston: Benjamin Perkins, 1842), 68.

2. Johann Friedrich Rochlitz, "Nachrichten: Leipzig," *AmZ* 6 (9 May 1804), 542: "Sie ist ein merkwürdiges, kolossales Werk, von einer Tiefe, Kraft, und Kunstgelehrsamkeit, wie sehr wenige—; von einer Schwierigkeit in Absicht auf Ausführung, sowohl durch den Komponisten, als durch ein grosses Orchester, (das sie freylich verlangt,) wie ganz gewiss keine von allen jemals bekannt gemachten Sinfonieen. Sie will, selbst von dem geschicktesten Orchester wieder und immer wieder gespielt seyn, bis sich die bewundernswürdige Summe origineller und zuweilen höchstseltsam gruppireter Ideen enge genug verbindet, abrundet, und nun als grosse Einheit hervorgehet, wie sie dem Geiste des Komponisten vorgeschwebt hat; sie will aber auch wieder und immer wieder gehört seyn, ehe der Zuhörer, selbst der gebildete, im Stande ist, das Einzelne im Ganzen und das Ganze im Einzelnen überall zu verfolgen und mit nöthiger Ruhe in der Begeisterung zu geniessen . . . " The attribution to Rochlitz is from Jin-Ah Kim, "Johann Friedrich Rochlitz und seine Konzertkritiken in der *Allgemeinen musikalischen Zeitung* bis 1807/08," *Archiv für Musikwissenschaft* 70 (2013), 202.

3. Anonymous. "Nachrichten: Wien, d. 1sten Dec.," *AmZ* 10 (16 December 1807), 184: ". . . über welche Ref. nach diesem ersten Anhören noch kein Urtheil fallen will."

4. Anonymous, "Schuppanzigh's Quartetten: Viertes Abonnement, eröffnet am 8ten February 1824," *Wiener Allgemeine musikalische Zeitung mit besonderer Rücksicht auf den österreichischen Kaiserstaat* 8 (27 March 1824), 45: "Diese Composition muß man öfter hören, um dieselbe gründlich beurtheilen zu können."

5. Anonymous, "Wien: Musikalisches Tagebuch vom Monat März," *AmZ* 28 (1826), 310–11: "Aber den Sinn des fugirten Finale wagt Ref. nicht zu deuten: für ihn war es unverständlich, wie Chinesisch. Wenn die Instrumente in den Regionen des Süd- und Nordpols mit ungeheuern Schwierigkeiten zu kämpfen haben, wenn jedes derselben anders figurirt und sie sich per transitum irregulärem unter einer Unzahl von Dissonanzen durchkreuzen, wenn die Spieler, gegen sich selbst misstrauisch, wohl auch nicht ganz rein greifen, freylich, dann ist die babylonische Verwirrung fertig."

6. Anonymous, "Wien: Musikalisches Tagebuch vom Monat März," *AmZ* 28 (1826), 311: "Doch wollen wir damit nicht voreilig absprechen: vielleicht kommt noch die Zeit, wo das, was uns beym ersten Blicke trüb und verworren erschien, klar und wohlgefälligen Formen erkannt wird."

NOTES TO PAGES 104–106

7. Triest, "Bemerkungen über die Ausbildung der Tonkunst in Deutschland," 300–01: "Da ihn nun sein *Dichtergeist* von gemeinen Ideen zurückhielt, wenn er frey komponiren durfte, so konnte es nicht fehlen, dass diejenigen, deren Geist dem seinigen nicht verwandt war, ihn nicht verstanden, und nur nach wiederholter Uebung kaum ahndeten, was für ein Gedankenreichthum darin verborgen wäre. Bach war ein andrer *Klopstock*, der Töne *statt* Worte gebrauchte. Ist es die Schuld des Odendichters, wenn seine lyrische Schwunge dem rohen Haufen Nonsens zu seyn scheinen?" Translation altered slightly from Triest, "Remarks on the Development of the Art of Music in Germany," 346.

8. See Hans-Henrik Krummacher, *Lyra: Studien zur Theorie und Geschichte der Lyrik vom 16. bis zum 19. Jahrhundert* (Berlin: De Gruyter, 2013), 81, 86, 92, 95, 97, 110, 113, 130.

9. Walter J. Ong, "The Province of Rhetoric and Poetic," *Modern Schoolman: A Quarterly Journal of Philsophy* 19 (1942), 27, 24.

10. William Wordsworth, Preface to *Lyrical Ballads, with Pastoral and other Poems*, 3rd ed., 2 vols. (London: T. N. Longman and O. Rees, 1802), 1: xxxiii–xxxiv.

11. Robert Fink, "Going Flat: Post-Hierarchical Music Theory and the Musical Surface," in *Rethinking Music*, ed. Nicholas Cook and Mark Everist (New York: Oxford University Press, 1999), 104. Holly Watkins documents the growing discourse around depth in music over the course of the nineteenth century in her *Metaphors of Depth in German Musical Thought: From E. T. A. Hoffmann to Arnold Schoenberg* (Cambridge: Cambridge University Press, 2011).

12. Johann Friedrich Reichardt, Review of J. N. Forkel, *Ueber die Theorie der Musik*, in *Allgemeine deutsche Bibliothek* 25–26 (1779–80), Abteilung 5, 3019–3024. The review, signed "Sk.", is ascribed to Reichardt in Gundula Schütz, *Vor dem Richterstuhl der Kritik: Die Musik in Friedrich Nicolais 'Allgemeiner deutscher Bibliothek' 1765–1806* (Tübingen: Niemeyer, 2007), 307.

13. Friedrich Rochlitz, "Die Verschiedenheit der Urtheile über Werke der Tonkunst," *AmZ* 1 (8 May 1799), 497–506. For many similar comments, see the writings surveyed in Daniel Fuhrimann, *"Herzohren für die Tonkunst": Opern- und Konzertpublikum in der deutschen Literatur des langen 19. Jahrhunderts* (Freiburg: Rombach, 2005).

14. Heinrich Christoph Koch, "Ueber den Modegeschmack in der Tonkunst," *Journal der Tonkunst* 1 (1795), 90: "So wenig man blos vermittelst eines gesunden Auges wahres Vergnügen an der bildenden Künsten empfinden, und die Schönheiten derselben beurtheilen kann, eben so wenig

NOTES TO PAGES 106–109

kann dieses in der Tonkunst blos vermittelst eines gesunden Ohres geschehen. Um Kunstwerke schön zu finden, und das Vergnügen zu genießen, welches sie gewähren, muß auch der bloße Liebhaber der Kunst sich einen gewissen Grad von Kunstgefühl eigen zu machen suchen."

15. Johann Friedrich Rochlitz, "Die Verschiedenheit der Urtheile über Werke der Tonkunst," 501–02: "... ohne Reize ... Virtuosen die nichts sind, als Virtuosen"; 503: "... welche blos mit dem Ohre hören—gute harmlose Leutchen"; 505: "diejenigen, welch mit *ganzer Seele* hören." A long tradition of listener taxonomies would follow: the most recent and in many respects most comprehensive is Christian Weining, "Listening Modes in Concerts: A Review and Conceptual Model," *Music Perception* 40/2 (2022), 112–34. On taxonomies of listeners in general, see Fuhrimann, *"Herzohren für die Tonkunst,"* 45–66.

16. Anonymous, Review of Emmanuel Aloys Förster, *Anleitung zum Generalbass* (Vienna: Johann Träg und Sohn, 1805), *AmZ* 9 (15 October 1806), 36: "Ganz recht hat Hr. F., wenn er behauptet, dass auch mittelmässige Klavierspieler, ja selbst das andere Geschlecht, Kenntniss der Harmonie besitzen sollten ... weil sie viel Vergnügen verschafft, indem man das Ganze der Kompositionen nun erst einsehen lernt—ja man könnte hinzusetzen: weil ohne diese Wissenschaft überhaupt an Produkten dieser Kunst dann nur ein sinnliches, ein blosser angenehmer Reiz, ein blosses Spiel der sogenannten niedern Seelenkräfte bleiben muss, aber nie zu dem Spiel werden kann, das die Kunst eigentlich beabsichtiget."

17. Anonymous, "Recension: *Grand Concerto pour le Pianoforte ... par Louis van Beethoven.* Oeuvre 37," *AmZ* 7 (10 April 1805), 445–57; Anonymous, "Recension: *Sinfonia eroica ... da Luigi van Beethoven. Op. 55,"* *AmZ* 9 (18 February 1807), 319–34.

18. E. T. A. Hoffmann, "Recension: *Sinfonie ... par Louis van Beethoven ... Oeuvre 67,"* 633: "Beethovens Musik bewegt die Hebel des Schauers, der Furcht, des Entsetzens, des Schmerzes, und erweckt jene unendliche Sehnsucht, die das Wesen der Romantik ist."

19. Adolph Bernhard Marx, "Ueber die Anfoderungen unserer Zeit an musikalische Kritik; in besonderem Bezuge auf diese Zeitung," *BAmZ* 1 (1824), 18: "... Erkenntnis der Natur jedes Kunstmittels, jedes Kunstwerkes, jedes Künstlers, endlich der ganzen Kunst." Ibid., 9–10.

20. On what William Weber calls the "explosion" of public music culture, see his *Music and the Middle Class: The Social Structure of Concert Life in London, Paris and Vienna between 1830 and 1848,* 2nd ed. (Aldershot: Ashgate, 2004), 19–34. See also Hanns-Werner Heister, *Das Konzert: Theorie einer Kulturform.* 2 vols. (Wilhelmshaven: Heinrichshofen,

180 NOTES TO PAGES 109–110

1983); Schleuning, *Der Bürger erhebt sich*; Axel Beer, *Musik zwischen Komponist, Verlag und Publikum: Die Rahmenbedingungen des Musikschaffens in Deutschland im ersten Drittel des 19. Jahrhunderts* (Tutzing: Schneider, 2000).

21. See Ulrich Tadday, *Die Anfänge des Musikfeuilleutons: Der kommunikative Gebrauchswert musikalischer Bildung in Deutschland um 1800* (Stuttgart: J. B. Metzler, 1993); and Axel Beer, *"Empfehlenswerthe Musikalien": Besprechungen musikalischer Neuerscheinungen ausserhalb der Fachpresse (Deutschland, 1. Hälfte des 19. Jahrhunderts): Eine Bibliographie*, 2 vols. (Göttingen: Hainholz, 2000).

22. *"Eben komme ich von Haydn...": Georg August Griesingers Korrespondenz mit Joseph Haydns Verleger Breitkopf & Härtel 1799–1809*, ed. Otto Biba (Zürich: Atlantis, 1987), 169. See also Christina Bashford, "Learning to Listen: Audiences for Chamber Music in Early Victorian London," *Journal of Victorian Culture* 4, no. 1 (1999), 39.

23. On the immense success of this book and its many editions and translations, see Peter Bloom, "*La Musique mise à la portée de tout le monde* by François-Joseph Fétis," *19CM* 10, no. 1 (1986), 84–88; and Renate Groth, "*La musique mise à la portée de tout le monde*: François-Joseph Fétis und der Musikhörer," in *Zwischen Wissenschaft und Kunst: Festgabe für Richard Jakoby*, ed. Peter Becker, Arnfried Edler, Beate Schneider (Mainz: Schott, 1995), 227–33.

24. Fétis, *La musique mise à la portée de tout le monde*, 1: "La musique peut se définir l'*art d'émouvoir par la combinaison des sons*."

25. Fétis, *La musique mise à la portée de tout le monde*, 345: "S'il n'y avait dans la musique qu'un principe de sensation vague, fondé seulement sur un rapport de convenance entre les sons, ayant pour unique résultat d'affecter plus ou moins agréablement l'oreille, cet art serait peu digne de l'attention publique; car n'étant destiné qu'à satisfaire un sens isolé, il ne mériterait pas plus de considération que l'art culinaire. Il y aurait en effet peu de différence entre le mérite d'un musicien et celui d'un cuisinier; mais il n'en est point ainsi. Ce n'est pas seulement l'oreille qui est affectée par la musique; si celle-ci réunit certaines qualités, elle émeut l'âme, d'une manière indéterminée à la vérité, mais plus puissamment que la peinture, la sculpture ou tout autre art." Translation from Fétis, *Music Explained to the World*, 279.

26. Fétis, *La musique mise à la portée de tout le monde*, 340, 357: "Sentir est la vocation de l'espèce humaine entière; juger appartient aux habiles." "A la vérité, ces effets n'ont lieu que pour ceux dont l'éducation est faite." Translation altered from Fétis, *Music Explained to the World*, 276, 288.

NOTES TO PAGES 110–111

27. Fétis, *La musique mise à la portée de tout le monde*, vi: "Toutefois il y a bien loin de ce sentiment vague, qui n'a d'autre origine que des sensations irréfléchies, à la sûreté de jugement qui résulte de connaissances positives. Chaque art a ses principes qu'il faut étudier, pour augmenter ses jouissances en formant son goût." Translation from Fétis, *Music Explained to the World*, xi.

28. Fétis, *La musique mise à la portée de tout le monde*, 369: "Indiquer les moyens d'augmenter les jouissances et de diriger le jugement sans être obligé de se soumettre à un long noviciat qu'on a rarement le temps et la volonté de faire, tel est mon but." Translation from Fétis, *Music Explained to the World*, 297.

29. Fétis, *La musique mise à la portée de tout le monde*, 343: "Parler de ce qu'on ignore est une manie dont tout le monde est atteint, parce que personne ne veut avoir l'air d'ignorer quelque chose. Cela se voit en politique, en littérature, en sciences, et surtout en beaux-arts." Translation from Fétis, *Music Explained to the World*, 278.

30. See the epigraph to the present chapter.

31. Fétis, *La musique mise à la portée de tout le monde*, 396: "Ces analyses, dis-je, se font avec la rapidité de l'éclair, dès qu'on en a contracté l'habitude; elles deviennent inhérentes à notre manière de sentir, au point de se transformer elles-mêmes en sensations." Translation altered from Fétis, *Music Explained to the World*, 317.

32. Fétis, *La musique mise à la portée de tout le monde*, 396–97: "Il ne se borne point, lui, à saisir quelques détails de formes, à distinguer des mélodies plus ou moins bien rhythmées, une expression plus ou moins dramatique, etc.: le musicien entend tous les détails de l'harmonie, remarque un son qui. dans un accord, ne se résout pas convenablement . ou un heureux emploi d'une dissonance inattendue, d'une modulation inusitée, et de toutes les finesses de la simultanéité ou de la succession des sons; il distingue les diverses sonorités d'instrumens, applaudit ou censure des innovations de formules ou des abus de moyens: enfin, les immenses détails de tout ce qui compose les grandes masses musicales sont présens à son esprit comme s'il les examinait avec réflexion sur le papier. Croit-on qu'il fasse péniblement toutes ces remarques, que cela l'empêche de goûter l'effet général de la composition, et qu'il en éprouve moins de plaisir que celui qui s'abandonne en aveugle à ses sensations? Nullement. Il ne pense seulement pas à toutes ces choses; elles sont présentes à sa pensée, mais comme par enchantement, sans qu'il le sache, sans même qu'il s'en occupe. Merveilleux effet d'une organisation perfectionnée par l'étude et par l'observation! Tout ce qui semblerait devoir affaiblir la sensation, pour augmenter la part de l'intelligence,

182 NOTES TO PAGES 111–112

tourne au profit de cette même sensation." Translation altered from Fétis, *Music Explained to the World*, 317–18.

33. Fétis, *La musique mise à la portée de tout le monde*, 373: "Que si l'on parvient à se défendre de toutes les faiblesses qui faussent le jugement et gâtent les sensations, alors commencera réellement l'action de l'intelligence pour l'analyse des sensations, et pour juger de leur nature." Translation altered from Fétis, *Music Explained to the World*, 300.

34. Fétis, *La musique mise à la portée de tout le monde*, 341: "Il y a tant d'exemples d'erreurs occasionnées par elles que l'on devrait toujours s'abstenir de juger avant d'avoir examiné sa conscience, et d'avoir écarté de son coeur et de son esprit tout ce qui peut paralyser l'action de l'intelligence." Translation from Fétis, *Music Explained to the World*, 276.

35. Fétis, *La musique mise à la portée de tout le monde*, 74–75: "Qu'un homme du monde, au lieu de s'abandonner sans réserve au plaisir vague que lui cause un air, un duo, se décide à en examiner l'ordonnance, à considérer la disposition et le retour des phrases, les rhythmes principaux, la cadence, etc.: d'abord ce travail lui sera pénible et troublera ses jouissances; mais insensiblement l'habitude suppléera l'attention, et bientôt elle sera telle que l'attention même sera moins nécessaire. Alors, ce qui n'aura paru d'abord qu'un calcul aride deviendra l'origine d'un jugement facile et la source des plus vives jouissances." Translation altered from Fétis, *Music Explained to the World*, 67.

36. Fétis, *La musique mise à la portée de tout le monde*, 399: "Apprendre à faire des analyses du principe des sensations musicales est sans doute une étude qui détourne l'attention de ce qui pourrait flatter les sens; cette étude trouble le plaisir qu'on éprouverait à entendre de la musique; mais qu'importe, si l'on ne fait que suspendre ce plaisir pour le rendre plus vif? Chaque jour l'étude deviendra moins pénible, dès qu'on en aura contracté l'habitude, et le moment viendra où l'analyse se fera sans qu'on y prenne garde, et sans que les sensations en soient troublées." Translation altered from Fétis, *Music Explained to the World*, 317.

37. Fétis, *La musique mise à la portée de tout le monde*, 394: "Je dirai de la musique instrumentale ce que j'ai déjà eu occasion de répéter plusieurs fois: il faut avoir la patience de l'écouter sans prévention, bien même qu'on ne s'y plaise pas; avec de la persévérance on finira par la goûter, et dès lors on pourra commencer à l'analyser; car ce genre de musique a aussi ses mélodies, son rhythme, ses quantités symétriques, ses variétés de forme, ses effets d'harmonie et ses modes d'instrumentation." Translation from Fétis, *Music Explained to the World*, 316.

NOTES TO PAGES 113–117   183

38. Fétis, *La musique mise à la portée de tout le monde*, 395–96: "Je suis certain que beaucoup de lecteurs, en parcourant le chapitre qui précède, se seront dit: "Que prétend cet homme avec ses analyses? Veut-il donc gâter nos jouissances par un travail continuel, incompatible avec ce les plaisirs que procurent les arts? Ceux-ci ce doivent être sentis et non analysés. Loin de ce nous ces observations et ces comparaisons, ce bonnes tout au plus pour ceux dont l'âme ce sèche ne peut trouver autre chose dans la musique, ou pour des professeurs de contrece point. Nous voulons jouir et non juger; donc nous n'avons pas besoin de raisonnemens. C'est fort bien. A Dieu ne plaise que je veuille troubler vos plaisirs . . .

    "Se persuaderait-on, par hasard, que je suis assez privé de sens pour vouloir qu'on substitue l'analyse des produits des arts aux plaisirs qu'ils donnent? Non, non, telle n'a point été ma pensée; mais certain qu'on ne voit que ce qu'on a appris à regarder, qu'on n'entend que ce qu'on sait écouter, que nos sens enfin, et par suite nos sensations, ne se développent que par l'exercice, j'ai voulu démontrer comment on dirige celui de l'ouïe pour le rendre plus habile à saisir toutes les impressions de la musique . . ." Translation altered from Fétis, *Music Explained to the World*, 316, 317.

39. Alexandra Hui, *The Psychophysical Ear: Musical Experiments, Experimental Sounds, 1840–1910* (Cambridge, MA: MIT Press, 2012), 23.

40. Johann Christian Lobe, *Musikalische Briefe: Wahrheit über Tonkunst und Tonkünstler*, 2 vols. (Leipzig: Baumgärtner, 1852), 1:12: ". . . man soll bei der Musik nicht *denken*, sondern fühlen, *geniessen*."

41. A comprehensive history of the genre of the music appreciation text remains to be written. For the moment, see Julia J. Chybowski, "Developing American Taste: A Cultural History of the Early Twentieth-century Music Appreciation Movement" (PhD diss., University of Wisconsin-Madison, 2008); and Kate Guthrie, *The Art of Appreciation: Music and Middlebrow Culture in Modern Britain* (Berkeley and Los Angeles: University of California Press, 2021).

42. Hermann Kretzschmar, *Führer durch den Konzertsaal: Abtheilung: Sinfonie und Suite, 1. Band* (Leipzig: Breitkopf & Härtel, 1898), v: ". . . mindestens die Fähigkeit, Türen und Fenster zu unterscheiden."

43. See Christian Thorau, "'What Ought to be Heard': Touristic Listening and the Guided Ear," in *OHML*, 207–27; and Christian Thorau, "From Program Leaflets to Listening Apps: A Brief History of Guided Listening," in *Classical Concert Studies: A Companion to Contemporary Research and Performance*, ed. Martin Tröndle (New York: Routledge, 2020), 61–80.

44. Krehbiel, *How to Listen*, ix.

184   NOTES TO PAGES 117–119

45. See Leon Botstein, "Listening through Reading: Musical Literacy and the Concert Audience." *19CM* 16 (1992): 129–45; Melanie Unseld, *Biographie und Musikgeschichte: Wandlungen biographischer Konzepte in Musikkultur und Musikhistoriographie* (Cologne: Böhlau, 2014); Bonds, *The Beethoven Syndrome*.

46. Charles H. Purday, "To the Editor of *The Musical World*," *The Musical World* (12 December 1836), 191.

47. Pierre Baillot, *L'art du violon: Nouvelle methode* (Mainz: Schott, 1834), 259: "Il ne suffit pas que l'artiste soit bien préparé pour le public, il faut aussi que le public le soit à ce qu'on va lui faire entendre." See also Christina Bashford, *The Pursuit of High Culture: John Ella and Chamber Music in Victorian Culture* (Woodbridge, Suffolk: Boydell, 2007); Anselma Lanzendörfer, "Designated Attention: The Transformation of Music Announcements in Leipzig's Concert Life, 1781–1850," in *OHML*, 163–85.

48. Christina Bashford, "Concert Listening the British Way? Program Notes and Victorian Culture," *OHML*, 188–89. See also Christina Bashford, "Not Just 'G': Towards a History of the Programme Note," in *George Grove, Music and Victorian Culture*, ed. Michael Musgrave (Basingstoke: Macmillan, 2003), 115–42. For a reproduction of one of Ella's synoptic summaries (of Mozart's String Quartet in D Major, K. 575), see Thorau, "From Program Leaflets to Listening Apps," 68.

49. On the social implications of taste in general, see Pierre Bourdieu, *Distinction: A Social Critique of the Judgement of Taste*, trans. Richard Nice (Cambridge, MA: Harvard University Press, 1984), and Terry Eagleton, *The Ideology of the Aesthetic* (Oxford: Blackwell, 1990). See also Anne-Marie Link, "The Social Practice of Taste in Late Eighteenth-century Germany: A Case Study," *Oxford Art Journal* 15/2 (1992), 3–14. Although Link is concerned primarily with the visual arts, the mechanisms by which this ideology spread to a wider public are equally applicable to music.

50. Bourdieu, *Distinction*, 488, 491. The passage in the *KdU* to which Bourdieu refers is 5:210 (§5).

51. Georg von Weiler, "Ueber den Begriff der Schönheit," 120.

52. E. T. A. Hoffmann, "Beethovens Instrumentalmusik" (1813), in his *Sämtliche Werke in sechs Bänden*, ed. Wulf Segebrecht and Hartmut Steinecke (Frankfurt/Main: Deutscher Klassiker Verlag, 1985–2004), 2/1:54–55: "Den musikalischen Pöbel drückt Beethovens mächtiger Genius; er will sich vergebens dagegen auflehnen . . . Wie ist es aber, wenn nur *Eurem* schwachen Blick der innere tiefe Zusammenhang jeder

NOTES TO PAGES 119–120

Beethovenschen Komposition entgeht? Wenn es nur an *Euch* liegt, daß Ihr des Meisters, dem Geweihten verständliche Sprache nicht versteht, wenn Euch die Pforte des innersten Heiligtums verschlossen blieb?"

53. E. T. A. Hoffmann, "Des Kapellmeisters, Johannes Kreislers, Dissertatiuncula über den hohen Werth der Musik," *AmZ* 14 (29 July 1812), 503–04: "Der Zweck der Kunst überhaupt ist doch kein anderer, als dem Menschen eine angenehme Unterhaltung zu verschaffen und ihn so von den ernstern oder vielmehr den einzigen ihm anständigen Geschäften, nämlich solchen, die ihm Brot und Ehre im Staat erwerben, auf eine angenehme Art zu zerstreuen, so daß er nachher mit gedoppelter Aufmerksamkeit und Anstrengung zu dem eigentlichen Zweck seines Daseins zurückkehren, d.h. ein tüchtiges Kammrad in der Waldmühle des Staats sein und (ich bleibe in der Metapher) haspeln und sich trillen lassen kann. Nun ist aber keine Kunst zur Erreichung dieses Zwecks tauglicher, als die Musik. Das Lesen eines Romans oder Gedichts, sollte auch die Wahl so glücklich ausfallen, daß es durchaus nichts phantastisch Abgeschmacktes, wie mehrere der allerneuesten, enthält, und also die Phantasie, die eigentlich der schlimmste und mit aller Macht zu ertödtende Theil unserer Erbsünde ist, nicht im mindesten anregt—dieses Lesen, meine ich, hat doch das Unangenehme, daß man gewissermaßen genötigt wird, an das zu denken, was man liest: dies ist aber offenbar dem Zweck der Zerstreuung entgegen."

54. Hans Georg Nägeli, *Vorlesungen über Musik mit Berücksichtigung der Dilettanten* (Stuttgart and Tübingen: J. G. Cotta, 1826), 12: "wer ... sich nicht in geistigen Anstrengungen erhoben hält, der lauft Gefahr, die Kraft des Aufschwunges zu verlieren, und in eine tiefere Sphäre der Sinnlichkeit hinabzusinken ... Das höchste Kunstgefühl ist nur dann ein beseligendes Wonnegefühl, wenn ihm die Sehnsucht nach Idealen beywohnt. Diese Sehnsucht wird aber nur befriediget durch das Vermögen, die Töne in ihrer Zusammenverbindung zum Kunstwerk aufzufassen."

55. Nägeli, *Vorlesungen über Musik*, 15: "Sein geistiges Streben geht daher bey jedem Kunstwerk darauf aus, jedes Einzelne mit Allem im Zusammenhang aufzufassen; sein Streben geht nur auf Zusammenhang, Planmäßigkeit, Mannigfaltigkeit in Einheit, Ideenreichthum. Seine Geistesthätigkeit bestehet dabey in steten Vergleichen, Unterscheiden, Beziehen, Bey-, Unter- und Ueberordnen."

56. Friedrich Louis Bührlen, "Soll man bei der Instrumentalmusik Etwas denken?" *AmZ* 29 (1 August 1827), 549: "Ein Geistesverwandter des Künstlers, wenn Sie Kunstreiches fassen wollen ... "

NOTES TO PAGES 121–122

57. Friedrich Rochlitz, "Der Geschmack: Schreiben an einen Tonkünstler." See Carolin Krahn, *Topographie der Imaginationen: Johann Friedrich Rochlitz' musikalisches Italien um 1800* (Vienna: Hollitzer, 2021), 84–86.

58. Adolph Bernhard Marx, *Die alte Musiklehre im Streit mit unserer Zeit* (Leipzig: Breitkopf & Härtel, 1841), vi: "Die Lebensfrage für unsre Kunst . . . ist einfach die: *ob ihre geistige, oder sinnliche Seite vorwalten. . .* " For two impressive accounts of the growing polarization of "serious" and "popular" music over the course of the nineteenth century, see Sponheuer, *Musik als Kunst und Nicht-Kunst*, and Knapp, *Making Light*.

59. August Wilhelm Ambros, *Culturhistorische Bilder aus dem Musikleben der Gegenwart* (Leipzig: Heinrich Matthes, 1860), 33–34: "Wenn wir an Beethoven das Bild einer großen Seele haben, die sich in Musik und durch Musik ausspricht, und dadurch die Töne, die sie nach dem Maß und Gesetze der Schönheit ordnet, mit höchstem geistigen Gehalte füllet,—so ist Beethovens Zeitgenosse Rossini sein gerader Gegensatz: der Tonkünstler, der zuerst das Prinzip des blos sinnlichen Genusses in der Musik zur unbedingten Geltung erhoben hat . . . Rossini ist entschieden der Tonkünstler, mit dessen Laufbahn, so glänzend sie an sich ist, die Zeit des Verfalles der Tonkunst anfängt. Wenn das Dessert an die Reihe kommt, ist die Tafel zu Ende."

60. Franz Brendel, *Geschichte der Musik in Italien, Deutschland und Frankreich* (Leipzig: Bruno Hinze, 1852), 370–71: "ein Versinken in Sinnlichkeit." See also the essays in *The Invention of Beethoven and Rossini: Historiography, Analysis, Criticism*, ed. Nicholas Mathew and Benjamin Walton (Cambridge: Cambridge University Press, 2013).

61. Stendhal, *Vie de Rossini*, 2:453. Ibid., 1:13–14: "Ce qui fait de la musique le plus entraînant des plaisirs de l'âme, et lui donne une supériorité marquée sur la plus belle poésie . . . c'est qu'il s'y mêle un plaisir physique estrêmement vif . . . Elle donne un plaisir extrême, mais de peu de durée, et de peu de fixité." Translation altered slightly from Stendhal, *Life of Rossini*, rev. ed., trans. Richard N. Coe (New York: Orion, 1970), 15.

62. Adolphe Adam, *Souvenirs d'un musicien* (Paris: Michel Levy frères, 1857), 164: ". . . l'unique but de la musique est de charmer l'oreille et d'émouvoir le coeur . . . "

63. See Bonds, *Absolute Music*, 157–72. On the complicated relationship of Hanslick's treatise to Kantian thought, see Alexander Wilfing, "Hanslick, Kant, and the Origins of *Vom Musikalisch-Schönen*," *Musicologica Austriaca: Journal for Austrian Music Studies* (June 18, 2018).

64. See Karl Homann, "Zum Begriff Einbildungskraft nach Kant," *Archiv für Begriffsgeschichte* 14 (1970), 290. For examples of the use of "Phantasie,"

NOTES TO PAGES 122–124 187

see Hanslick, *Vom Musikalisch-Schönen: Ein Beitrag zur Revision der Ästhetik der Tonkunst* (Leipzig: Rudolph Weigel, 1854), 4, 52, 78.

65. Hanslick, *Vom Musikalisch-Schönen*, 78–79: "Ohne geistige Thätigkeit gibt es überhaupt keinen ästhetischen Genuß . . . Zum Berauschtwerden brauchts nur der Schwäche, aber es gibt *eine Kunst des Hörens*." Translations from *Eduard Hanslick's On the Musically Beautiful: A New Translation*, ed. and trans. Lee Rothfarb and Christoph Landerer (New York: Oxford University Press, 2018), 89–90, altered slightly to reflect the wording of the first edition.

66. Hanslick, *Vom Musikalisch-Schönen*, 81:"Eine ästhetische Anschauung hat Musik niemals als Ursache, sondern stets als Wirkung aufzufassen, nicht als Producirendes, sondern als Product." Translation from *Eduard Hanslick's On the Musically Beautiful*, 92, altered slightly to reflect wording of the first edition.

67. Hanslick, *Vom Musikalisch-Schönen*, 71–72: "Halbwach in ihren Fauteuil geschmiegt, lassen jene Enthusiasten von den Schwingungen der Töne sich tragen und schaukeln, statt sie scharfen Blickes zu betrachten. Wie das stark und stärker anschwillt, nachläßt, aufjauchzt oder auszittert, das versetzt sie in einen unbestimmten Empfindungszustand, den sie für rein geistig zu halten so unschuldig sind. Sie bilden das 'dankbarste' Publikum und dasjenige, welches geeignet ist, die Würde der Musik am sichersten zu discreditiren. Das ästhetische Merkmal des geistigen Genusses geht ihrem Hören ab; eine feine Cigarre, ein pikanter Leckerbissen, ein laues Bad leistet ihnen unbewußt, was eine Symphonie. Vom gedankenlos gemäch-lichen Dasitzen der Einen bis zur tollen Verzückung der Andern ist das Princip dasselbe: die Lust am *Elementarischen* der Musik." Translation from *Eduard Hanslick's On the Musically Beautiful*, 82–83.

68. Hanslick, *Vom Musikalisch-Schönen*, 81: "J. Strauß hat reizende, ja geist-reiche Musik in seinen bessern Walzern niedergelegt,—sie hören auf es zu sein, sobald man lediglich dabei im Tact tanzen will." Translation from *Eduard Hanslick's On the Musically Beautiful*, 92.

69. Katharine Ellis, "Researching Audience Behaviors in Nineteenth-Century Paris: Who Cares if You Listen?" in *OHML*, 37, 41.

EPILOGUE

1. Wagner to Franz Liszt, letter of 2 October 1850, in *Sämtliche Briefe*, ed. Gertrud Strobel and Werner Wolf (Leipzig: Verlag für Musik, 1967–), 3:431: "[S]eitdem es kunstkenner giebt, ist die kunst zum teufel gegan-gen. Durch einpauken von kunstintelligenz können wir das publikum nur

188   NOTES TO PAGES 124–127

vollends stupid machen. Ich sagte: nichts weiter fordere ich vom publikum als *gesunde sinne und ein menschliches herz.*"

2. Wackenroder, "Das merkwürdige musikalische Leben des Tonkünstlers Joseph Berglinger," in his *Sämtliche Werke und Briefe,* 1:133, 139–40: "Seine . . . Seele war ganz ein Spiel der Töne . . . Wie war mir zu Muth, als ich hinter den Vorhang trat! . . . Daß ich, statt frei zu fliegen, erst lernen mußte, in dem unbehülflichen Gerüst und Käfig der Kunstgrammatik herumzuklettern! . . . Die prächtige Zukunft ist eine jämmerliche Gegenwart geworden."

3. Ibid., 1:140: "Und wenn mich einmal irgendeiner, der eine Art von halber Empfindung hat, loben will und kritisch rühmt und mir kritische Fragen vorlegt,—so möcht ich ihn immer bitten, daß er sich doch nicht soviel Mühe geben möchte, das Empfinden aus den Büchern zu lernen."

4. Ibid., 1:144: "Ach! daß eben seine *hohe Phantasie* es sein mußte, die ihn aufrieb?—Soll ich sagen, daß er vielleicht mehr dazu geschaffen war, Kunst zu *genießen* als *auszuüben?*—Sind diejenigen vielleicht glücklicher gebildet, in denen die Kunst still und heimlich wie ein verhüllter Genius arbeitet und sie in ihrem Handeln auf Erden nicht stört?"

5. See Abigail Zitin, "Thinking Like an Artist: Hogarth, Diderot, and the Aesthetics of Technique," *Eighteenth-Century Studies* 46 (2013), 555–70. On the implications of Diderot's perspective for music, see Elisabeth Le Guin, "'One Says That One Weeps, but One Does Not Weep': *Sensible,* Grotesque, and Mechanical Embodiments in Boccherini's Chamber Music," *JAMS* 55 (2002): 207–54.

6. Alison, *Essays on the Nature and Principles of Taste,* 8–9.

7. See Bonds, *Music as Thought,* 44–59.

8. Schopenhauer, *Die Welt als Wille und Vorstellung* (1818/1844), in his *Sämtliche Werke,* 7 vols., ed. Julius Frauenstädt and Arthur Hübscher (Wiesbaden, E. Brockhaus, 1948–61), 2:210 (§34): " . . . indem man, nach einer sinnvollen deutschen Redensart, sich gänzlich in diesen Gegenstand *verliert,* d. h. eben sein Individuum, seinen Willen, vergißt und nur noch als reines Subjekt, als klarer Spiegel des Objekts bestehend bleibt." Translation from Schopenhauer, *The World as Will and Representation,* 2 vols, ed. Christopher Janaway, trans. Judith Norman, Alistair Welchman (Cambridge: Cambridge University Press, 2010), 1:201.

9. Schopenhauer, *Die Welt als Wille und Vorstellung,* in his *Sämtliche Werke,* 2:312 (§52): "Das unaussprechlich Innige aller Musik, vermöge dessen sie als ein so ganz vertrautes und doch ewig fernes Paradies an uns vorüberzieht, so ganz verständlich und doch so unerklärlich ist . . . ." Translation from Schopenhauer, *The World as Will and Representation,* 1:292.

NOTES TO PAGES 127–128

10. Schopenhauer, *Die Welt als Wille und Vorstellung*, in his *Sämtliche Werke* 2:309 (§52): "Wenn also die Musik zu sehr sich den Worten anzuschließen und nach den Begebenheiten zu modeln sucht, so ist sie bemüht, eine Sprache zu reden, welche nicht die ihrige ist. Von diesem Fehler hat Keiner sich so rein gehalten, wie *Rossini*: daher spricht seine Musik so deutlich und rein ihre *eigene* Sprache, daß sie der Worte gar nicht bedarf und daher auch mit bloßen Instrumenten ausgeführt ihre volle Wirkung thut." Translation from Schopenhauer, *The World as Will and Representation*, 1:289.

11. Schopenhauer, *Die Welt als Wille und Vorstellung*, in his *Sämtliche Werke*, 2:307 (§52): "Der Komponist offenbart das innerste Wesen der Welt und spricht die tiefste Weisheit aus, in einer Sprache, die seine Vernunft nicht versteht; wie eine magnetische Somnambule Aufschlüsse giebt über Dinge, von denen sie wachend keinen Begriff hat." Translation from Schopenhauer, *The World as Will and Representation*, 1:288.

12. Lydia Goehr, "Schopenhauer and the Musicians: An Inquiry into the Sounds of Silence and the Limits of Philosophizing about Music," in *Schopenhauer, Philosophy and the Arts*, ed. Dale Jacquette (Cambridge: Cambridge University Press, 1996), 216–17.

13. Richard Wagner, *Beethoven* (Leipzig: E. W. Fritzsch, 1870), 15: "das sympathische Gehör . . . jener traumartige Zustand."

14. Wagner to Liszt, letter of 2 October 1850, in *Sämtliche Briefe*, ed. Gertrud Strobel and Werner Wolf (Leipzig: Verlag für Musik, 1967–), 3:431: "Ich will nur verkehrte anforderungen nicht gelten lassen, daß man an das publikum stellt; ich will nicht gelten lassen, das man dem publikum seine *kunstunverständigkeit* vorwirft, und dagegen alles heil der kunst davon erwartet, daß man diesem publikum von oben herein kunstintelligenz einpfropfe: seitdem es kunstkenner giebt, ist die kunst zum teufel gegangen. Durch einpauken von kunstintelligenz können wir das publikum nur vollends stupid machen. Ich sagte: nichts weiter fordere ich vom publikum als *gesunde sinne und ein menschliches herz*." Wagner had expressed a similar sentiment in a letter 9 September 1850 to the Freiherr von Zigesar (Wagner, *Sämtliche Briefe*, 3:397–98).

15. Franz Liszt, *Lohengrin et Tannhäuser de Richard Wagner* (Leipzig: F. A. Brockhaus, 1851); Anonymous ("Y"), "Signale aus Weimar," *Signale für die musikalische Welt*, 9 (1851), 236: " . . . ein Vademecum, mit dem jeder sich in dem Labyrinth der Wagner'schen Doppeldichtung zurechtfinden kann." On Liszt's pamphlet, see Christian Thorau, *Semantisierte Sinnlichkeit: Studien zu Rezeption und Zeichenstruktur der Leitmotivtechnik Richard Wagners* (Stuttgart: Steiner, 2003), 38–58, 258.

190   NOTES TO PAGES 128–129

16. Wagner, *Oper und Drama* (1851), in his *Gesammelte Schriften und Dichtungen*, 11 vols., ed. Wolfgang Golter (Berlin: Bong, 1913), 4:78. On *Gefühlverständnis*, see Udo Bermbach, *Der Wahn des Gesamtkunstwerks: Richard Wagners politisch-ästhetische Utopie* (Stuttgart: Metzler, 2004), 185–90.

17. Wagner, *Oper und Drama*, in his *Gesammelte Schriften und Dichtungen*, 4:78: "Im Drama müssen wir Wissende werden durch das Gefühl. Der Verstand sagt uns: *so ist es* erst, wenn uns das Gefühl gesagt hat: *so muß es sein*."

18. Richard Wagner, "Eine Mitteilung an meine Freunde" (1851), in his *Gesammelte Schriften und Dichtungen*, 4:232: "Der Künstler wendet sich an das Gefühl, und nicht an den Verstand: wird ihm mit dem Verstande geantwortet, so wird hiermit gesagt, daß er eben nicht *verstanden* worden ist, und unsere Kritik ist in Wahrheit nichts anderes als das Geständnis des Unverständnisses des Kunstwerkes, das nur mit dem Gefühle verstanden werden kann—allerdings mit dem gebildeten und dabei nicht verbildeten Gefühle." In the closing line, Wagner plays on the similarity of the words for "refined" (*gebildet*, with overtones of "educated") and "deformed" (*verbildet*), the latter of which carries the whiff of over-sophistication.

19. See Thorau, *Semantisierte Sinnlichkeit*, 258–61. On Wagner's attitude toward listening in general, see David Trippett, *Wagner's Melodies: Aesthetics and Materialism in German Musical Identity* (Cambridge: Cambridge University Press, 2013), 198–202.

20. Wagner, *Beethoven*, 19: "Die Musik . . . kann an und für sich einzig nach der Kategorie des Erhabenen beurteilt werden, da sie, sobald sie uns erfüllt, die höchste Exstase des Bewußtseins der Schrankenlosigkeit erregt . . . [D]iese übt die Musik *sofort* bei ihrem ersten Eintritte aus, indem sie den Intellekt sogleich von jedem Erfassen der Relationen der Dinge außer uns abzieht, und als reine, von jeder Gegenständlichkeit befreite Form uns gegen die Außenwelt gleichsam abschließt, dagegen nun uns einzig in unser Inneres, wie in das innere Wesen aller Dinge blicken läßt."

21. Friedrich Nietzsche, *Menschliches, Allzumenschliches* (1880), in his *Sämtliche Werke: Kritische Studienausgabe*, 15 vols., ed. Giorgio Colli and Mazzino Montinari (Berlin: Walter de Gruyter, 1980), 2:177: "Unsere Ohren sind, vermöge der außerordentlichen Übung des Intellekts durch die Kunstentwicklung der neuen Musik, immer intellektualer geworden. Deshalb ertragen wir jetzt viel größere Tonstärke, viel mehr 'Lärm,' weil wir viel besser eingeübt sind, auf die *Vernunft in ihm* hinzuhorchen, als unsere Vorfahren. Tatsächlich sind nun alle unsere Sinne eben dadurch, daß sie sogleich nach der Vernunft, also nach dem 'es bedeutet' und nicht

NOTES TO PAGES 129–131

mehr nach dem 'es ist' fragen, etwas abgestumpft worden . . . Was ist von alledem die Konsequenz? Je gedankenfähiger Auge und Ohr werden, um so mehr kommen sie an die Grenze, wo sie unsinnlich werden: die Freude wird ins Gehirn verlegt, die Sinnesorgane selbst werden stumpf und schwach, das Symbolische tritt immer mehr an Stelle des Seienden—und so gelangen wir auf diesem Wege so sicher zur Barbarei, wie auf irgendeinem anderen."

22. Nietzsche, *Zur Genealogie der Moral* (1887), in his *Sämtliche Werke*, 5:346: "Mit dieser außerordentlichen Werthsteigerung der Musik, wie sie aus der Schopenhauer'schen Philosophie zu erwachsen schien, stieg mit einem Male auch *der Musiker* selbst unerhört im Preise: er wurde nunmehr ein Orakel, ein Priester, ja mehr als ein Priester, eine Art Mundstück des 'An-sich' der Dinge, ein Telephon des Jenseits— er redete fürderhin nicht nur Musik, dieser Bauchredner Gottes,—er redete Metaphysik: was Wunder, daß er endlich eines Tages *asketische Ideale* redete? . . ." Ellipsis in original. Translation altered slightly from *Basic Writings of Nietzsche*, ed. and trans. Walter Kaufmann (New York: Modern Library, 2000), 539.

23. Nietzsche, *Der Fall Wagner* (1888), in his *Sämtliche Werke*, 6:14–15: "Sie baut, organisirt, wird fertig: damit macht sie den Gegensatz zum Polypen in der Musik, zur 'unendlich Melodie'." Translation from *Basic Writings of Nietzsche*, 613.

24. Nietzsche, *Der Fall Wagner*, in his *Sämtliche Werke*, 6:16: "Il faut méditerraniser la musique: . . . Die Rückkehr zur Natur, Gesundheit, Heiterkeit, Jugend, *Tugend*!" Translation from *Basic Writings of Nietzsche*, 615–16. On Nietzsche's turn to Bizet and "southern" music in general, see Sander L. Gilman, "Nietzsche, Bizet, and Wagner: Illness, Health, and Race in the Nineteenth Century," *Opera Quarterly* 23 (2007), 247–64.

25. See, for example, Ted Gioia, *How to Listen to Jazz* (New York: Basic Books, 2016), 46–47: "If you learn anything from this guide to listening, let it be a respect for the demands of the music . . . The work of art always requires us to adapt to it—and in this manner can be distinguished from escapism or shallow entertainment, which instead aims to adapt to the audience, to give the public *exactly* what it wants. We can tell that we are encountering a real work of art by the degree to which it *resists* our subjectivity."

26. Rose Rosengard Subotnik, "Toward a Deconstruction of Structural Listening: A Critique of Schoenberg, Adorno, and Stravinsky," in her *Deconstructive Variations: Music and Reason in Western Society* (Minneapolis: University of Minnesota Press, 1996), 148–76, a slightly altered version of an essay that had originally appeared in 1988.

27. See the essays in *Beyond Structural Listening? Postmodern Modes of Hearing*, ed. Andrew Dell'Antonio (Berkeley and Los Angeles: University of California Press, 2004), including Subotnik's response to them (p. 279–302).
28. Abbate, "Music—Drastic or Gnostic?" (and see above, p. 14); Karol Berger, "Musicology According to Don Giovanni, or: Should We Get Drastic?" *JM* 22 (2005), 490–501; Michael Gallope, *Deep Refrains: Muisc, Philosophy, and the Ineffable* (Chicago: University of Chicago Press, 2017); Martin Scherzinger, "Event or Ephemeron? Music's Sound, Performance, and Media: A Critical Reflection on the Thought of Carolyn Abbate," *Sound Stage Screen* 1 (2021), 145–92.
29. Andreas Dorschel, "Der Welt abhanden kommen: Über musikalischen Eskapismus," *Merkur* 66, no. 2 (2012), 135–42.
30. For an accessible summary of recent developments, see Nina Kraus, *Of Sound Mind: How the Brain Constructs a Meaningful Sonic World* (Cambridge, MA: MIT Press, 2021).

Works Cited

Abbate, Carolyn. *In Search of Opera*. Princeton, NJ: Princeton University Press, 2001.

Abbate, Carolyn. "Music—Drastic or Gnostic?" *Critical Inquiry* 30 (2004): 505–36.

Adam, Adolphe. *Souvenirs d'un musicien*. Paris: Michel Levy frères, 1857.

d'Alembert, Jean Leronde. *Oeuvres*. 5 vols. Paris: Belin, 1821–22.

Alison, Archibald. *Essays on the Nature and Principles of Taste*. Edinburgh: Bell and Bradfute, 1790.

Ambros, August Wilhelm. *Culturhistorische Bilder aus dem Musikleben der Gegenwart*. Leipzig: Heinrich Matthes, 1860.

Ammon, Frieder von. "Opera on Opera (on Opera): Self-Referential Negotiations of a Difficult Genre." In *Self-Reference in Literature and Music*, 65–85. Ed. Walter Bernhart and Werner Wolf. Amsterdam and New York: Rodopi, 2010.

Anonymous. "Ankündigung." *Wiener Zeitung*, 23 February 1791: 463.

Anonymous. "Arts. Musique." *L'Avantcoureur*, 16 January 1764: 38–39.

Anonymous. "Aufschlüsse über Musik aus den Werken der Philosophen." *AmZ* 5 (17 November 1802): 129–36.

Anonymous. "Gedanken über die Oper." *AmZ* 1 (3 and 17 October 1798): 1–9, 33–38.

Anonymous. "Hayden (in Salzburg)." *Musikalischer Almanach auf das Jahr 1782* ("Alethinopel": s.n., 1782): 19–21.

Anonymous. "Nachrichten: Auszüge aus Briefen, Todesfälle: Wien, den 29. January 1787." *Magazin der Musik* 2 (1787): 1273–74.

Anonymous. "Nachrichten: Wien, am April." *AmZ* 7 (1 May 1805): 500–04.

Anonymous. "Nachrichten: Wien, d. 1sten Dec." *AmZ* 10 (16 December 1807): 183–85.

Anonymous. "Philharmonic Concerts. Eighth Concert, Monday, June 6, 1825." *The Harmonicon*, no. 31 (July 1825): 118.

Anonymous. "Recension: *Grand Concerto pour le Pianoforte . . . par Louis van Beethoven*. Oeuvre 37." *Amz* 7 (10 April 1805): 445–57.

WORKS CITED

Anonymous. "Recension: *Sinfonia eroica . . . da Luigi van Beethoven. Op. 55.*" *AmZ* 9 (18 February 1807): 319–34.

Anonymous. "Recensionen. *Variations tirés des derniers Quatuors de Mr. Joseph Haydn, arrangés pour le Clavecin ou Pianof. par Mr. l'Abbé Gelinek.* Vienna: Cappi etc." *AmZ* 4 (15 June 1802): 618–19.

Anonymous. Review of *Anleitung zum Generalbass* by Emmanuel Aloys Förster (Vienna: Johann Träg und Sohn, 1805). *AmZ* 9 (15 October 1806): 35–40.

Anonymous. "Schuppanzigh's Quartetten: Viertes Abonnement eröffnet am 8ten February 1824." *Wiener Allgemeine musikalische Zeitung mit besonderer Rücksicht auf den österreichischen Kaiserstaat* 8 (27 March 1824): 45–46.

Anonymous ("Y"). "Signale aus Weimar." *Signale für die musikalische Welt* 9 (1851): 236–37.

Anonymous. "Tre Sonate per il Clav. o Foretpiano con un Violino . . . dal S. Luigi van Beethoven. Op. 12." *AmZ* 1 (5 June 1799): 570–71.

Anonymous. "Wien. 17 April 1805. Fortsetzung." *Der Freimüthige* 3 (17 April 1805): 332.

Anonymous. "Wien in Junius 1783." *Magazin der Musik* 1 (1783): 842–44.

Anonymous. "Wien: Musikalisches Tagebuch vom Monat März." *AmZ* 28 (1826): 301–04, 309–15.

Aristotle. *Rhetoric.* Trans. W. Rhys Roberts. London: Oxford University Press, 1924.

Asper, Helmut G. *Hanswurst: Studien zum Lustigmacher auf der Berufsschauspielerbühne in Deutschland im 17. und 18. Jahrhundert.* Emsdetten: Lechte, 1980.

Bacht, Nikolaus. "Jean Paul's Listeners." *Eighteenth-Century Music* 3 (2006): 201–12.

Baillot, Pierre. *L'art du violon: Nouvelle methode.* Mainz: Schott, 1834.

Ballstaedt, Andreas. "'Humor' und 'Witz' in Joseph Haydns Musik." *Archiv für Musikwissenschaft* (1998): 195–219.

Bartel, Dietrich. *Musica Poetica: Musical-rhetorical Figures in German Baroque Music.* Lincoln: University of Nebraska Press, 1997.

Bashford, Christina. "Concert Listening the British Way? Program Notes and Victorian Culture." *OHML*, 187–206.

Bashford, Christina. "Learning to Listen: Audiences for Chamber Music in Early Victorian London." *Journal of Victorian Culture* 4, no. 1 (1999): 25–51.

Bashford, Christina. "Not Just 'G': Towards a History of the Programme Note." In *George Grove, Music and Victorian Culture*, 115–42. Ed. Michael Musgrave. Basingstoke: Macmillan, 2003.

WORKS CITED

Bashford, Christina. *The Pursuit of High Culture: John Ella and Chamber Music in Victorian Culture.* Woodbridge, Suffolk: Boydell, 2007.

Batteux, Charles. *Les beaux-arts réduits à un même principe.* 2nd ed. Paris: Durand, 1747.

Bauer, Elisabeth Eleonore."Beethoven—unser musikalischer Jean Paul: Anmerkungen zu einer Analogie." In *Beethoven: Analecta varia,* 83–105. Ed. Heinz-Klaus Metzger and Reiner Riehn. Munich: edition text + kritik, 1987.

Beattie, James. *Essays: On Poetry and Music as they Affect the Mind.* 3rd ed. London: E. and C. Dilly, 1779.

Beck, Hamilton H. H. *The Elusive "I" in the Novel: Hippel, Sterne, Diderot, Kant.* New York: Peter Lang, 1987.

Becker, Judith. *Deep Listeners: Music, Emotion, and Trancing.* Bloomington: Indiana University Press, 2004.

Beer, Axel. *"Empfehlenswerthe Musikalien": Besprechungen musikalischer Neuerscheinungen ausserhalb der Fachpresse (Deutschland, 1. Hälfte des 19. Jahrhunderts): Eine Bibliographie.* 2 vols. Göttingen: Hainholz, 2000.

Beer, Axel. *Musik zwischen Komponist, Verlag und Publikum: Die Rahmenbedingungen des Musikschaffens in Deutschland im ersten Drittel des 19. Jahrhunderts.* Tutzing: Schneider, 2000.

Beghin, Tom, and Sander M. Goldberg, eds. *Haydn and the Performance of Rhetoric.* Chicago: University of Chicago Press, 2007.

Berger, Karol. *Bach's Cycle, Mozart's Arrow: An Essay on the Origins of Musical Modernity.* Berkeley and Los Angeles: University of California Press, 2007.

Berger, Karol. "Beethoven and the Aesthetic State." *Beethoven Forum* 7 (1999): 17–44.

Berger, Karol. "Musicology According to Don Giovanni, or: Should We Get Drastic?" *JM* 22 (2005): 490–501.

Berger, Karol. "Toward a History of Hearing: The Classic Concerto, a Sample Case." In *Convention in Eighteenth- and Nineteenth-Century Music: Essays in Honor of Leonard G. Ratner,* 405–29. Ed. Wye J. Allanbrook, Janet M. Levy, William P. Mahrt. Stuyvesant, NY: Pendragon, 1992.

Berlioz, Hector. *À travers chants.* Paris: Michel Lévy frères, 1862.

Bermbach, Udo. *Der Wahn des Gesamtkunstwerks: Richard Wagners politisch-ästhetische Utopie.* Stuttgart: Metzler, 2004.

Besseler, Heinrich. "Grundfragen des musikalischen Hörens." *Jahrbuch der Musikbibliothek Peters* 32 (1925–26): 35–52.

Besseler, Heinrich. "Fundamental Issues of Musical Listening (1925)." Trans. Matthew Pritchard with Irene Auerbach. *Twentieth-Century Music* 8, no. 1 (2011): 49–70.

Biba, Otto, ed. *"Eben komme ich von Haydn . . . ": Georg August Griesingers Korrespondenz mit Joseph Haydns Verleger Breitkopf & Härtel 1799–1809.* Zürich: Atlantis, 1987.

Bloom, Peter. "*La Musique mise à la portée de tout le monde* by François-Joseph Fétis." *19CM* 10, no. 1 (1986): 84–88.

Bonds, Mark Evan. *Absolute Music: The History of an Idea.* New York: Oxford University Press, 2014.

Bonds, Mark Evan. *The Beethoven Syndrome: Hearing Music as Autobiography.* New York: Oxford University Press, 2020.

Bonds, Mark Evan. "The Court of Public Opinion: Haydn, Mozart, Beethoven." In *Beethoven und andere Hofmusiker seiner Generation*, 7–24. Ed. Birgit Lodes, Elisabeth Reisinger, and John D. Wilson. Bonn: Beethoven-Haus, 2018.

Bonds, Mark Evan. "Irony and Incomprehensibility: Beethoven's 'Serioso' String Quartet in F minor, Op. 95, and the Path to the Late Style." *JAMS* 70 (2017): 285–356.

Bonds, Mark Evan. "Life, Liberty, and the Pursuit of Happiness: Revolutionary Ideals in Narratives of the 'Farewell' Symphony." In *Joseph Haydn & die "Neue Welt": Musik- und Kulturgeschichtliche Perspektiven*, 283–301. Ed. Walter Reicher and Wolfgang Fuhrmann. Vienna: Hollitzer, 2019. (Eisenstädter Haydn Berichte, 11.)

Bonds, Mark Evan. *Listen to This.* Upper Saddle River, NJ: Prentice-Hall, 2009.

Bonds, Mark Evan. *Music as Thought: Listening to the Symphony in the Age of Beethoven.* Princeton, NJ: Princeton University Press, 2006.

Bonds, Mark Evan. "Turning Liebhaber into Kenner: Johann Nikolaus Forkel's Lectures on the Art of Listening, ca. 1780–1785." In *OHML*, 145–62.

Bonds, Mark Evan. *Wordless Rhetoric: Musical Form and the Metaphor of the Oration.* Cambridge, MA: Harvard University Press, 1991.

Booth, Wayne C. "The Self-conscious Narrator in Comic Fiction before *Tristram Shandy*." *Publications of the Modern Language Association* 67 (1952): 163–85.

Botstein, Leon. "The Consequences of Presumed Innocence: The Nineteenth-century Reception of Joseph Haydn." In *Haydn Studies*, 1–34. Ed. W. Dean Sutcliffe. Cambridge: Cambridge University Press, 1998.

Botstein, Leon. "Listening through Reading: Musical Literacy and the Concert Audience." *19CM* 16 (1992): 129–45.

Botstein, Leon. "Toward a History of Listening." *Musical Quarterly* 82, nos. 3–4 (1998): 427–31.

Bourdieu, Pierre. *Distinction: A Social Critique of the Judgement of Taste.* Trans. Richard Nice. Cambridge, MA: Harvard University Press, 1984.

WORKS CITED 197

Boyé. *L'expression musicale, mise au rang des chimères*. Amsterdam: s.n., 1779.

Brendel, Franz. *Geschichte der Musik in Italien, Deutschland und Frankreich*. Leipzig: Bruno Hinze, 1852.

Brown, A. Peter. *Joseph Haydn's Keyboard Music: Sources and Style*. Bloomington: Indiana University Press, 1986.

Bührlen, Friedrich Louis ("F.L.B."). "Reflexionen über das Wesen der Musik." *AmZ* 17 (1815): 761–67, 777–85.

Bührlen, Friedrich Louis. "Soll man bei der Instrumentalmusik Etwas denken?" *AmZ* 29 (1827): 529–38, 545–54.

Bunzel, Anja, and Natasha Loges, eds. *Musical Salon Culture in the Long Nineteenth Century*. Woodbridge, Suffolk, and Rochester, NY: Boydell Press, 2019.

Bürger, Christa, et al., eds. *Zur Dichotomisierung von hoher und niederer Literatur*. Frankfurt am Main: Suhrkamp, 1982.

Burney, Charles. *A General History of Music*. 4 vols. London: Author, 1776–89.

Burney, Charles. *The Present State of Music in Germany, the Netherlands, and United Provinces*. 2nd ed. 2 vols. London: T. Becket, J. Robson, and G. Robinson, 1775.

Burnham, Scott. "Haydn and Humor." In *The Cambridge Companion to Haydn*, 61–76. Ed. Caryl Clark. Cambridge: Cambridge University Press, 2005.

Burwick, Frederick. "Greek Drama: Coleridge, de Quincey, A. W. Schlegel." *Wordsworth Circle* 44 (2013): 3–12.

Burwick, Frederick. *Illusion and the Drama: Critical Theory of the Enlightenment and Romantic Era*. University Park: Pennsylvania State University Press, 1991.

du Châtelet, Gabrielle Emilie le Tonnelier de Breteuil, Marquise de. *Discours sur le bonheur*. In *Huitième Recueil philosophique et littéraire de la Société Typographique de Bouillon*, 8:1–78. Bouillon: Société Typographique de Bouillon, 1779.

Chew, Geoffrey. "The Night-Watchman's Song Quoted by Haydn and Its Implications." *Haydn-Studien* 3 (1973–74): 106–24.

Chua, Daniel K. L. "Haydn as Romantic: A Chemical Experiment with Instrumental Music." In *Haydn Studies*, 120–51. Ed. W. Dean Sutcliffe. Cambridge: Cambridge University Press, 1998.

Chybowski, Julia J. "Developing American Taste: A Cultural History of the Early Twentieth-century Music Appreciation Movement." PhD diss., University of Wisconsin-Madison, 2008.

Cicero, Marcus Tullius. *Rhetorica ad Herennium*. Trans. Harry Caplan. Cambridge, MA: Harvard University Press, 2014.

WORKS CITED

Connor (Swietlicki), Catherine. "*Postmodernism avant la lettre*: The Case of *Early Modern Spanish Theater.*" *Gestos* 9 (1994): 43–59.

Cook, Nicholas. *Beyond the Score: Music as Performance.* New York: Oxford University Press, 2014.

Cook, Nicholas. *Music, Imagination, and Culture.* Oxford: Clarendon Press, 1990.

Copland, Aaron. *Music and Imagination.* Cambridge, MA: Harvard University Press, 1952.

Corda, Tiziana. *E. T. A. Hoffmann und Carlo Gozzi: Der Einfluss der Commedia dell'Arte und der Fiabe Teatrali in Hoffmanns Werk.* Würzburg: Königshausen & Neumann, 2012.

Cowart, Georgia. "Sense and Sensibility in Eighteenth-Century Musical Thought." *Acta musicologica* 56 (1984): 251–66.

Crousaz, Jean-Pierre. *Traité du beau.* Paris: François L'Honoré, 1715.

Csikszentmihalyi, Mihaly. *Flow: The Psychology of Optimal Experience.* New York: Harper & Row, 1990.

Cypess, Rebecca. *Women and Musical Salons in the Enlightenment.* Chicago: University of Chicago Press, 2022.

Cypess, Rebecca, and Nancy Sinkoff, eds. *Sara's World: Gender, Judaism, and the Bach tradition in Enlightenment Berlin.* Rochester, NY: University of Rochester Press, 2018.

Czerny, Johann. *Sterne, Hippel und Jean Paul: Ein Beitrag zur Geschichte des humoristischen Romans in Deutschland.* Berlin: Alexander Duncker, 1904.

D'Angelo, Paolo. *Sprezzatura: Concealing the Effort of Art from Aristotle to Duchamp.* Trans. Sarin Marchetti. New York: Columbia University Press, 2018.

Danuser, Hermann. "Das imprévu in der Symphonik: Aspekte einer musikalischen Formkategorie in der Zeit von Carl Philipp Emanuel Bach bis Hector Berlioz." *Musiktheorie* 1 (1986): 61–81.

Danuser, Hermann. "Robert Schumann und die romantische Idee einer selbstreflexiven Kunst." In Henriette Herwig et al., eds. *Übergänge zwischen Künsten und Kulturen: Internationaler Kongress zum 150. Todesjahr von Heinrich Heine und Robert Schumann,* 471–91. Stuttgart: Metzler, 2007.

Darnton, Robert. *The Great Cat Massacre and Other Episodes in French Cultural History.* New York: Basic Books, 1984.

De Bolla, Peter. *The Education of the Eye: Painting, Landscape, and Architecture in Eighteenth-century Britain.* Stanford, CA: Stanford University Press, 2003.

Dell'Antonio, Andrew. *Listening as Spiritual Practice in Early Modern Italy.* Berkeley and Los Angeles: University of California Press, 2011.

WORKS CITED

Dell'Antonio, Andrew, ed. *Beyond Structural Listening? Postmodern Modes of Hearing*. Berkeley and Los Angeles: University of California Press, 2004.

Descartes, René. *Compendium musicae*. Utrecht: à Zÿll und ab Ackers dÿck, 1650.

Deutsch, Otto Erich, ed. *Mozart: Die Dokumente seines Lebens*. Kassel: Bärenreiter, 1961.

Dewey, John. *Art as Experience*. New York: Minton, Balch, 1934.

Dickinson, Edward. *The Education of a Music Lover: A Book for Those who Study or Teach the Art of Listening*. New York: C. Scribner's Sons, 1911.

Diergarten, Felix. "'At Times Even Homer Nods Off': Heinrich Christoph Koch's Polemic against Joseph Haydn." *Music Theory Online* 14, no. 1 (2008), https://www.mtosmt.org/issues/mto.08.14.1/mto.08.14.1.diergar ten.html.

Dies, Albert Christoph. *Biographische Nachrichten von Joseph Haydn*. Vienna: Camesina, 1810.

Dittersdorf, Karl Ditters von. *Lebensbeschreibung: Seinem Sohne in die Feder diktiert*. Leipzig: Breitkopf & Härtel, 1801.

Dolan, Emily. *The Orchestral Revolution: Haydn and the Technologies of Timbre*. Cambridge: Cambridge University Press, 2013.

Dorschel, Andreas. "Der Welt abhanden kommen: Über musikalischen Eskapismus." *Merkur* 66, no. 2 (2012): 135–42.

Dresdner, Albert. *Die Entstehung der Kunstkritik im Zusammenhang der Geschichte des europäischen Kunstlebens*. Munich: F. Bruckmann, 1915.

Du Bos, Jean-Baptiste. *Réflexions critiques sur la poésie et sur la peinture*. 2 vols. Paris: Jean Mariette, 1719.

Du Bos, Jean-Baptiste. *Critical Reflections on Poetry and Painting*. Trans. Thomas Nugent. 2 vols. London: John Nourse, 1748.

Duncan, D. A. "Persuading the Affections: Mersenne's Advice to the Harmonic Orator." In *French Musical Thought, 1600–1800*, 149–75. Ed. Georgia Cowart. Ann Arbor, MI: UMI Research Press, 1989.

Eagleton, Terry. *The Ideology of the Aesthetic*. Oxford: Blackwell, 1990.

Eliot, T. S. *The Complete Poems and Plays, 1909–1950*. New York: Harcourt, Brace & World, 1962.

Ellis, Katharine. "Music Criticism, Speech Acts and Generic Contracts." In *Nineteenth-Century Music Criticism*, 3–21. Ed. Teresa Cascudo García-Villaraco. Turnhout: Brepols, 2017.

Ellis, Katharine. "Researching Audience Behaviors in Nineteenth-Century Paris: Who Cares if You Listen?" In *OHML*, 37–54.

Engell, James. *The Creative Imagination: Enlightenment to Romanticism*. Cambridge, MA: Harvard University Press, 1981.

WORKS CITED

Erlmann, Veit. *Reason and Resonance: A History of Modern Aurality*. New York: Zone Books, 2010.

Fétis, François-Joseph. *La musique mise à la portée de tout le monde: Exposé succinct de tout ce qui est nécessaire pour juger de cet art, et pour en parler sans l'avoir étudié*. Paris: Alexandre Mesnier, 1830.

Fétis, François-Joseph. *Music Explained to the World, or: How to Understand Music and Enjoy its Performance*. Boston, MA: Benjamin Perkins, 1842.

Fink, Robert. "Going Flat: Post-Hierarchical Music Theory and the Musical Surface." In *Rethinking Music*, 102–37. Ed. Nicholas Cook and Mark Everist. New York: Oxford University Press, 1999.

Finney, Gretchen L. "Ecstasy and Music in Seventeenth-Century England." *Journal of the History of Ideas* 8 (1947): 153–86.

Forkel, Johann Nikolaus. *Allgemeine Geschichte der Musik*. 2 vols. Leipzig: Schwickert, 1788–1801.

Forkel, Johann Nikolaus. *Ankündigung seines akademischen Winter-Concerts von Michaelis 1779 bis Ostern 1780*. Göttingen: Dietrich, 1779.

Forkel, Johann Nikolaus. "Genauere Bestimmung einiger musikalischer Begriffe: Zur Ankündigung des academischen Winterconcerts von Michaelis 1780 bis Ostern 1781." *Magazin der Musik* 1 (1783): 1039–72.

Forkel, Johann Nikolaus. *Ueber die Theorie der Musik, insofern sie Liebhabern und Kennern nothwendig und nützlich ist: Eine Einladungschrift zu musikalischen Vorlesungen*. Göttingen: Wittwe Vandenhoeck, 1777.

Forkel, Johann Nikolaus. "Vorrede." In his *Musikalisch-Kritische Bibliothek* 1:iii–xxvi. Gotha: Karl Wilhelm Ettinger, 1778.

Fuhrimann, Daniel. *"Herzohren für die Tonkunst": Opern- und Konzertpublikum in der deutschen Literatur des langen 19. Jahrhunderts*. Freiburg: Rombach, 2005.

Fuhrmann, Wolfgang. "Haydn und sein Publikum." Habilitationsschrift, Bern, 2010.

Fuhrmann, Wolfgang. "Originality as Market-Value: Remarks on the Fantasia in C Hob. XVII:4 and Haydn as Musical Entrepreneur." *Studia Musicologica* 51 (2010): 303–16.

Fux, Johann Joseph. *Gradus ad Parnassum*. Vienna: Joannis Petri van Gehlen, 1725.

Gabrielsson, Alf. *Strong Experiences with Music: Music is Much More than Just Music*. Trans. Rod Bradbury. Oxford: Oxford University Press, 2011.

Gallope, Michael. *Deep Refrains: Music, Philosophy, and the Ineffable*. Chicago: University of Chicago Press, 2017.

Gerard, Alexander. *An Essay on Taste*. London: A. Millar; Edinburgh: A. Kincaid and J. Bell, 1759.

WORKS CITED

Gilman, Sander L. "Nietzsche, Bizet, and Wagner: Illness, Health, and Race in the Nineteenth Century." *Opera Quarterly* 23 (2007): 247–64.

Ginsborg, Hannah. "Kant." In *The Routledge Companion to Philosophy and Music*, 328–29. Ed. Theodore Gracyk and Andrew Kania. London and New York: Routledge, 2011.

Gioia, Ted. *How to Listen to Jazz*. New York: Basic Books, 2016.

Goehr, Lydia. *The Imaginary Museum of Musical Works: An Essay in the Philosophy of Music* Oxford: Clarendon Press, 1992.

Goehr, Lydia. "Schopenhauer and the Musicians: An Inquiry into the Sounds of Silence and the Limits of Philosophizing about Music." In *Schopenhauer, Philosophy and the Arts*, 200–28. Ed. Dale Jacquette. Cambridge: Cambridge University Press, 1996.

Grant, Roger Mathew. *Peculiar Attunements: How Affect Theory Turned Musical*. New York: Fordham University Press, 2020.

Griesinger, Georg August. "Apologie der Tafelmusik." *AmZ* 2 (22 January 1800): 291–94.

Griesinger, Georg August. *Biographische Notizen über Joseph Haydn*. Leipzig: Breitkopf & Härtel, 1810.

Gritten, Anthony. "Does the Performer Have to Listen?" *Music & Practice* 6 (2022): 1–20.

Gritten, Anthony. "Resonant Listening." *Performance Research* 15, no. 3 (2010): 115–22.

Groth, Renate. "*La musique mise à la portée de tout le monde*: François-Joseph Fétis und der Musikhörer." In *Zwischen Wissenschaft und Kunst: Festgabe für Richard Jakoby*, 227–33. Ed. Peter Becker, Arnfried Edler, Beate Schneider. Mainz: Schott, 1995.

Gumbrecht, Hans Ulrich. *Production of Presence: What Meaning Cannot Convey*. Stanford, CA: Stanford University Press, 2004.

Guthrie, Kate. *The Art of Appreciation: Music and Middlebrow Culture in Modern Britain*. Berkeley and Los Angeles: University of California Press, 2021.

Habermas, Jürgen. *The Structural Transformation of the Public Sphere: An Inquiry into a Category of Bourgeois Society*. Trans. Thomas Burger. Cambridge, MA: MIT Press, 1989.

Hadow, William Henry. "Introduction." In Percy Scholes, *The Listener's Guide to Music*, v–vii. London: Oxford University Press, 1919.

Hanslick, Eduard. *Vom Musikalisch-Schönen: Ein Beitrag zur Revision der Ästhetik der Tonkunst*. Leipzig: Rudolph Weigel, 1854.

Hanslick, Eduard. *Eduard Hanslick's On the Musically Beautiful: A New Translation*. Ed. and trans. Lee Rothfarb and Christoph Landerer. New York: Oxford University Press, 2018.

Harloe, Katherine. *Winckelmann and the Invention of Antiquity: History and Aesthetics in the Age of Altertumswissenschaft*. Oxford: Oxford University Press, 2013.

Hass, Ole, ed. *Répertoire international de la presse musicale: Allgemeine musikalische Zeitung, 1798–1848*. 14 vols. Baltimore: RIPM, 2009.

Haydn, Joseph. *Gesammelte Briefe und Aufzeichnungen*. Ed. Dénes Bartha. Kassel: Bärenreiter, 1965.

Heister, Hanns-Werner. *Das Konzert: Theorie einer Kulturform*. 2 vols. Wilhelmshaven: Heinrichshofen, 1983.

Herder, Johann Gottfried. *Werke in zehn Bänden*. 10 vols. Ed. Martin Bollacher et al. Frankfurt am Main: Deutscher Klassiker Verlag, 1985–2000.

Heusinger, Johann Heinrich Gottlieb. *Handbuch der Ästhetik*. 2 vols. Gotha: Justus Perthes, 1797.

Hiller, Johann Adam. "Abhandlung von der Nachahmung der Natur in der Musik. *Historisch-kritische Beyträge zur Aufnahme der Musik* 1 (1754–55): 515–43.

Hiller, Johann Adam. "Verzeichnis der im Jahr 1766 in Italien aufgeführten Singspiele." *Wöchentliche Nachrichten und Anweisungen, die Musik betreffend* 2 (13 July 1767): 13–14.

Hiller, Johann Adam. "Zehnte Fortsetzung des Entwurfs einer musikalischen Bibliothek." *Wöchentliche Nachrichten und Anmerkungen die Musik betreffend* 3 (3 October 1768): 103–08.

Hoeckner, Berthold. "Schumann and Romantic Distance." *JAMS* 50 (1997): 55–132.

Høffding, Simon. "Performative Passivity: Lessons on Phenomenology and the Extended Musical Mind with the Danish String Quartet." In *Music and Consciousness 2: Worlds, Practices, Modalities*, 127–42. Ed. Ruth Herbert, David Clarke, and Eric Clarke. New York: Oxford University Press, 2019.

Hoffmann, Ernst Theodor Amadeus. "Beethovens Instrumentalmusik" (1813). In his *Sämtliche Werke in sechs Bänden*, vol. 2/1: 52–61. Ed. Wulf Segebrecht and Hartmut Steinecke. Frankfurt/Main: Deutscher Klassiker Verlag, 1993.

Hoffmann, Ernst Theodor Amadeus. "Des Kapellmeisters, Johannes Kreislers, Dissertatiuncula über den hohen Werth der Musik." *AmZ* 14 (29 July 1812): 503–09.

Hoffmann, Ernst Theodor Amadeus. "Recension: *Sinfonie . . . par Louis van Beethoven . . . Oeuvre 67 . . .* " *AmZ* 12 (1810): 630–42, 652–59.

Homann, Karl. "Zum Begriff Einbildungskraft nach Kant." *Archiv für Begriffsgeschichte* 14 (1970): 266–302.

WORKS CITED

Hosler, Bellamy. *Changing Aesthetic Views of Instrumental Music in 18th-century Germany*. Ann Arbor, MI: UMI Research Press, 1981.

Hui, Alexandra. *The Psychophysical Ear: Musical Experiments, Experimental Sounds, 1840–1910*. Cambridge, MA: MIT Press, 2012.

Hume, David. *A Treatise of Human Nature* (1739–40). Ed. Lewis Amherst Selby-Bigge and P. H. Niddich. 2nd ed. Oxford: Oxford University Press, 2014.

Hunter, Mary. "Self-Reflexivity." In *The Cambridge Haydn Encyclopedia*, 348–49. Ed. Caryl Clark and Sarah Day-O'Connell. Cambridge: Cambridge University Press, 2019.

Iser, Wolfgang. *Laurence Sterne: Tristram Shandy*. Trans. David Henry Wilson. Cambridge: Cambridge University Press, 1988.

Janz, Tobias. "'Music about Music': Metaization and Intertextuality in Beethoven's *Prometheus Variations* op. 35." In *Metareference across Media: Theory and Case Studies*, 211–33. Ed. Werner Wolf. Amsterdam and New York: Rodopi, 2009.

Johnson, James H. *Listening in Paris: A Cultural History*. Berkeley and Los Angeles: University of California Press, 1995.

Johnson, Julian. *Mahler's Voices: Expression and Irony in the Songs and Symphonies*. New York: Oxford University Press, 2009.

Johnson, Julian. "Narrative Strategies in E. T. A. Hoffmann and Robert Schumann." In *Resounding Concerns*, 55–70. Ed. Rüdiger Görner. Munich: Iudicium, 2003.

Junker, Carl Ludwig. *Über den Werth der Tonkunst*. Bayreuth and Leipzig: Johann Andreas Lübecks sel. Erben, 1786.

Junker, Carl Ludwig. *Zwanzig Componisten: Eine Skizze*. Bern: Typographische Gesellschaft, 1776.

Kaltenecker, Martin. *L'oreille divisée: Les discours sur l'écoute musicale aux XVIIIe et XIXe siècles*. Paris: Musica falsa, 2010.

Kames, Henry Home, Lord. *Elements of Criticism*. 4th ed. 2 vols. Edinburgh: J. Kincaid and J. Bell, 1769.

Kamien, Roger. *Music: An Appreciation*, 12th ed. New York: McGraw-Hill, 2018.

Kant, Immanuel. *Anthropology from a Pragmatic Point of View*. Ed. and trans. Robert B. Louden, Manfred Kuehn. Cambridge: Cambridge University Press, 2006.

Kant, Immanuel. "Fragmente über musikalische Gegenstände aus neuen, wichtigen, nichtmusikalischen Schriften: Aus Kants Anthropologie." *AmZ* 2 (9 December 1799): 23–25.

WORKS CITED

Kant, Immanuel. *Gesammelte Schriften*. Ed. Königlich Preußische Akademie der Wissenschaften. Berlin: Georg Reimer, 1900–.

Kant, Immanuel. [*Kritik der Urteilskraft*. English] *Critique of Judgment*. Trans. Werner S. Pluhar. Indianapolis and Cambridge: Hackett, 1987.

Kant, Immanuel. [*Kritik der Urteilskraft*. English] *Critique of the Power of Judgment*. Ed. Paul Guyer. Trans. Paul Guyer and Eric Matthews. Cambridge: Cambridge University Press, 2000.

Kant, Immanuel. *Metaphysics of Morals*. Trans. Mary Gregor. Cambridge: Cambridge University Press, 1996.

Kant, Immanuel. "Von der Methodenlehre des Geschmacks." *Musikalisches Kunstmagazin* 2 (1791): 65.

Kavanagh, Thomas M. *Enlightened Pleasures: Eighteenth-century France and the New Epicureanism*. New Haven, CT: Yale University Press, 2010.

Keymer, Thomas, ed., *Laurence Sterne's Tristram Shandy: A Casebook*. Oxford and New York: Oxford University Press, 2006.

Kennedy, George A. *Classical Rhetoric and Its Christian and Secular Tradition from Ancient to Modern Times*. Chapel Hill: University of North Carolina Press, 1980.

Kim, Jin-Ah. "Johann Friedrich Rochlitz und seine Konzertkritiken in der *Allgemeinen musikalischen Zeitung* bis 1807/08." *Archiv für Musikwissenschaft* 70, no. 3 (2013): 191–208.

Klorman, Edward. *Mozart's Music of Friends: Social Interplay in the Chamber Works*. Cambridge: Cambridge University Press, 2016.

Knapp, Raymond. *Making Light: Haydn, Musical Camp, and the Long Shadow of German Idealism*. Durham, NC: Duke University Press, 2018.

Kneller, Jane. *Kant and the Power of Imagination*. Cambridge: Cambridge University Press, 2007.

Kobbé, Gustav. *How to Appreciate Music*. New York: Moffat, Yard, 1906.

Koch, Heinrich Christoph. "Ueber den Modegeschmack in der Tonkunst." *Journal der Tonkunst* 1 (1795): 63–121.

Koch, Heinrich Christoph. *Versuch einer Anleitung zur Composition*. 3 vols. Rudolstadt: Löwische Erben und Schirach; Leipzig: A.F. Böhme, 1782–93.

Kopitz, Klaus Martin, and Rainer Cadenbach, eds. *Beethoven aus der Sicht seiner Zeitgenossen in Tagebüchern, Briefen, Gedichten und Erinnerungen*. 2 vols. Munich: G. Henle, 2009.

Körner, Christian Gottfried. "Über Charakterdarstellung in der Musik" (1795). In his *Aesthetische Ansichten: Ausgewählte Aufsätze*, 24–47. Ed. Joseph P. Bauke. Marbach: Schiller-Nationalmuseum, 1964.

Krahn, Carolin. *Topographie der Imaginationen: Johann Friedrich Rochlitz' musikalisches Italien um 1800*. Vienna: Hollitzer, 2021. (Wiener Veröffentlichungen zur Musikwissenschaft, 54.)

WORKS CITED

Kranefeld, Ulrike. *Der nachschaffende Hörer: Rezeptionsästhetische Studien zur Musik Robert Schumanns.* Stuttgart: J. B. Metzler, 2000.

Kraus, Nina. *Of Sound Mind: How the Brain Constructs a Meaningful Sonic World.* Cambridge, MA: MIT Press, 2021.

Krause, Christian Gottfried. *Von der musikalischen Poesie.* Berlin: Johann Friedrich Voss, 1752.

Krehbiel, Henry Edward. *How to Listen to Music: Hints and Suggestions to Untaught Lovers of the Art.* New York: C. Scribner's Sons, 1896.

Kretzschmar, Hermann. *Führer durch den Konzertsaal, I. Abtheilung: Sinfonie und Suite, 1. Band.* 3rd ed. Leipzig: Breitkopf & Härtel, 1898.

Kristeller, Paul Oskar. "The Modern System of the Arts: A Study in the History of Aesthetics." *Journal of the History of Ideas* 12 (1951): 496–527, and 13 (1952): 17–46.

Krummacher, Hans-Henrik. *Lyra: Studien zur Theorie und Geschichte der Lyrik vom 16. bis zum 19. Jahrhundert.* Berlin: De Gruyter, 2013.

Kuplen, Mojca. "Reflective and Non-reflective Aesthetic Ideas in Kant's Theory of Art." *BJA* 61 (2021): 1–16.

Kurze, Fabian Oliver. "In die Stille geleiten: Darstellungsprinzipien und Erfahrungsweisen eines musikalischen Grundphänomens." PhD diss., Tübingen, 2018.

Lamy, Bernard. *La rhétorique ou l'art de parler.* 4th ed. Paris: Florentin & Pierre Delaulne, 1701.

Landon, H. C. Robbins. *Haydn: Chronicle and Works.* 5 vols. London: Thames and Hudson, 1976–80.

Lanham, Richard A. *Tristram Shandy: The Games of Pleasure.* Berkeley: University of California Press, 1973.

Lanzendörfer, Anselma. "Designated Attention: The Transformation of Music Announcements in Leipzig's Concert Life, 1781–1850." In *OHML*, 163–85.

Le Guin, Elisabeth. "'One Says That One Weeps, but One Does Not Weep': *Sensible*, Grotesque, and Mechanical Embodiments in Boccherini's Chamber Music." *JAMS* 55 (2002): 207–54.

Lessing, Gotthold Ephraim. *Werke.* 5 vols. Ed. Franz Bornmüller. Leipzig and Vienna: Bibliographisches Institut, 1884.

Levinson, Jerrold. *Music in the Moment.* Ithaca, NY: Cornell University Press, 1997.

Levinson, Jerrold. "Musical Chills." In his *Contemplating Art: Essays in Aesthetics*, 220–36. Oxford: Clarendon Press, 2006.

Levinson, Jerrold. "Musical Frissons." *Revue française d'études américaines* 86 (2000): 64–76.

Lichtenthal, Peter. *Der musikalische Arzt, oder: Abhandlung von dem Einflusse der Musik auf den Körper, und von ihrer Anwendung in gewissen Krankheiten.*

Nebst einigen Winken, zur Anhörung einer guten Musik. Vienna: Christian Friedrich Wappler und Beck, 1807.

Lieske, Rudolf. *Tiecks Abwendung von der Romantik.* Berlin: E. Ebering, 1933.

Link, Anne-Marie. "The Social Practice of Taste in Late Eighteenth-century Germany: A Case Study." *Oxford Art Journal* 15, no. 2 (1992): 3–14.

Liszt, Franz. *Lohengrin et Tannhäuser de Richard Wagner.* Leipzig: F. A. Brockhaus, 1851.

Lobe, Johann Christian. *Musikalische Briefe: Wahrheit über Tonkunst und Tonkünstler.* 2 vols. Leipzig: Baumgärtner, 1852.

Locke, John. *An Essay concerning Human Understanding.* Ed. Peter H. Nidditch. Oxford: Clarendon Press, 1975.

Loughridge, Deirdre. *Haydn's Sunrise, Beethoven's Shadow: Audiovisual Culture and the Emergence of Musical Romanticism.* Chicago: University of Chicago Press, 2016.

Lowe, Melanie. *Pleasure and Meaning in the Classical Symphony.* Bloomington: Indiana University Press, 2007.

McAuley, Tomás. "Immanuel Kant and the Downfall of the *Affektenlehre.*" In *Sound and Affect: Voice, Music, World,* 342–60. Ed. Judith Lochhead, Eduardo Mendieta, Stephen Decatur Smith. Chicago: University of Chicago Press, 2021.

McAuley, Tomás. *The Music of Philosophy: German Idealism and Musical Thought.* New York: Oxford University Press, forthcoming.

Machlis, Joseph. *Music: Adventures in Listening.* New York: W. W. Norton, 1966.

Mäcklin, Harri. "Aesthetic Self-Forgetfulness." *BJA* 61 (2021): 527–41.

Marmontel, Jean-François. *Eléments de littérature.* Ed. Sophie Le Ménahèze. Paris: Desjonquères. 2005.

Marx, Adolph Bernhard. *Die alte Musiklehre im Streit mit unserer Zeit.* Leipzig: Breitkopf & Härtel, 1841.

Marx, Adolph Bernhard. "Ueber die Anfoderungen unserer Zeit an musikalische Kritik, in besonderem Bezuge auf diese Zeitung." *BAmZ* 1 (1824): 2–4, 9–11, 17–19.

Mathew, Nicholas, and Benjamin Walton, eds. *The Invention of Beethoven and Rossini: Historiography, Analysis, Criticism.* Cambridge: Cambridge University Press, 2013.

Mathews, W. S. B. *How to Understand Music: A Concise Course in Musical Intelligence and Taste.* Chicago: Author, 1880.

Mattheson, Johann ["Aristoxenus der jüngere"]. *Die neueste Untersuchung der Singspiele nebst beygefügter musikalischer Geschmacksprobe.* Hamburg: Christian Herold, 1744.

Mattheson, Johann. *Der vollkommene Capellmeister.* Hamburg: Christian Herold, 1739.

WORKS CITED

Mauzi, Robert. *L'idée du bonheur dans la littérature et la pensée françaises au XVIIIe siècle*. Paris: Armand Colin, 1960.

Meier, Georg Friedrich. *Anfangsgründe aller schönen Wissenschaften*. 3 vols. Magdeburg: Carl Hermann Hemmerde, 1748–50.

Mersenne, Marin. *Harmonie universelle, contenant la théorie et la pratique de la musique* (1636). 3 vols. Reprint. Paris: Centre national de la recherche scientifique, 1963.

Michaelis, Christian Friedrich. "Einige Gedanken über das Interessante und Rührende in der Musik." *Eunomia: Eine Zeitschrift des 19. Jahrhunderts* 4 (August 1804): 144–51.

Michaelis, Christian Friedrich. "Nachtrag zu den Ideen über die ästhetische Natur der Musik." *Eunomia: Eine Zeitschrift des 19. Jahrhunderts* 1 (1801): 343–48.

Michaelis, Christian Friedrich. *Ueber den Geist der Tonkunst, mit Rücksicht auf Kants Kritik der ästhetischen Urtheilskraft: Ein ästhetischer Versuch*. 2 vols. Leipzig: Schäferische Buchhandlung, 1795–1800.

Michaelis, Christian Friedrich. *Ueber den Geist der Tonkunst und andere Schriften*. Ed. Lothar Schmidt. Chemnitz: Gudrun Schröder, 1997.

Michaelis, Christian Friedrich. "Vermischte Bemerkungen über Musik." *Berlinische Musikalische Zeitung* 1 (1805): 13–14, 21–22, 25–26; and 2 (1806): 81–82, 93–94, 105–06.

Mikusi, Balázs. "The G Minor Minuet of Mozart's 'Haffner' Serenade: Yet Another Musical Joke?" *The Musical Times* 147 (2006): 47–55.

Miller, Hugh M. *Introduction to Music: A Guide to Good Listening*. New York: Barnes and Noble, 1958.

Mirka, Danuta. *Metric Manipulations in Haydn and Mozart: Chamber Music for Strings, 1787–1791*. New York: Oxford University Press, 2009.

Montesquieu. *Essai sur le goût* (published 1758). Ed. Charles-Jacques Beyer. Geneva: Librairie Droz, 1967.

Moritz, Karl Philipp. *Schriften zur Ästhetik und Poetik*. Ed. Hans Joachim Schrimpf. Tübingen: Max Niemeyer, 1962.

Morrow, Mary Sue. *German Music Criticism in the Late Eighteenth Century: Aesthetic Issues in Instrumental Music*. Cambridge: Cambridge University Press, 1997.

Mozart, Wolfgang Amadeus. *Briefe und Aufzeichnungen: Gesamtausgabe*. 2nd ed. 8 vols. Ed. Wilhelm A. Bauer, Otto Erich Deutsch, Ulrich Konrad. Bärenreiter: Deutscher Taschenbuch Verlag, 2005.

Müller-Kampel, Beatrice. *Hanswurst, Bernardon, Kasperl: Spasstheater im 18. Jahrhundert*. Paderborn: Ferdinand Schöningh, 2003.

Mullan, John. *Sentiment and Sociability: The Language of Feeling in the Eighteenth Century*. Oxford: Clarendon Press, 1988.

Nägeli, Hans Georg. *Vorlesungen über Musik mit Berücksichtigung der Dilettanten*. Stuttgart and Tübingen: J. G. Cotta, 1826.

Nancy, Jean-Luc. *Listening*. Trans. Charlotte Mandell. New York: Fordham University Press, 2007.

Neubauer, John. *The Emancipation of Music from Language: Departure from Mimesis in Eighteenth-century Aesthetics*. New Haven, CT: Yale University Press, 1986.

Nietzsche, Friedrich. *Basic Writings of Nietzsche*. Ed. and trans. Walter Kaufmann. New York: Modern Library, 1968.

Nietzsche, Friedrich. *Sämtliche Werke: Kritische Studienausgabe*. 15 vols. Ed. Giorgio Colli and Mazzino Montinari. Berlin: Walter de Gruyter, 1980.

November, Nancy. *Cultivating String Quartets in Beethoven's Vienna*. Woodbridge, Suffolk: Boydell, 2017.

November, Nancy. "Instrumental Arias or Sonic Tableaux: 'Voice' in Haydn's String Quartets Opp. 9 and 17." *M&L* 89 (2008): 346–72.

O'Connor, Thomas Austin. "Is the Spanish *Comedia* a Metatheater?" *Hispanic Review* 43 (1975): 275–89.

Oesterreich, Peter L. "Das Verhältnis von ästhetischer Theorie und Rhetorik in Kants *Kritik der Urteilskraft*." *Kant-Studien* 83 (1992): 324–35.

Ong, Walter J. "The Province of Rhetoric and Poetic." *Modern Schoolman: A Quarterly Journal of Philsophy* 19 (1942): 24–27.

Ottenberg, Hans-Günter. *C. P. E. Bach*. Trans. Philip J. Whitmore. Oxford: Oxford University Press, 1987.

"L'ouïe dans la pensée européene au XVIIIe siècle." Special issue of the *Revue germanique internationale* 27 (2018).

Panksepp, Jaak. "The Emotional Sources of 'Chills' Induced by Music." *Music Perception* 13, no. 2 (1995): 171–207.

Paul, Steven Everett. "Wit, Comedy, and Humour in the Instrumental Music of Franz Joseph Haydn." PhD diss., University of Cambridge, 1980.

Paulin, Roger. *Ludwig Tieck: A Literary Biography*. Oxford: Clarendon Press, 1985.

Pepys, Samuel. *The Diary of Samuel Pepys*. 11 vols. Ed. Robert Latham and William Matthews. Berkeley: University of California Press, 1970–83.

Pericolo, Lorenzo. "What is Metapainting? *The Self-Aware Image* Twenty Years Later." In *The Self-Aware Image: An Insight into Early Modern Metapainting*, 11–31. Ed. Victor I. Stoichita. Trans. Anne-Marie Glasheen. London: Harvey Miller, 2015.

Peyser, Ethel. *How to Enjoy Music: A First-Aid to Music Listeners*. New York: G. P. Putnam's Sons, 1933.

Plamper, Jan. *The History of Emotions: An Introduction*. Trans. Keith Tribe. New York: Oxford University Press, 2015.

WORKS CITED

Plato, *Republic*. Trans. G. M. A. Grube and C. D. C. Reeve. In *Plato: Complete Works*, 971–1223. Ed. John M. Cooper. Indianapolis and Cambridge: Hackett, 1997.

Pluche, Noël-Antoine. *Le spectacle de la nature... tome septième, contenant ce qui regarde l'homme en société, nouvelle édition*. Paris: Veuve Estienne et fils, 1751.

Pochat, Götz. "Aesthetic Illusion and the Breaking of Illusion in Painting (Fourteenth to Twentieth Centuries)." In *Immersion and Distance: Aesthetic Illusion in Literature and Other Media*, 237–61. Ed. Werner Wolf, Walter Bernhart, and Andreas Mahler. Amsterdam and New York: Radopi, 2013.

Preston, John. *The Created Self: The Reader's Role in Eighteenth-Century Fiction*. New York: Barnes & Noble, 1970.

Pritchard, Matthew. "Music in Balance: The Aesthetics of Music after Kant, 1790–1810." *JM* 36 (2019): 39–67.

Purday, Charles. "To the Editor of *The Musical World*." *The Musical World*, 12 December 1836: 191.

Quantz, Johann Joachim. *Versuch einer Anweisung die Flöte traversiere zu spielen*. Berlin: J. F. Voss, 1752.

Quintilian, Marcus Fabius. *The Institutio oratoria of Quintilian*. 3 vols. Trans. H. E. Butler. London: William Heinemann; Cambridge, MA: Harvard University Press, 1953.

Ranum, Patricia M. *The Harmonic Orator: The Phrasing and Rhetoric of the Melody in French Baroque Airs*. Hillsdale, NY: Pendragon, 2001.

Reddy, William M. *The Navigation of Feeling: A Framework for the History of Emotions*. Cambridge: Cambridge University Press, 2001.

Reichardt, Johann Friedrich. "Fingerzeige für den denkenden und forschenden deutschen Tonkünstler." *Musikalisches Kunstmagazin* 2 (1791): 87–89.

Reichardt, Johann Friedrich. "Neue merkwürdige musikalische Werke." *Musikalisches Kunstmagazin* 1 (1782): 69–87.

Reichardt, Johann Friedrich. Review of J. N. Forkel, *Ueber die Theorie der Musik. Allgemeine deutsche Bibliothek* 25–26 (1779–80), Abteilung 5: 3019–24.

Reiman, Erika. *Schumann's Piano Cycles and the Novels of Jean Paul*. Rochester, NY: University of Rochester Press, 2004.

Rellstab, Ludwig. "Ueber Beethovens neuestes Quartett." *BAmZ* 2 (25 May 1825): 165–66.

Richards, Annette. *The Free Fantasia and the Musical Picturesque*. Cambridge: Cambridge University Press, 2001.

Richter, Jean Paul Friedrich. *Flegeljahre: Eine Biographie*. 4 vols. Tübingen: Cotta, 1804–05.

Richter, Jean Paul Friedrich. *Vorschule der Ästhetik*. Ed. Norbert Miller. Hamburg: Felix Meiner, 1990.

WORKS CITED

Riedel, Friedrich Just. *Theorie der schönen Künste*. 2nd ed. Vienna and Jena: Cuno, 1774.

Riepel, Joseph. *Gründliche Erklärung der Tonordnung insbesondere, zugleich aber für die mehresten Organisten insgemein*. Frankfurt: s. n., 1757.

Riggs, Robert. "'On the Representation of Character in Music': Christian Gottfried Körner's Aesthetics of Instrumental Music." *Musical Quarterly* 81 (1997): 599–631.

Riley, Matthew. "Johann Nikolaus Forkel on the Listening Practices of 'Kenner' and 'Liebhaber'." *Music & Letters* 84 (2003): 414–33.

Riley, Matthew. *Musical Listening in the German Enlightenment: Attention, Wonder and Astonishment*. Aldershot: Ashgate, 2004.

Ringer, Mark. *Electra and the Empty Urn: Metatheater and Role-Playing in Sophocles*. Chapel Hill: University of North Carolina Press, 1998.

Robertson, Ritchie. *The Enlightenment: The Pursuit of Happiness, 1680–1790*. New York: Harper, 2021.

Rochlitz, Friedrich. "Der Geschmack: Schreiben an einen Tonkünstler." *AmZ* 33 (1831): 477–83, 501–10.

Rochlitz, Friedrich. "Nachrichten: Leipzig." *AmZ* 6 (9 May 1804): 541–43.

Rochlitz, Friedrich. "Die Verschiedenheit der Urtheile über Werke der Tonkunst." *AmZ* 1 (8 May 1799): 497–506.

Rosa, Hartmut. *Resonance: A Sociology of Our Relationship to the World*. Trans. James C. Wagner. Cambridge: Polity Press, 2019.

Rothstein, Eric. "'Ideal Presence' and the 'Non Finito' in Eighteenth-Century Aesthetics." *Eighteenth-Century Studies* 9 (1976): 307–32.

Rouget, Gilbert. *Music and Trance: A Theory of the Relations Between Music and Possession*. Trans. Derek Coltman, Gilbert Rouget, and Brunhilde Biebuyck. Chicago: University of Chicago Press, 1985.

Ruetz, Caspar. "Sendschreiben eines Freundes an den andern über einige Ausdrücke des Herrn Batteux von der Musik." *Historisch-kritische Beyträge zur Aufnahme der Musik* 1 (1754): 273–311.

de Ruiter, Jacob. *Der Charakterbegriff in der Musik: Studien zur deutschen Ästhetik der Instrumentalmusik 1740–1850*. Stuttgart: Franz Steiner, 1989.

Salmen, Walter. *Johann Friedrich Reichardt: Komponist, Schriftsteller, Kapellmeister und Verwaltungsbeamter der Goethezeit*. 2nd ed. Hildesheim: Georg Olms, 2002.

Scarlatti, Domenico. *Essercizi per gravicembalo* [London: B. Fortier, 1738].

Scheibe, Johann Adolph. *Critischer Musikus*. 2nd ed. Leipzig: Bernhard Christoph Breitkopf, 1745.

Scherzinger, Martin. "Event or Ephemeron? Music's Sound, Performance, and Media: A Critical Reflection on the Thought of Carolyn Abbate." *Sound Stage Screen* 1 (2021): 145–92.

WORKS CITED

Schiller, Friedrich. *On the Aesthetic Education of Man in a Series of Letters.* Trans. Elizabeth M. Wilkinson and L. A. Willoughby. Oxford: Clarendon Press, 1967.

Schiller, Friedrich. *Werke und Briefe in zwölf Bänden.* 12 vols. Ed. Ott Dann et al. Frankfurt am Main: Deutscher Klassiker Verlag, 1988–2004.

Schiltz, Katelijne. *Music and Riddle Culture in the Renaissance.* Cambridge: Cambridge University Press, 2015.

Schlegel, August Wilhelm. *Ueber dramatische Kunst und Litteratur: Vorlesungen.* 2 vols. Heidelberg: Mohr und Zimmer, 1809–11.

Schlegel, Friedrich. *Kritische Friedrich-Schlegel-Ausgabe.* Ed. Ernst Behler et al. Munich: F. Schöningh, 1958–.

Schleuning, Peter. *Der Bürger erhebt sich: Geschichte der deutschen Musik im 18. Jahrhundert.* 2nd ed. Stuttgart: Metzler, 2000.

Schopenhauer, Arthur. *Sämtliche Werke.* 7 vols. Ed. Julius Frauenstädt and Arthur Hübscher. Wiesbaden, E. Brockhaus, 1948–61.

Schopenhauer, Arthur. *The World as Will and Representation.* 2 vols. Ed. Christopher Janaway. Trans. Judith Norman, Alistair Welchman. Cambridge: Cambridge University Press, 2010.

Schulte-Sasse, Jochen. "Aesthetic Illusion in the Eighteenth Century." In *Aesthetic Illusion: Theoretical and Historical Approaches,* 105–21. Ed. Frederick Burwick and Walter Pape. Berlin and New York: Walter de Gruyter, 1990.

Schulte-Sasse, Jochen. *Die Kritik an der Trivialliteratur seit der Aufklärung: Studien zur Geschichte des modernen Kitschbegriffs.* Munich: Wilhelm Fink, 1971.

Schütz, Gundula. *Vor dem Richterstuhl der Kritik: Die Musik in Friedrich Nicolais 'Allgemeiner deutscher Bibliothek' 1765–1806.* Tübingen: Niemeyer, 2007.

Senner, Wayne M., Robin Wallace, and William Meredith, eds. *The Critical Reception of Beethoven's Compositions by His German Contemporaries.* Trans. Wayne M. Senner. 2 vols. Lincoln: University of Nebraska Press, 1999–2001.

Shiner, Larry. *The Invention of Art: Cultural History.* Chicago: University of Chicago Press, 2001.

Sisman, Elaine. "Haydn, Shakespeare, and the Rules of Originality." In *Haydn and His World,* 3–36. Ed. Elaine Sisman. Princeton, NJ: Princeton University Press, 1997.

Sisman, Elaine. "Haydn's Theater Symphonies." *JAMS* 43 (1990): 292–352.

Small, Christopher. *Musicking: The Meanings of Performing and Listening.* Middletown, CT: Wesleyan University Press, 1998.

Smith, Adam. "Of the Nature of that Imitation which Takes Place in What Are Called the Imitative Arts." In his *Essays on Philosophical Subjects,* 169–213.

Ed. W. P. D. Wightman and J. C. Bryce. Oxford: Clarendon Press, 1980. (The Glasgow Edition of the Works and Correspondence of Adam Smith, 3.)

Smith, Bruce R. "Early Modern Period." In *OHWMP*, 157–79.

Spazier, Carl. "Über Menuetten in Sinfonien." *Musikalisches Wochenblatt* 2 (1791): 91–92.

Sponheuer, Bernd. *Musik als Kunst und Nicht-Kunst: Untersuchungen zur Dichotomie von "hoher" und "niederer" Musik im musikästhetischen Denken zwischen Kant und Hanslick*. Kassel: Bärenreiter, 1987.

Steinbeck, Wolfram. "Witz und Werk: Zur Konstitution musikalischer Form in Haydns Symphonik." In *Joseph Haydn im 21. Jahrhundert: Bericht über das Symposium der Osterreichischen Akademie der Wissenschaften, der Internationalen Joseph Haydn Privatstiftung Eisenstadt und der Esterhazy Privatstiftung vom 14. bis 17. Oktober 2009 in Wien und Eisenstadt*, 231–63. Ed. Christine Siegert, Gernot Gruber, Walter Reicher. Tutzing: Hans Schneider, 2013.

Stendhal [Henri Beyle]. *Vie de Rossini*. 2 vols. Paris: Auguste Boulland, 1824.

Stendhal. *Life of Rossini*. Rev. ed. Trans. Richard N. Coe. New York: Orion, 1970.

Stephan, Sigmund Jakob-Michael. "The Early Romantic Comedy of Aesthetic Disobedience." *Oxford German Studies* 50, no. 3 (2021): 350–64.

Stockhausen, Johann Christoph. *Critischer Entwurf einer auserlesenen Bibliothek für die Liebhaber der Philosophie und schönen Wissenschaften*. 4th ed. Berlin: Haude und Spener, 1771.

Stoichita, Victor I. *The Self-Aware Image: An Insight into Early Modern Metapainting*. Trans. Anne-Marie Glasheen. London: Harvey Miller, 2015.

Stone-Davis, Férdia J. "Music and World-Making: Haydn's String Quartet in E-flat Major (op. 33 no. 2)." In Stone-Davis, ed. *Music and Transcendence*, 125–45. Farnham, Surrey: Ashgate, 2015.

Stone-Davis, Férdia J., ed., *Music and Transcendence*. Farnham, Surrey: Ashgate, 2015.

Styan, John L. *Drama, Stage and Audience*. Cambridge: Cambridge University Press, 1975.

Subotnik, Rose Rosengard. *Deconstructive Variations: Music and Reason in Western Society*. Minneapolis: University of Minnesota Press, 1996.

Sulzer, Johann Georg. *Allgemeine Theorie der schönen Künste*. 2 vols. Leipzig: M. G. Weidemanns Erben und Reich, 1771–74.

Sutcliffe, W. Dean. *Instrumental Music in an Age of Sociability: Haydn, Mozart and Friends*. Cambridge: Cambridge University Press, 2020.

Szendy, Peter. *Écoute: Une histoire de nos oreilles*. Paris: Editions L'Harmattan, 2000.

WORKS CITED

Szendy, Peter. *Listen: A History of Our Ears.* Trans. Charlotte Mandell. New York: Fordham University Press, 2008.

Tadday, Ulrich. *Die Anfänge des Musikfeuilleutons: Der kommunikative Gebrauchswert musikalischer Bildung in Deutschland um 1800.* Stuttgart: J. B. Metzler, 1993.

Talbot, Michael. "The Work-Concept and Composer-Centredness." In *The Musical Work: Reality or Invention?*, 168–86. Ed. Michael Talbot. Liverpool: Liverpool University Press, 2000.

Tan, Leonard, and Hui Xing Sin. "Flow Research in Music Contexts: A Systematic Literature Review." *Musicae Scientiae* 25, no. 4 (2021): 399–428.

Taplin, Oliver. "Fifth-Century Tragedy and Comedy: A Synkrisis." *Journal of Hellenic Studies* 106 (1986): 163–74.

Taruskin, Richard. *The Oxford History of Western Music.* 5 vols. Oxford: Oxford University Press, 2010.

Taylor, Benedict. *Music, Subjectivity, and Schumann.* Cambridge: Cambridge University Press, 2022.

Thorau, Christian. "From Program Leaflets to Listening Apps: A Brief History of Guided Listening." In *Classical Concert Studies: A Companion to Contemporary Research and Performance*, 61–80. Ed. Martin Tröndle. New York: Routledge, 2020.

Thorau, Christian. *Semantisierte Sinnlichkeit: Studien zu Rezeption und Zeichenstruktur der Leitmotivtechnik Richard Wagners.* Stuttgart: Steiner, 2003.

Thorau, Christian. "'What Ought to be Heard': Touristic Listening and the Guided Ear." In *OHML*, 207–27.

Thorau, Christian, and Hans-Jakob Ziemer, eds. *The Oxford Handbook of Music Listening in the 19th and 20th Centuries.* New York: Oxford University Press, 2019.

Tieck, Ludwig. *Sämmtliche Werke.* 2 vols. Paris: Baudry, 1841.

Todd, Janet. *Sensibility: An Introduction.* London: Methuen, 1986.

Triest, Johann Karl Friedrich. "Bemerkungen über die Ausbildung der Tonkunst in Deutschland im achtzehnten Jahrhundert." *AmZ* 3 (1801): 225–35, 241–49, 257–64, 273–86, 297–308, 321–31, 369–79, 389–401, 405–10, 421–32, 437–45.

Triest, Johann Karl Friedrich. "Remarks on the Development of the Art of Music in Germany in the Eighteenth Century." Trans. Susan Gillespie. In *Haydn and His World*, 321–94. Ed. Elaine Sisman. Princeton, NJ: Princeton University Press, 1997.

Trippett, David. *Wagner's Melodies: Aesthetics and Materialism in German Musical Identity.* Cambridge: Cambridge University Press, 2013.

Turino, Thomas. *Music as Social Life: The Politics of Participation*. Chicago: University of Chicago Press, 2008.

Unseld, Melanie. *Biographie und Musikgeschichte: Wandlungen biographischer Konzepte in Musikkultur und Musikhistoriographie*. Cologne: Böhlau, 2014.

Vogler, Georg Joseph. "Thätige Geschmaks-Bildung für die Beurtheiler der Tonstücken." In his *Betrachtungen der Mannheimer Tonschule* 1 (1778): 277–312.

Wackenroder, Wilhelm Heinrich. *Sämtliche Werke und Briefe: Historisch-kritische Ausgabe*. 2 vols. Ed. Silvio Vietta and Richard Littlejohns. Heidelberg: Winter, 1991.

Wagner, Richard. *Beethoven*. Leipzig: E. W. Fritzsch, 1870.

Wagner, Richard. *Gesammelte Schriften und Dichtungen*. 11 vols. Ed. Wolfgang Golter. Berlin: Bong, 1913.

Wagner, Richard. *Sämtliche Briefe*. Ed. Gertrud Strobel and Werner Wolf. Leipzig: Deutscher Verlag für Musik, 1967–.

Wallrup, Erik. *Being Musically Attuned: The Act of Listening to Music*. Farnham, Surrey: Ashgate, 2015.

Waltham-Smith, Naomi. *Music and Belonging: Between Revolution and Restoration*. New York: Oxford University Press, 2017.

Watkins, Holly. *Metaphors of Depth in German Musical Thought: From E. T. A. Hoffmann to Arnold Schoenberg*. Cambridge: Cambridge University Press, 2011.

Weber, William. "Did People Listen in the 18th Century?" *Early Music* 25 (1997): 678–91.

Weber, William. *Music and the Middle Class: The Social Structure of Concert Life in London, Paris and Vienna between 1830 and 1848*. 2nd ed. Aldershot: Ashgate, 2004.

Webster, James. "Haydn and the Rhetoric of Improvisation." In *Haydn and the Performance of Rhetoric*, 172–212. Ed. Tom Beghin and Sander M. Goldberg. Chicago: University of Chicago Press, 2007.

Webster, James. *Haydn's "Farewell" Symphony and the Idea of Classical Style: Through-Composition and Cyclic Integration in His Instrumental Music*. Cambridge: Cambridge University Press, 1991.

Weiler, Georg von. "Ueber den Begriff der Schönheit, als Grundlage einer Aesthetik der Tonkunst." *AmZ* 13 (13 February 1811): 117–24.

Weining, Christian. "Listening Modes in Concerts: A Review and Conceptual Model." *Music Perception* 40, no. 2 (2022): 112–34.

Weiss, Piero, and Richard Taruskin, eds. *Music in the Western World: A History in Documents*. 2nd ed. Belmont, CA: Schirmer, 2008.

WORKS CITED

Wheelock, Gretchen A. *Haydn's Ingenious Jesting with Art: Contexts of Musical Wit and Humor.* New York: Schirmer Books, 1992.

Wilfing, Alexander. "Hanslick, Kant, and the Origins of *Vom Musikalisch-Schönen.*" *Musicologica Austriaca: Journal for Austrian Music Studies* (June 18, 2018).

Winkler, Gerhard J. "Op. 33/2: Zur Anatomie eines Schlußeffekts." *Haydn-Studien* 6 (1994): 288–97.

Winkler, Klaus. "Alter und Neuer Musikstil im Streit zwischen den Berlinern und Wienern zur Zeit der Frühklassik." *Die Musikforschung* 33 (1980): 37–45.

Wollenberg, Susan. "A New Look at C. P. E. Bach's *Musical Jokes.*" In *C. P. E. Bach Studies,* 295–314. Ed. Stephen L. Clark. Oxford: Clarendon Press, 1988.

Wolf, Werner. "Metamusic? Potentials and Limits of 'Metareference' in Instrumental Music: Theoretical Reflections and a Case Study (Mozart's *Ein musikalischer Spaß*)." In *Self-reference in Literature and Music,* 1–32. Ed. Walter Bernhart and Werner Wolf. Amsterdam and New York: Rodopi, 2010.

Woodmansee, Martha. *The Author, Art, and the Market: Rereading the History of Aesthetics.* New York: Columbia University Press, 1993.

Wordsworth, William. *Lyrical Ballads, with Pastoral and other Poems.* 3rd ed. 2 vols. London: T. N. Longman and O. Rees, 1802.

Young, James O. "The 'Great Divide' in Music." *BJA* 45, no. 2 (2005): 175–84.

Zaminer, Frieder. "Über die Herkunft des Ausdrucks 'Musik verstehen'." In *Musik und Verstehen: Aufsätze zur semiotischen Theorie, Ästhetik und Soziologie der musikalischen Rezeption,* 314–19. Ed. Peter Faltin and Hans-Peter Reinecke. Cologne: Arno Volk, 1973.

Zitin, Abigail. *Practical Form: Abstraction, Technique, and Beauty in Eighteenth-century Aesthetics.* New Haven, CT: Yale University Press, 2020.

Zitin, Abigail. "Thinking Like an Artist: Hogarth, Diderot, and the Aesthetics of Technique." *Eighteenth-Century Studies* 46 (2013): 555–70.

Index

For the benefit of digital users, indexed terms that span two pages (e.g., 52–53) may, on occasion, appear on only one of those pages.

Abbate, Carolyn, 13, 14–15, 131
Adam, Adolphe, 121
Alembert, Jean Leronde d', 26
Alexander the Great, 7–8
Alison, Archibald, 41, 125
Ambros, August Wilhelm, 121
Aristophanes, 31
Aristotle, 38
Ars est celare artem, 40, 90

Bach, Carl Philipp Emanuel, 39, 58–59, 73, 96–97, 104
Baillot, Pierre, 118
Batteux, Charles, 26, 27
Beattie, James, 39–40
beauty, 5–6, 10–11, 22–23, 26, 38, 67–68, 77, 79–81, 83–84, 87–88, 90–91, 92–94, 96, 98, 99–100, 114, 115, 121, 122
Becker, Judith, 14
Beethoven, Ludwig van, 62–64, 105, 121
　Piano Concerto in C minor, op.37, 108
　Symphony no. 2 in D Major, op. 36, 101–2
　Symphony no. 3 in E♭ Major, op. 55 ("Eroica"), 60
　Symphony no 4 in B♭ Major, op. 68, 102
　Symphony no. 5 in C minor, op. 67, 29, 108, 113–14, 119, 126
　Symphony no. 6 in F Major, op. 68 ("Pastoral"), 9–10

　Symphony no. 7 in A Major, op. 92, 60–61
　String Quartet in F minor, op. 95 ("Serioso"), 61
　String Quartet in in B♭ Major, op. 130, 103
　String Quartet in C♯ minor, op. 131, 61
　String Quartet in E♭, op. 127, 62–63
　Violin Sonatas, op. 12, 61
Berger, Karol, 71–72, 99
Berglinger, Joseph, 18, 29, 124–25
Berio, Luciano, 9–10
Berlioz, Hector, 8, 9–10, 63, 113–14, 115–16
Bonds, Mark Evan, 116
Botstein, Leon, 71–72
Bourdieu, Pierre, 118–19
Boyé, 27–28
Brendel, Franz, 121
Bührlen, Friedrich Louis, 120
Burney, Charles, 25, 39, 51–52, 58–59, 70, 73–74

Cage, John, 9–10, 65–66
Calderón de la Barca, Pedro, 57
Campioni, Carlo Antonio, 53–54
Cannabich, Christian, 53–54, 73
Châtelet, Gabrielle Emilie le Tonnelier de Breteuil, du, Marquise de, 24–25
Chua, Daniel, 42–43
Cicero, Marcus Tullius, 36
Commedia dell'arte, 53, 57

INDEX

Copland, Aaron, 1–2
counterpoint, 35–36, 41, 73, 96, 106, 112–13
Crousaz, Jean-.Pierre, 69
Czerny, Carl, 62

Descartes, René, 71–72
Dewey, John, 23–24
Diderot, Denis, 63–64, 125
Dies, Albert Christoph, 48–49
distance, aesthetic, 1, 8–10, 11–12, 31, 43, 45–46, 51, 87–90, 126, 131
Dittersdorf, Karl Ditters von, 52–53, 56, 59
Dorschel, Andreas, 131
Du Bos, Jean-Baptiste, 26, 68–69

ecstasy, 3, 19, 128–29
Eichendorff, Joseph von, 65
Eliot, T. S., 2, 3–4
emotions, 1–2, 8, 9–10, 14–15, 21–22, 27–28, 32, 33, 39–40, 45–47, 62, 86, 97, 110, 125, 128
Erlmann, Veit, 14–15
Esterházy, Prince Nicholas, 47, 58

fantasy. *See* imagination
Fétis, François-Joseph, 11, 101, 109–14
Fils (Filtz), Johann Anton, 52–53
fine arts, 10–11, 24, 67–68, 76–77, 80–81, 82, 95–96, 97, 110–11
Fontenelle, Bernard Le Bovier de, 5–6, 37–38, 41
Forkel, Johann Nikolaus, 6, 70–71, 74, 97–98, 106
fourth wall, 1–2, 7, 8–10, 12, 15, 22, 42–66, 88, 94, 105, 109–10, 113–14, 117, 130
Fux, Johann Joseph, 35–36

Genzinger, Marianne von, 58
Gerard, Alexander, 80
Gijsbrechts, Cornelius Norbertus, 32
gnostic listening, 14–15, 17, 131
Goehr, Lydia, 13, 127
Goethe, Johann Wolfgang, 32, 87, 89–90
Gottsched, Johann Christoph, 53
Gozzi, Carlo, 57
grammar, musical, 34–35, 124–25

Griesinger, Georg August, 55–56, 58–59, 99–100, 109
Gumbrecht, Hans Ulrich, 18

Hadow, William Henry, 115–16
Hanslick, Eduard, 122–23
Hanswurst, 31, 53
happiness, 24–25, 89
harmony, 23, 25, 74, 94, 107, 111
Haydn, Joseph, 31, 42–59, 94
    Keyboard Sonata in D Major, Hob. XVI:42, 57
    Keyboard Sonata in C Major, Hob. XVI:50, 44–45
    Piano Trio in E♭, Hob. XV:29, 51
    String Quartet in G Major, op. 17, no. 5, 50
    String Quartet op. 33, no. 2 ("Joke"), 12, 43, 67, 74, 87–88
    String Quartet in G Major, op. 33, no. 5, 45
    String Quartet in B♭, op. 50, no. 1, 44
    String Quartet in E♭, op. 50, no. 3, 44
    String Quartet in C Major, op. 54, no. 2, 47–48
    String Quartets, op. 64, 56
    Symphony no. 45 in F# minor ("Farewell"), 47, 55–56
    Symphony no. 46 in B Major, 47
    Symphony no. 60 in C Major ("Il distratto"), 45–47
    Symphony no. 67 in F Major 47–48
    Symphony no. 68 in B♭, 49
    Symphony no. 79 in F Major, 48
    Symphony no. 80 in D minor, 50–51
    Symphony no. 83 in G minor ("La Poule"), 49
    Symphony no. 90 in C Major, 44
    Symphony no. 93 in D Major 49–50
    Symphony no. 94 in G Major ("Surprise"), j 48–49
    Symphony no. 98 in B♭ Major, 48
Hegel, Georg Friedrich Wilhelm, 58
Herder, Johann Gottfried, 20–21
Heusinger, Johann Heinrich Gottlieb, 90–91
Hiller, Johann Adam, 26–27, 36, 52–54
Hippel, Theodor Gottlieb von, 63–64, 65

INDEX

Hoffmann, Ernst Theodor Amadeus, 29, 57, 63–64, 65, 108, 119–20, 126
Hofmann, Leopold, 52–53
Hugo, Victor, 89–90
Humboldt, Alexander, 87
Hume, David, 25
humor (incl. *Laune*), 12, 31, 43, 54–57, 59–60, 94

ideal presence (Kames), 21–23
imagination (incl. fantasy), 16, 22–23, 71–72, 79, 80, 81–83, 89–90, 91–94, 95–96, 99, 103, 119, 122, 125
improvisation, 51, 62
instrumental music vs. vocal music, 5–7, 10–11, 16, 26, 28–29, 34–35, 42–43, 68, 70–71, 75, 76–79, 80–83, 86, 92–93, 95–100
Ives, Charles, 9–10, 65–66

Jankélévitch, Vladimir, 14–15
Joseph II, Holy Roman Emperor, 56, 59–60
Junker, Carl Ludwig, 27–28, 54

Kames, Henry Home, Lord, 21–22, 25, 41
Kamien, Roger, 95–96, 116
Kant, Immanuel, 6–7, 10–11, 68, 76–83, 85–86, 90–92, 95–99
Klopstock, Friedrich Gottlieb, 97, 104
Kobbé, Gustav, 115
Koch, Heinrich Christoph, 39, 46–47, 106–7
Körner, Christian Gottfried, 86–87
Krause, Christian Gottfried, 26
Krehbiel, Henry Edward, 115, 117
Kreidler, Johannes, 9–10
Kretzschmar, Hermann, 117

Lachenmann, Helmut, 9–10
Lamy, Bernard, 38
Laune. See humor
Lessing, Gotthold Ephraim, 42
Lichtenthal, Peter, 84–85
Liszt, Franz, 63, 113–14, 127–28
Lobe, Johann Christian, 114
Locke, John, 24–25
Longinus, 48
Lope de Vega, Félix, 57

Machlis, Joseph, 116
Mahler, Gustav, 9–10, 65–66
Marmontel, Jean-François, 28
Marx, Adolf Bernhard, 61, 108–9, 121, 123
Mathews, W. S. B., 114
Mattheson, Johann, 25, 39–40, 69–70
Meier, Georg Friedrich, 38, 40
Mersenne, Marin 34
Michaelis, Christian Friedrich, 67, 92–94
mimesis, 26, 27
Montesquieu, 24
Moritz, Karl Philipp, 22–23
Mozart, Leopold, 36–37
Mozart, Wolfgang Amadeus, 25, 36–37, 41, 59–60

Nägeli, Hans Georg, 120
Nietzsche, Friedrich, 11–12, 126, 129–30
November, Nancy, 12

oratory
    decline of image in relation to music, 13
    framework of, 13, 34–40, 83–85
    Kant's objection to, 78–79, 82–88
    relation to poetry, 104
    relation to rhetoric, 34
Orpheus, 7–8, 19
Ovid, 40

Pepys, Samuel, 7–8
performers, musical, 16, 35, 39, 45
Peyser, Ethel, 116
Pindar, 90
Plato, 23–24, 28, 78–79, 126
pleasure, 6–7, 8, 10–11, 21–23, 24–30, 35–36, 39–40, 67–69, 70, 72–74, 76, 77–78, 79–80, 89, 92, 93–94, 97–98, 99, 104–7, 109–10, 111–13, 114–17, 118–19, 121–22
Pleyel, Ignaz, 53–54, 59, 109
Pluche, Noël-Antoine, 5–6, 26
poetry vs. oratory, 62, 82–83, 97, 103, 104, 105
program music, 46–47, 96
program notes, 117–18, 130
Prokofiev, Sergei, 9–10, 12, 65–66
Pugnani. Gaetano, 53–54
Purday, Charles, 117–18

INDEX

Quantz, Johann Joachim, 35–36, 41, 73
Quintilian, Marcus Fabius, 35–36, 38, 40

Rattle, Sir Simon, 44
reading, modes of, 21–22, 35–36, 38, 41, 63–64, 89, 100
reflective listening, defined 3–4
Regnard, Jean-François, 45–46
Reichardt, Johann Friedrich, 56, 72–73, 91, 92, 106
Rellstab, Ludwig, 62–63
resonant listening, defined, 2–3
rhetoric, 34–36, 62, 78–79, 83–84, 85, 89, 104, 105
Richardson, Samuel, 32
Richter, Jean Paul Friedrich, 31, 57, 63–64, 95
Riedel, Friedrich Just, 22–23
Riepel, Joseph, 40
Rochlitz, Friedrich, 91–92, 101–2, 106–7, 121
Rousseau, Jean Jacques, 32
Ruetz, Caspar, 27

salons, 15
Satie, Eric, 9–10, 65–66
Scarlatti, Domenico, 52
Scheibe, Johann Adolph, 69–70
Schelling, Friedrich Wilhelm, 29
Schiller, Friedrich, 85–89
Schlegel, August Wilhelm, 89–90
Schlegel, Friedrich, 29, 90, 94–95
Schopenhauer, Arthur, 19, 126–27, 129–30
Schubert, Franz, 63, 102
Schumann, Robert, 9–10, 63, 65, 113–14
silence in music, 44–45
Smetana, Bedřich, 63
Sonnenfels, Joseph von, 53
Spazier, Carl, 53–54

Stamitz, Johann 73
Stamitz, Karl, 73
Stendhal (Henri Beyle), 16, 121
Sterne, Laurence, 31, 32–33, 56–57, 63–64, 65
Stockhausen, Johann Christoph, 53–54
Stravinsky, Igor, 9–10, 65–66
structural listening, 3–4, 71–72, 131
sublime, 92–93, 128–29
Subotnik, Rose Rosengard, 131
Sulzer, Johann Georg, 6
synoptic listening, 71–73, 76, 96, 108, 120

taste, 69–70, 77–78, 79, 80, 91, 99, 101, 108–9, 118–19, 121, 125
Tieck, Ludwig, 23, 63–65
time, cyclical vs. linear, 99
Tirso di Molina, 57
Toeschi, Carlo (Carl Joseph), 53–54
Tondichter (Tone poet), 62, 105
trance, 3, 14
Triest, Johann Karl Friedrich, 95–97

Valéry, Paul, 2–3
Vanhal, Johann Baptist, 59
virtuosity, 39–40, 107
vocal music. *See* instrumental vs. vocal music
Vogler, Georg Joseph, 22–23

Wackenroder, Wilhelm Heinrich, 18, 23, 29–30, 124–25
Wagner, Richard, 11–12, 113–14, 124, 127–29, 130
Weiler, Georg von, 98–99, 119
Weill, Kurt, 9–10, 65–66
Winckelmann, Johann Joachim, 100
Woodmansee, Martha, 100
Wordsworth, William, 104–5